Interpreting Charismatic Experience

David Middlemiss

Interpreting
Charismatic Experience

SCM PRESS LTD

0334 026520

First published 1996
by SCM Press Ltd
9–17 St Albans Place London N1 0NX

Typeset at The Spartan Press Ltd
Lymington, Hants
Printed in Great Britain by
Biddles Ltd, Guildford and King's Lynn

Contents

Preface

This book is the product of my own confusion. This confusion resulted from having been a minister for eight years and having to assess charismatic phenomena, such as the claims of 'prophets' who would tell me with such certainty 'what God is saying to the church'. During church services I had to interpret the varied and sometimes dramatic physical manifestations associated with charismatic experience. Is this person on the floor of our church 'slain in the Spirit', hypnotized or hyper-ventilating? Why does God give such a confused system of 'guidance' to his people? Why do people look for 'the demonic' in heavy metal music or obscure corners of people's personalities when there is so much evident evil in the world; the killing in Serbia and Rwanda spring to mind. Does the charismatic movement have any intellectual or biblical credibility? In the end I left the church and spent three years writing a Ph.D thesis in the Divinity Faculty of Glasgow University so that I could attempt to find answers to my questions.

The search to resolve such issues has not been undertaken in order to justify a previously held position, but to find out how things really are. Consequently, it has been profoundly disturbing to write because the issues on which it impinges affect the foundations of my entire belief system, and this system was turned upside down by writing the thesis.

My central question is: 'If a person claims to have encountered God in his or her experience, how can one tell if this is what has really occurred?' I didn't realize quite how far-reaching this issue is, and how hard it is to resolve until I had the opportunity to research the question properly. It led me on a long personal journey through church history, theology and on into philosophy. Although it is a long and exhausting journey, once embarked on there is no way back. In the middle it left me sitting by the road despairing of the possibility of ever finding any answer to the question, and therefore sceptical that any Christian understanding of experience is justified. After a lifetime of involvement with the church this is like losing the horizon, spinning through the abyss without any fixed points to determine which way is 'up' and which is 'down'. When eventually I did find a way in which I could in principle resolve my questions, it became possible to rebuild a more knowable universe.

From the point of view of a person who has just travelled on such a journey, this book is overwhelmingly positive because it does argue that there are rational means of interpreting Christian experience. To one who does not ask such questions, however, it may appear to be negative and over-critical of charismatic experience.

However, although the book may appear to be critical of charismatic experience, this is because I believe that in order to preserve that which is of value in a context of this kind, there is a need to be ruthless in cutting out the nonsense. If the charismatic movement is not able to do this, then there are strong historical grounds to suppose that the good will be driven out by the bad with resultant disillusionment and confusion.

The relevance of the work is illustrated by the fact that as this preface is being written, parts of England are experiencing what is called the 'Toronto Blessing'. This is precisely the kind of experience for which this book should be able to provide the means of assessment.

One last point is that I normally use the masculine pronoun in my writing. This is personal habit, and I do not in any way mean it to be exclusive or offensive. I use it as a shorthand which includes the feminine.

Acknowledgments

I would like to thank my Ph.D. supervisor Dr Houston for giving me so much time, help and criticism. Thanks also to Norman Shanks for allowing me the space to develop my initial ideas. I would like to thank Liz and Richard for looking after the home while I have been away in Scotland, along with family in Lowestoft who were such a help during this time. Thanks also go to my friends and flatmates who kept me sane, and had such good parties, during the months in Glasgow.

I particularly acknowledge a debt to Basil Mitchell's work, especially *The Justification of Religious Belief*. His arguments have pushed this book in the direction in which it travelled, and in significant sections I have used his means of justifying religious belief in application to charismatic experience.

Many thanks to John and Lynn Wallis for supplying me with a computer and for bailing me out when there were problems to solve. I am also indebted to Andrew Tucker and Marie Page who were prepared to offer criticism of the book from within the charismatic movement. Also thanks to those who helped with seemingly endless proof reading; particularly to John Woods, Joyce Ogden and to Mavis Wallis for all the effort and care with which they corrected my work. I am also grateful to Jo Herrington for her help with psychological aspects of the book.

Finally my thanks go to the Dr Williams Bursary. Before the days when dissenters were allowed to go to English universities, Dr Williams died and left money to educate dissenting English ministers in Scotland at Glasgow University. Although the law has now changed, the legacy hasn't, and it was this which made it possible for me to spend three gloriously traumatic years studying in Glasgow.

Introduction

He that would seriously set upon the search of truth, ought in the first place to prepare his Mind with a love of it. For he that Loves it not, will not take much pains to get it; nor be much concerned when he misses it.[1]

One of the most striking features of the charismatic movement, which has influenced the church to such a large extent during the second half of the twentieth century, is its confusing diversity of theology and experience. During the first half of the century charismatic experience was much more straightforward to grasp, with the dominant model of practice and theology being derived directly from traditional Pentecostalism. This resulted in an easily definable theology, which predicted specific experiences in a specific order; conversion, baptism in the Spirit, and then as a sign, speaking in tongues and other gifts of the Spirit. Following this there were character changes to be expected as the fruit of the Spirit grew along with a renewed consecration to God. This theology would also broadly typify the early charismatic writers, such as Dennis Bennet and Arthur Wallis.

However, the significant problems raised by this traditional Pentecostalism, in terms of questionable exegesis, shallow theology and dubious implications of these doctrines, have led to dissatisfaction with this approach. Consequently the theological interpretation of Pentecostal experiences has been modified to a considerable degree by writers such as David Watson, Michael Harper, and Tom Smail. They typify what became known as 'Neo-Pentecostalism', and it was this that became more typical of charismatic theology through the 1970s. Part of this development was a social shift, and so a charismatic is playfully, but accurately, described by Dr A.Walker as 'a middle-class Pente-costal'.²

Subsequent to this we have been offered a 'Third wave' model which has developed through the 'Vineyard Fellowships' who follow John Wimber's teaching. Vineyard churches began in California, but have now been established in many parts of the world. One of the distinctive features of these churches is a 'time of ministry' where one can observe trembling, crying, laughing, screaming, shaking, falling to the ground, people with sensations of electricity, heat and cold, and so on.

Out of one such church, the 'Airport Vineyard Fellowship' in Toronto, has come the 'Toronto Blessing'. This has become the dominant issue in the English charismatic churches during the mid 1990s, and has spread in a contagious way to different parts of the world. It is accompanied by profound effects on individuals and unusually dramatic phenomena such as barking like a dog, clucking like a chicken, roaring like a lion. There have been strong feelings over whether or not such phenomena are indicators of the Holy Spirit's work.

This wide variation in almost every area of theology, experience and style has created something of a supermarket level of choice within the charismatic movement. For example, the focus on tongues associated with Pentecostalism has been replaced by a focus on healing. One can now choose between many alternative manners of healing; healing of memories, laying on of hands, calling for the elders, anointing with oil and public healing meetings. There are also many differing demonologies which influence the way both physical and mental health is viewed.

There is a diversity in theology, and in the popular understanding of experience. 'Baptism in the Spirit', which was viewed as a necessary second stage of initiation by traditional Pentecostals, has gathered a variety of alternative descriptions; being 'slain in the Spirit', 'receiving the Spirit', the 'second blessing', 'receiving the Spirit of adoption', or the 'fullness of the Spirit'.

There is an application of aspects of Old Testament theology such as 'claiming the land', walking around cities, 'curses and blessings', and illness being attributed to sin inherited from parents.³

There are differing personalities involved in leading and teaching, each with their own distinctive styles, styles which are not always compatible. The new ideas of such people are all easily accessible through the explosion of Christian literature, in the form of books and magazines, and 'tape ministries', as well as at the Christian conferences such as Spring Harvest or Stoneleigh. The 'Downs' and 'Dales' conferences drew people primarily from the emerging house churches, but Spring Harvest draws a cross section from all denominations. All of this has a dramatic effect on members of the local church, as the members' ideas are not primarily shaped by the pastor, but by these diverse sources.

There is a strong cross-denominational aspect, which has added to the diversity in styles of worship, as the charismatic forms have been adapted to differing church cultures. The charismatic movement has crossed denominational boundaries between Protestant sects. There has also been an extensively developing Catholic charismatic movement.

This diversity is magnified by an inter-continental mix of ideas in which the English church is influenced by other parts of the world. There are numerous American writers and preachers with their own Western emphases, often advocating wealth and success as being indicators of God's blessing. On the other side of the world are people such as Paul Yonggi Cho in Korea who is minister of the 'biggest church in the world' and an advocate of his own brand of Pentecostalism which includes such ideas as imagining specific items during prayer as a means of getting what is desired.[4]

Clearly there is a tremendous diversity within the charismatic movement, and one of the consequences of this is that to describe a person as being 'charismatic' can mean so much that is not only varied, but even contradictory, both in experience and theology that it is therefore in danger of becoming a meaningless description.

We are not dealing any longer with a situation where there is a single and easily definable theology and experience, but with a bewildering breadth and variety, which leads to a mix of what could be described from any point of view as being good and bad. It is a mix which is extremely difficult to define and sift. In fact, it is the vagueness of definition and the sheer diversity of experience within the movement which has created the need for this book. It is this complex mix of 'charismatic' experience and theology for which I am aiming to find means of assessment.

Before I can scrutinize this mix, difficult questions have to be answered. What are the distinguishing marks of experience which comes from God, as distinct from that which does not? Can one ever know that an experience did in reality have its source in God? Underlying this is the more basic question of how to verify any sort of religious interpretation of experience.

The issue I am aiming to resolve is 'How can one assess the claim that a person has encountered God in charismatic experience?' This is one of the themes taken up by the great American philosopher and theologian Jonathan Edwards (1703–1758) in *A Treatise Concerning The Religious Affections*. What are the distinguishing marks of a work of the Spirit of God? What is the nature of true religion?[5]

Edwards is a useful source, because in him we find the unusual combination of an excellent enlightenment philosopher who presides over a church which might be described as charismatic in modern terms. One of the distinguishing features of Edwards' work is that he straddles the balance between reason and emotion with such delicacy. It is the loss of such balance that creates so much of the division associated with revival, and preserving an equilibrium in this context is a feat which is rarely achieved for long.

One of the reasons why Edwards gave a high priority to the assessment of religious experience was because he was aware of how crucial the answers to these questions were, and of how much damage could be done if they were not dealt with properly. Indeed, he attributed the eventual disintegration of the seventeenth-century revival in New England primarily to this failing:

It is by the mixture of counterfeit religion with true, not discerned and distinguished, that the devil has had his greatest advantage against the cause of the kingdom of Christ all along hitherto. It is by this means principally, that he has prevailed against all revivings of religion that ever have been since the founding of the Christian Church.[6]

One has good historical grounds to expect the same disintegration, if the current charismatic movement does not find adequate means to assess its claims.

This book is not a piece of historical theology or sociology, or anthropology, or psychology, or church history, though these fields contribute to discussion and they will be used to illustrate the central argument of the book which is focussed on charismatic epistemology. What this means is that we are searching to see how one could justify a claim that one could *know* that God has intervened in experience.

To use an analogy, my aim is to draw a map of the territory, and to outline the main features. If one does want to assess theological claims which are made on the basis of charismatic experience, then these are the culs-de-sac, these are the dangerous areas, these are the best roads, and these are the kind of guidelines which will help to get through to a justification of one's views. In order to demonstrate the relevance of these issues, I will illustrate them with reference to a variety of charismatic experiences, but my aim is to look for the means of assessment, and not primarily to assess.

This is important because, as will become evident, by its very nature, this movement is in a state of rapid and continuous change. Consequently, if I were to write a straightforward assessment of a particular part of this movement, then I would have done a piece of work which was of limited value because by the time it had been read, it would already be out of date. This makes it particularly significant to discover how such experience should and should not be assessed in principle, because, if it can be done, this will leave us with the means of evaluating continually whatever charismatic experience presents itself, however varied its form.

Consequently, this is not a book which is committed to any particular claim, or section of the charismatic movement. It is written with a theoretical passion, and its commitment is not to 'prove' one particular viewpoint, but to find out how things really are. In an analysis of charismatic experience, such a starting point is essential, because, as will be ascertained, there are significant obstacles to a simple search for truth in this context.

At times this emphasis on what is true can appear destructive, because it means undermining interpretations of experiences which are of great significance to people. However, this must still be done. First, because its primary aim is to search for the means of distinguishing those beliefs about charismatic claims which are true from those which are false. There is no intention of defending misguided beliefs for fear of being offensive or hurting people's feelings. This would be a misleading distraction from an attempt to discover whether these beliefs are justified or not. Secondly, this apparent destructiveness is quite superficial. In the long term the wisest course is to avoid any false belief, because the safest way to prevent disillusionment is to ensure that one does not take on beliefs which are illusory.

This distinction between reality and illusion is not made as rigorously as it ought to be in the current charismatic movement. For example, I have discovered through personal conversation with them that some of those involved in Wimber conferences estimate that between 75% and 90% of apparent experiences of the Spirit are purely of a psychological nature. It would be interesting to discover on what basis such a figure is reached, but leaving this issue aside, the concern remains that an acceptance of this undistinguished mix of experience is sometimes seen as being permissible. There is a strong historical precedent to suppose that this is a seed which could easily grow into widespread disillusionment within this movement.

> And by what is seen of the terrible consequences of this counterfeit religion, when not distinguished from true religion, God's people in general have their minds unhinged and unsettled in things of religion, and know not where to set their foot, or what to think or do; and many are brought into doubts, whether there be anything in religion; and heresy and infidelity and atheism greatly prevail.[7]

Consequently, demonstrating that a person does not know that which he thought he did know is to make a positive step closer to wisdom. It clears the ground to make way for genuine knowledge. To paraphrase both Russell and Wittgenstein, any wall which is parted from the truth must be pulled down. The book inevitably involves demolishing some poorly justified claims to knowledge, but this is of itself both useful and important.

We will also endeavour to move beyond demolition work to see if it is possible to build an overtly constructive argument which could support genuine interpretation of charismatic experience. Whether this is possible or not remains to be seen. If it is not, then we may be forced to share a conclusion with the *Tractatus* that

What we cannot speak about we must pass over in silence.[8]

I

History Repeats Itself

Enthusiasm and charismatic experience

What is called 'charismatic' in the present day is part of a long strand of apparently common experience which reaches back into the New Testament. The people who approve of such experience describe it as 'refreshment' 'renewal', 'revival', 'the movement of the Spirit', or 'restoration of the church'. Those who dislike what they observe (or hear about) call it 'emotionalism', 'enthusiasm', or even 'occult'. It consists of such a wide variety of experience and theology that labels are almost meaningless and it is sometimes difficult to see what holds it together at all.

Consequently, we ought to begin the search by defining what kind of experience we are talking about. In order to do this it is helpful to put charismatic experience into its historical context to see what can be learned from the experience of previous generations. Similarities with the phenomena of revivals, for example, have often been pointed out, and there are some apparent family connections between these areas of experience. The possibility which I would like to explore here, however, is that the experience of what was called 'enthusiasm' (in the seventeenth- and eighteenth-century sense of the word) could be the charismatic movement's closest ancestral relative.

The word 'enthusiasm' itself was first coined to describe the religious fervour of the 'Anabaptistical Sect' of Nicholas Stork of Silesia.[1] No religious group would have chosen the word to describe itself because it was a term of outright abuse. It meant that while a person was fanatically committed to a belief, his or her rational faculties had been switched off and the belief itself was an unjustified delusion. Consequently a comparison between charismatic experience and enthusiasm needs to be made with care because enthusiasm, in this sense, is a loaded term to use. According to George Hickes in 1680, enthusiasm is a 'demonic spirit' which needs to be exorcised,[2] and according to Wesley, 'Every enthusiast, then, is properly a madman.'[3]

> Enthusiasm, in general, may, then, be described in some such manner as this: A religious madness arising from some falsely imagined influence or inspiration of God; at least, from imputing something to God, which ought not to be expected from him.[4]

Charles Wesley was himself described as an enthusiast by other writers; Henry Fielding wrote Methodism off as a lot of 'Nonsense and enthusiasm'.[5] Wesley certainly would not have agreed with Fielding's description of himself; nobody in their right mind would apply it to themselves.

Dr Johnson's dictionary defines enthusiasm as follows:

(1) A vain belief of private revelation; a vain confidence of divine favour,
(2) Heat of imagination; violence of passion,
(3) Elevation of fancy; exaltation of ideas.[6]

Numerous movements were described as being enthusiastic during the time of Wesley and Dr Johnson, and some of them do appear to have a family resemblance to the charismatic movement.

The Montanist movement of the second century was one of the earliest. It was a movement in reaction against (what Montanus saw as) the dead spirituality and formalism of the early church. It aimed to reinstate the gifts of the Spirit and so it moved out of the main church and met in the houses of its own people. It had its own strong leaders, and inspired the same kind of opposition from mainstream Christianity that enthusiasts always experience. The Montanists are in the unhappy position that all of the surviving written material on their movement was written by those who disliked them most and denounced them as heretics. However, it does seem that the movement sank into confusion along with its erroneous prophecies of the imminent return of Christ, as is the way with movements which allow themselves to be directed by prophets.

Many of the Catholic saints were described as 'extravagant enthusiasts' by Warton in *The Enthusiasm of the Church of Rome* (1688). According to Warton, these saints believed themselves to be in direct communication with God and claimed to be able to perform miracles, but they were simply demonstrating 'the exercise of a blind enthusiasm'. Warton includes Saint Ignatius, Thomas à Kempis and Francis of Assisi in the category of enthusiast, because of their claims that God spoke directly to them and for their 'folly' of supporting the doctrines of Purgatory and Transubstantiation.

Following the Reformation there was an explosion of enthusiastic movements: Jansenism, Quietism, Malaval, Petrucci, Molinos, The French Prophets, Methodism, and many others.

For example, the Anabaptists were described as enthusiasts on the grounds that they claimed to receive new revelation.[7] They attempted to restore biblical ethics in their entirety, including the polygamy of Old Testament days. In 1527 they were condemned for heresy and experienced violent opposition from the mainstream church for the next twenty-five years. If they lived in Catholic territories they were burned to death, and those in Protestant areas were drowned or put to the sword. The most infamous incident was the siege of Münster, in which the combined forces of Catholics and Lutherans butchered the defenders of the city and tortured the leaders to death. Enthusiasts always experience 'opposition from the mainstream church', though few face such severe opposition as this.

The early Quaker James Naylor was also considered to be an enthusiast. In a foretaste of the current charismatic trend for doing 'praise marches' through cities, he called on the people to 'join the lambs war' and in 1656 he marched into Bristol on a donkey while people waved palm branches along the road, an event which was intended to illustrate the 'inward comming of christ into the heart'. Unfortunately for Naylor, the symbolism was missed by most people in Bristol, who rather considered it to be blasphemy. They whipped him, branded him with a 'B' on the forehead, bored a hole in his tongue and put him in prison.[8] This did somewhat dampen his enthusiasm. Enthusiasts were not generally popular people.

What is difficult for the average twentieth-century person to appreciate is the impact that these movements had on the whole of English society in the seventeenth and eighteenth centuries. During this time the society was still largely 'Christian', at least in a broad sense that the culture was shaped and affected significantly by the church, rather than the church being a peculiar minority enclave. Consequently, enthusiastic movements were discussed in all parts of the country, and in all parts of society. There are essays and books on the theme written by a wide variety of people which include journalists, philosophers, theologians, ministers, and *belle lettristes*.[9]

In the academic world the most perceptive discussion of enthusiasm was written by the Empiricist philosopher John Locke in the *Essay Concerning Human Understanding* (1690). There was perhaps a degree of irritation with enthusiasts because they made so many claims to speak on behalf of God, and to know with *certainty* that they were correct, but without having good reasons to support these beliefs. According to Locke, enthusiasm:

> which though founded neither on reason, nor Divine Revelation, but rising from the Conceits of a warmed or overweening Brain, works yet, where it once gets a footing, more powerfully on the Perswasions and Actions of Men, than either of those two, or both together:[10]

Locke is concerned about the detachment from reason, which he considers to be the crucial issue in understanding the nature of enthusiasm.

> Every conceit that thoroughly warms our fancies must pass for an inspiration, if there be nothing but the strength of our perswasions, whereby to judge of our perswasions; if reason must not examine their truth by something extrinsical to the perswasions themselves, inspirations and delusions, truth and falsehood, will have the same measure, and will not be possible to be distinguished.[11]

In the literary world, Jonathan Swift wrote a satirical essay on enthusiasm entitled *A Discourse Concerning the Mechanical Operation of the Spirit, in A Tale of a Tub*. Its glorious central image is of an enthusiastic preacher who is represented as an ass trying to climb a rocky path on the way up to heaven while a whole denomination of people sit precariously on his back and rely on him to get them to their destination.

> Instead of the term, Ass, we shall make use of gifted, or enlightened teacher; And the Word Rider, we will exchange for that of Fanatic Auditory, or any other Denomination of the like import.[12]

Swift considers that enthusiastic belief is as justifiable as the belief that other planets are inhabited by aliens, for which there is no evidence; and with the belief in the possiblity of 'the squaring of the circle', which is quite impossible. He states that enthusiasm claims to be 'A lifting up of the Soul or its Faculties above Matter', and that this is normally seen to be achieved through three 'mechanisms'; God, the devil, or the flesh.

1. 'Prophecy or Inspiration' which is the 'immediate act of God'.
2. Possession, which is the 'immediate act of the Devil'.
3. Natural causes 'strong Imagination, Spleen, violent Anger, Fear, Grief, Pain, and the like'.

Swift intends to take a fourth 'less well understood mechanism', and argues facetiously that 'it is purely an Effect of Artifice and Mechanic Operation'. In other words, enthusiasm is a deliberate hoax.

As we travel forward through the centuries the term 'enthusiasm' gradually changes in meaning. By the middle of the nineteenth century, the word had become ambiguous as to whether it implied approval or disapproval. It had also diverged from the religious context and had begun to be used also in application to literature and politics. By the time we reach 1964, 'enthusiasm' has lost its negative connotations, and the OED defines it more straightforwardly as 'ardent zeal'.

What 'enthusiasm' refers to in this book, however, is a label for the numerous movements which have the tendencies outlined below. They are movements which contain a wide variety of different views, and yet underneath they are remarkably united by the same collection of tendencies.

The most thorough analysis of them has been done by R.A. Knox in his book *Enthusiasm*. He defines enthusiasm as follows.

> I have called this book 'Enthusiasm', not meaning thereby to name (for name it has none) the elusive thing that is its subject. I have only used a cant term, pejorative, and commonly misapplied, as a label for a tendency.[13]

This entire and apparently confused jumble of 'tendencies' and experiences do combine to form a startlingly recurrent situation throughout church history. 'The pattern is always repeating itself, not in outline merely but in detail.'[14]

What is this pattern like? According to Knox it consists of the following traits. The enthusiastic movement will claim to be restoring the primitive spirituality of the church, but is usually denounced and opposed, both by the mainstream of the church, and by those with no spirituality of any sort. Almost always there will be schism which creates rival groups and prophets. Eventually the movement will be absorbed into the institutional as the initial fervour dies out.

Enthusiastic spirituality is described as 'Ultraspiritualism' by Knox, by which he means that the supernatural becomes an expected part of everyday life. One aspect of this is that total transformation of the personality is expected as the norm, rather than the exception.

There is a single-minded desire to live a life of 'angelic purity', which tends towards a separation from all 'worldly' amusements. In the situation where a group develops the idea of its own impeccability:

> actions which bring damnation to the worldling may be inculpable in the children of light. We must be prepared for strange alterations of rigourism and anti-nomianism.[15]

The main stream of religion is condemned as being an affair of simply outward form and ordinances, whereas authentic Christianity is now being restored as an affair of the heart through the enthusiastic group, who claim direct and immediate access to God. The inward experiences of peace, joy and assurance are craved for, and expressed in simple 'heart worship'. There is a distinctly subjective emphasis.

According to Knox the implications of enthusiasm go even deeper than this, as at its root is a different theology of grace. The traditional doctrine sees nature as being perfected in eternity, whereas enthusiastic grace is rather less patient and expects heaven on earth. The saved man considers himself to have entered a new order of being, and to possess a whole new set of faculties or 'gifts', which allow a direct insight into God's will.

> 'David must not wear the panoply of Saul.' Especially, he decries the use of human reason as a guide to any sort of religious truth.[16]

The enthusiast claims to have a new status and authority in the kingdom of God, and this creates a distinct separation between the 'elect', and the 'sons of perdition'. There will be a reluctant submission to what are considered as sinful worldly governments, but at the same time, 'always the enthusiast hankers after a theocracy'. A group of people will sometimes separate themselves into the wilderness and set up a theocracy of their own.

The enthusiast often has a conviction that the second coming is shortly to be expected. Another trait is an experience of 'ecstasy', and a host of accompanying abnormal phenomena.

> We read of people breaking out into unintelligible utterance, or utterance identified by expert evidence as a language unknown to themselves; of remaining destitute of their senses in a holy trance, or, more often, shaken by convulsive movements from head to foot, for hours at a time. The unbeliever hesitates whether to explain all this as hysteria or as diabolic; the faithful are puzzled, some inclined to welcome and some to reprobate it. But, whatever the explanation, beyond doubt the

phenomena occur; we should throw over all belief in human evidence if we denied it.[17]

It is enthusiasm in this sense that is explored by Knox in *Enthusiasm*. The accuracy of his description of the nature of 'enthusiasm' is confirmed by the many such movements throughout church history which can be recognized because they have the same recurring jumble of tendencies. Consequently it is possible to use this generally accepted analysis as a useful base line to see if the current charismatic movement ought to be described as 'enthusiasm', and therefore placed into this historical context. Knox consistently resists the attempt to assess the experience and phenomena he describes, but in our case, we are attempting to discover the means of assessment. A description of enthusiasm is only the starting point.

I shall be gathering together diverse aspects of the charismatic movement, some of which may appear incompatible with one another in respect of their theology. It is still acceptable to consider them to be connected, however, because there may be the underlying pattern of an 'enthusiastic' movement which holds these traits and varying theologies together. Perhaps not all of these traits are represented in each particular group, and certainly not to the same extent, but each has found its expression in some aspect of the charismatic movement.

I shall also be referring to 'revival' as being enthusiasm, because each revival has been described by its opponents in this way. Whether they are inspired by God or not is not the issue at this point.

'Enthusiasm' is the term I am suggesting may be a description of the charismatic movement. I shall therefore compare the current charismatic movement with the traits of 'enthusiasm' as outlined by Knox, and determine whether this is indeed an acceptable term to apply.

The movement claims to be restoring the primitive spirituality of the church

> The Waldenses' ambition was to live the Sermon on the Mount; they would have no treasure on earth, they contested the right of the secular powers to inflict capital punishment, they would take no oaths.[18]

The desire to restore the primitive spirituality of the early church permeates the charismatic movement. Its aim is to be like the church of the New Testament in its simplicity, commitment, radicalism and power.

One extreme current expression of this trait comes from the Restoration movement, as the claim is not just to restore the primitive spirituality of the church, but to surpass it.[19] The Restoration view of church history is that spirituality deteriorated disastrously after the completion of the New Testament. The Montanists made an unsuccessful attempt to put this right, but the church hit rock bottom by AD 600. By this time the church has (putatively) abandoned scripture and taken on superstitious sacramental doctrines which distorted the gospel. The power of the Spirit was consequently withdrawn and nothing of positive spiritual significance seems to have happened for almost a thousand years

According to *Restoration* (the official magazine of the Restoration Churches) there is something positive to be said for movements such as the Reformation and the Anabaptist movement, because at least they revived the use of scripture and baptism. Religious fervour has been restored at differing times by groups such as the Methodists, Brethren, and Salvation Army. They created stepping stones towards the ultimate movement at the end of time. Those of delicate sensibilities may perhaps detect a tiny element of arrogance in this view of church history.

> That Restorations churches ... are seen as the foci of God's final chapter in the history of His people – and thus the whole world – can be seen in the list of recovered truths of the twentieth century as declared in *Restoration* magazine.[20]

Although this is the extreme end of the spectrum, the concept of restoring the primitive church in some form does permeate the whole charismatic movement. It is fundamentalist in its attitude to the Bible, and critical of the mainline church for taking on unbiblical traditions, which in their view should be rejected on the grounds that they are not taught in the New Testament. Also for ignoring parts of the Bible which are of a more charismatic nature, such as I Corinthians 14, or for spiritualizing passages which are literal descriptions of miraculous events. This particular trait gives impetus to the resurgence of spiritual gifts, and the particular emphasis on healing which permeates the whole movement. They are practised because they were part of the New Testament church.

The phenomena associated with the 'Toronto Blessing' are sometimes justified on the grounds that it is a restoration of the supernatural character of the ministry of the early church, an aspect which has been edited out by insipid contemporary Christianity. As with all enthusiastic movements, the charismatic movement is claiming to restore the primitive spirituality of the church.

The movement is denounced and opposed by the mainstream churches

> They grew also (many of them) very loose, and degenerate in their practices (for their opinions will certainly produce a filthy life by degrees); such as no Prayer in their Families, no Sabbath, insufferable Pride, frequent and hideous Lying.[21]

This theme of opposition will be explored more thoroughly in the next chapter. For the moment all we need to point out is that this is a feature of the contemporary charismatic movement. It lives in uneasy tension with the mainstream churches, often with mutual distrust and misunderstanding. Part of the church wishes to pull back and retain traditional forms of worship, and the other wishes for the spontaneity and freshness of the new. The mainstream denominations write cautious and sometimes threatened documents on the new movements, with accusations of splitting churches, theological naiveté, exaggerated subjectivity, or even heresy.

The 'Toronto Blessing' has also polarized attitudes, filling church newspapers with discussion on whether it is a movement which is 'of the Spirit' or not. It is frequently treated in categorical terms, where it is considered to be genuine experience of the Spirit *as a whole*, or else *all* emotional manipulation or evil. Such thinking forces outright acceptance or rejection of the 'Toronto Blessing' in its entirety.

Having said this, it would be unfair to say that the charismatic movement is always opposed by mainstream denominations. In England a common reaction has come to be an absorption of the aspects of the new which are seen as helpful; such as the new music, or the emphasis on using the gifts of all the believers, rather than just centring on the minister. The degree of opposition, however, is roughly in proportion to the level of radicalism in the movement, and an antagonistic reaction becomes inevitable with more developed enthusiasm. The more different it is from the traditional, the harder it will be to accept new views and to cope with change. Consequently there is a sympathetic attitude towards the moderate aspects of charismatic experience, but when there are more extreme views, the argument becomes more vicious. According to *Restoration* magazine, for example, denominations are 'made up of people who are not Christian at all',[22] they are 'apostate', 'out of step with the Spirit', and 'failing to repent'.[23] On the other hand, the 'charismatic extremists' are described by Peter Masters as: 'surely one of the greatest triumphs of Satan our malicious enemy.'[24]

It is justifiable to argue that the charismatic movement is often opposed by the mainstream church.

The movement becomes schismatic

No one is unaware of the schism which, after the consecration of Caecilian, was effected at Carthage through a certain mischief making woman named Lucilla . . . It was said that she kissed a bone of some martyr or other – if he was a martyr –

before she received the spiritual food and drink. Having then been corrected for thus touching, before she touched the sacred chalice, the bone of a dead man (if he was a martyr, at least he had not been acknowledged as such), she went away in confusion full of wrath . . .

In this way it came to pass that at the time the schism was brought to birth by the anger of a disgraced woman, was fed by ambition, and received its strength from avarice.[25]

This enthusiastic schismatic tendency is also evident in the charismatic movement. Splits permeate it back to its roots in Pentecostalism, which was itself divided into various sects, such as Elim and Assemblies of God. Classical Pentecostal churches also lived with a sharp distinction between mainline churches and themselves. Their doctrine implied fundamental inadequacies in those who had neither been 'baptized in the Spirit', nor 'spoken in tongues', i.e. those who had not were not Christian. These implications were not lost on the other denominations.

It continues to be a common criticism, that charismatic experience leads to division in churches. Even where a church does not split, there is still an inbuilt division between those with a 'charismatic experience' and those without. This leads to different spiritualities and consequently, even though they may meet in the same church, there is still a breach between the two groups.

Within the charismatic movement there is also a variety of strong figures, whose style, emphases and doctrine are not always compatible. Each has its own following, often becoming popular for a few years, before fading from popularity as the next set of ideas arrives. The 'Toronto Blessing' has very rapidly become divided, and there has been a split between Wimber's 'Vineyard' churches and the Airport Vineyard church in Toronto where the 'Toronto Blessing' originated.

The house church movement at the radical end of the spectrum proved to be divisive and vehement accusations of church splitting were aimed at the 'Bradford' house churches. Having split off from the old denominations, they have themselves been afflicted by internal divisions. For these house churches, there is no difficulty in separating from the traditional churches. Indeed, true believers really ought to leave the 'old wineskins', in the form of dead denominations; as one of their songs puts it, 'The Spirit won't be hindered by division'. God has finished with, and departed from, such structures.

In its divisiveness, then, the charismatic movement can be described as 'enthusiastic'.

The supernatural becomes an expected part of life

> Some of them leaped up many times, men and women several feet from the ground; they clapped their hands with the utmost violence; they shook their heads, they distorted their features, they threw their arms and legs to and fro, in a variety of postures; they sung, roared, shouted, screamed with all their might . . . The person of the house was delighted above measure, and said, Now is the power of God come indeed.[26]

The very word *charismata*, or 'gifts of grace' contains this sense of the imminence of the beyond; of grace impinging on human experience through the 'gifts of the Spirit'. In this sense 'supernatural' describes, for example, direct revelation where God is seen as speaking through 'tongues', 'interpretation' and 'prophecy'. The sense of having direct revelation from God tends towards an attitude in which direct guidance has to come from God before decisions can be made.

The other gifts such as 'healing' or 'miracles' are all seen as supernatural. According to the charismatic movement these ought to be a part of the life of every church. Different gifts have been given a central place at different times. For example, the Pentecostal church considered that tongues was an essential sign of the baptism in the Spirit; healing is currently emphasized by large areas of the charismatic movement. More recently prophecy has become increasingly important, as a result of groups such as the 'Kansas City Prophets'. There are claims that the unusual and dramatic phenomena associated with the 'Toronto Blessing' are also supernatural in origin. Two examples will illustrate the expectation of the supernatural.

The first example is a distinct emphasis on supernatural healing which exists throughout the charismatic movement, taking the form of claims to both physical and emotional healing. Illness is part of the kingdom of Satan, and therefore to be opposed; it is never God's will for his people to be ill. This is a common assumption of the entire spectrum of the movement.

> One of Satans most effective works is disease . . . Regardless of the cause, though, Christians have power over disease.[27]

> God wants us well, and does everything he can to ensure it.[28]

Anticipating miraculous healing is a particular way of expecting the supernatural to be a part of normal life.

The second example of 'supernatural immanence' is an emphasis put on the demonic by the charismatic movement. To those outside, this emphasis can appear extreme and obsessive, with a paranoid way of looking at the universe.

> For those who are disposed to accept the reality of the power of darkness it then becomes possible to be drawn into a world which has its own form of credibility and consistency which cannot for the most part be verified. The possibilities for credulity are enormous. It becomes difficult to disentangle fact from fantasy.[29]

This supernatural demonic concept can become an all-pervading way of thinking which attributes that which is strange to the direct intervention of God or to Satan. There are no neutral areas, but two kingdoms at war with each other; all events have a moral and spiritual dimension. It is a variation of a 'God-of-the-Gaps' thought pattern, which attributes unexplained (and much explicable) phenomena to the supernatural. In this case, however, it is more of a 'Devil of the Gaps' who is conjured up as an explanation of areas of experience which are not understood.

The effect of this is that mental states, illness, and all kinds of common events in every area of life are considered to be capable of being influenced by the demonic. If one is tired, it is 'the spirit of tiredness' which needs to be cast out; a hard-going service in a church needs 'the spirit of heaviness' casting out; a murderer is influenced by the 'Spirit of murder', and so on. Anger, sin, and unforgiveness are entry points for 'demonization'. Both people and every-day inanimate objects can be carriers of demons. Superman is a Satanic substitute for Jesus, as are 'Super Ted' and 'He Man'. Incredibly, tooth-fairies, Teddy Ruxpin, My Little Pony, and Care Bears are all children's toys which have been seen by some as being demonic.[30] This appears more like outright superstition than the immanent supernatural.

Some groups begin with the assumption that all Christians are 'demonized' by many different demons. According to Peter Horrobin these demons enter through the eyes, through any form of sin, through inheritance from parents, through emotions, through the area one lives in, or through church,[31] etc. This leaves no neutral areas of life which are free from the influence of the supernatural in the form of demons. Even if one is unaware of it, this supernatural influence is seen as shaping and infiltrating a person's life.

It would be grossly unfair to attribute these more extreme views to the whole charismatic movement, though it is still true that in less extreme form there is a widespread emphasis on the demonic. What is common throughout is a way of thinking which emphasizes a day-to-day supernatural experience, the 'Natural Supernatural', to quote John Wimber. In this sense, the charismatic movement can be described as 'enthusiastic' because it expects the supernatural to be part of everyday life.

Total transformation of the personality is expected as the norm

Many notoriously vicious persons have been reformed, and become externally quite new creatures. Some that are wealthy, and of fashionable, gay education; some great beaus and fine ladies, that seemed to have their minds swallowed up with nothing but the vain shows and pleasures of the world, have been wonderfully altered, have relinquished these vanities, and are become serious, mortified and humble in their conversation.[32]

Transformation of the personality has always been a Pentecostal theme, and a central claim for the 'baptism in the Spirit'. There are many paperbacks produced with testimonies to increased joy, peace, happiness, assurance, healing and so on. The pattern of such books is to tell what happened personally, and then attempt to theologize the experience in terms of the work of the Spirit. This stress on alteration of the personality is such a central theme of the charismatic movement that it is accused of using experience to justify theology, or of being an experience in search of a theology.

Another common example of a claim to achieve personality transformation is by the 'healing of memories'. It is a good example to consider, as it has the usual charismatic assumption that God's will is always to transform people into physically and mentally healthy, happy, and psychologically well-adjusted people.

When a person is ill and there is no evident physical healing even after prayer, this is sometimes explained by invoking a supplementary hypothesis that the illness is the expression of emotional trauma, and that this must be healed first.

> Deep hurts and fears often manifest themselves physically as back aches, headaches, skin rashes, asthma, and other illnesses. When we pray for healing of physical symptoms, we often see no change because we are praying for and expecting God to heal the symptom rather than to make us whole . . .
>
> We must realize that it is God's will for us to be whole and understand that our Father really desires to heal our attitudes.[33]

There is an assumption that God wants all Christians to have a standard level of personality and psychological smoothness. Whether this is justified or not is a separate issue; at this point what should be noted is that transformation of the personality (and the body) is perceived to be the norm.

There are indications that this expectation of personality transformation is moulded by particular cultural influences before being absorbed into the charismatic movement, for example in the widespread use of psychiatric language, aims, and therapeutic models. However, this essential characteristic of enthusiasm is still prevalent; transformation of the personality is expected as the norm.

A single minded desire to live a life of 'angelic purity', which tends towards a separation from all 'worldly' amusement

> After being deeply convinced of inbred sin, particularly of pride, anger, self-will and unbelief, in a moment they feel all faith and love, no pride, no self-will, no anger; and from that moment they have continual fellowship with God.[34]

Most enthusiastic movements are typified by a stress on holiness, particularly the revivals surrounding Wesley, Whitfield and Edwards. Whether this holiness is achieved or not is a different question, but a stress on and desire for holiness has often gone along with enthusiasm from the seventeenth century, through the 'Keswick' experience and into the present day.

As one would expect, this was also part of the Pentecostal claim for the nature of baptism in the Spirit.

> With the Baptism of the Spirit come such experiences as an overflowing fullness of the Spirit (John 7.37–39; Acts 4.8), a deeper reverence for God (Acts 2.42; Heb. 12.28), and intensified consecration to God and dedication to his work (Acts 2.42), and a more active love for Christ, for his word, and for the lost (Mark 16.20).[35]

This doctrine implies that holiness is the sudden result of a second experience:

> A crucial theme of holiness teaching is that there is available to believers, for them to possess immediately, a spiritual condition which is distinct from secular existence and markedly like the ideal life portrayed in the New Testament.[36]

Charismatic churches have not always been noted for holiness which is expressed in a concern for practical social issues, such as third-world poverty, or altering injustice in Western society. Charismatic holiness can tend towards a more introverted form. It is a spirituality which turns its back on the world, an attitude which is the consequence of a theology which sees the world as the kingdom of Satan. This world is what one is being saved from, one's neighbours are enemies of the kingdom, and Christians are soldiers who fight those who are not for the Gospel. It is a holiness which will consequently consist of purity in thought, of avoiding 'demonic influences' and steeping oneself in Christian literature and music, of the passive virtues of not doing or thinking the wrong things, and of feeling the right things. It is an introverted and subjective concept of being holy.

Though there do not seem to be any particular examples of groups which would claim 'impeccability', the stress on holiness is another 'enthusiastic' trait which, though of an introverted pattern, does still form a part of the charismatic movement and marks it out as being enthusiastic.

A *restoration of religion as an affair of the heart, as opposed to the outward form of traditional religion*

> I was to bring them off from all the worlds fellowships, and prayings, and singings, which stood in forms without power; that their fellowship might be in the Holy Ghost and in the Eternal Spirit of God; that they might pray in the Holy Ghost and sing in the Spirit and with the grace that comes by Jesus.[37]

It may well be the case that religion does deteriorate into outward formalism; certainly it was a recurring theme of the Old Testament Prophets. Whether true or not, though, the purpose at this stage is simply to observe that an attempt to restore the religion of the heart is another trait which links the charismatic movement with 'enthusiasm'.

One of the central foci of the charismatic movement is on the affairs 'of the heart', beginning with baptism in the Spirit. It is a movement in reaction to (what is considered to be) the dead *external* formalism of mainline denominations, and so its thinking and worship became dominated by *internal* conviction. Just as the Plymouth Brethren began in reaction against Anglican doctrine and liturgy, so the charismatic movement reacted against externals, such as buildings, theology or written liturgy, and these became comparatively irrelevant. What matters is how one feels about God.

This emphasis on the 'religion of the heart' is expressed in charismatic worship. What distinguishes these choruses from traditional hymns is an emphasis on feeling rather than theological content. When compared to hymns, they are intensely subjective. They are written to express a felt love for a personal God who has dramatically changed the worshippers. There is therefore an intimacy reflected in the music. Simply to look down the contents of a charismatic chorus book reveals that the largest section of songs will begin with 'I', or 'we'. They are characteristically intimate, personal, emotional, and subjective.

Charismatic renewal has a focus on the worship of the heart, and this creates an emotional intensity in worship. It is this, rather than particular musical styles, that makes its style of worship distinctive. It is another link between enthusiasm and the current charismatic movement.

The impatience of enthusiastic grace

'And if your faith be true, it will give you victory over sin and the devil, purify your hearts and consciences (for the true faith is held in true conscience), and bring you to please God, and give you access to him again.' But they could not endure to hear of purity, and of victory over sin and the devil; for they said they could not believe that any could be free from sin on this side of the grave.[38]

The immanence of grace is one of the fundamental traits of an enthusiastic movement. What I mean by this is that much is expected in *this* world, in terms of transformation of the personality; sense of well-being; material, social, mental and emotional prosperity. God is 'restoring the kingdom' on earth.

There are many examples of this impatience. The following quotation is from a magazine article entitled 'The right to choose', and tells the story of a couple whose son was seriously injured in a shooting incident. After casting out the 'Spirit of Death':

> The lord told me to lay hands on him and pray. I put my hands on his chest, and Linda put her hands on his head. The attendant squeezing the breathing bag looked at me, and I could read her expression. 'Don't you realize he's dead? There's nothing you can do . . .'
>
> I didn't pray loudly or boldly. My voice was shaky. I said 'Father, in the name of Jesus, we claim total healing for our son. We will not accept anything less, not because of who we are, but because of what your word says. We are standing on your word.'
>
> Then I talked to Satan. I took authority over him in the name of Jesus, and I called his assignment on my son null and void.[39]

What should be noted are the assumptions that perfect healing is a right which can be demanded, and that it can be expected immediately. The thrust of the article is that the Christian has the right to this at all times. All facets of God's Grace are for now, and one need wait for nothing.

Another example of impatient grace is an interpretation of the section of the 'The Lords Prayer' which says 'thy will be done on earth as it is in heaven'. On the basis of this it is argued that all that occurs in heaven is therefore the will of God on earth. As there are no tears, crying, pain or illness in heaven, it must be God's will that none of these things should occur now on earth. Therefore we should expect everything that is true of heaven to be true of life on earth. Clearly there are glaring problems with this view, not the least being the reality of death. However, for the present we are supposed to be simply observing traits, and this is one example of 'impatient grace' which links the charismatic movement to enthusiasm.

A set of gifts which allow a direct insight into God's will, with an accompanying degrading of human reason

> These things I did not see by the help of man, nor by the letter, though they are written in the letter, but I saw them in the light of the Lord Jesus Christ, and by his immediate Spirit and power, as did the holy men of God by whom the Holy Scriptures were written.[40]

> Reason is lost upon them, they are above it; they see the light infused into their understandings, and cannot be mistaken.[41]

There are two issues contained in this heading. One is the reliance on direct revelation, and the other is the degradation of reason. However, they are so closely linked together in an enthusiastic movement that it is more convenient to discuss these two traits in conjunction.

The degradation of reason will be examined in detail in the next chapter because of its crucial importance to understanding charismatic experience. What I want us to note here is that this is a distinct trait which typifies the whole spectrum of the charismatic movement, to varying extremes.

One example of this is in Wimber's approach to healing which depends on being able to hear directly what God wants to do in any particular situation.

> The most fundamental skill required for healing is openness to the Holy Spirit, emptying oneself and receiving his leading and power.[42]

> The only way, then, that one can believe God will heal in a given situation is to be told by God that this time he will heal; that is to his glory. We must depend on words of knowledge to provide us with the faith that God will heal.[43]

Listening to the Father is a noble starting point for prayer. However, this dependence on immediate revelation is directly linked to a departure from reason, because anyone would be foolish not to submit limited human reason to instructions given by God. Though such a claim to knowledge constitutes a circular argument, it does have its own internal logic, and this is why these two elements are always linked. Consequently the following statement from Wimber is predictable: 'God wants to woo us from our minds to our spirits,' you must 'watch out for evaluating what is going on with your mind'.[44]

The preference for direct revelation at the expense of reason is another enthusiastic trait which is evident in the charismatic movement. Indeed, I intend to argue that this is the fundamental trait of enthusiasm, and becomes the primary basis of its distinctive message. It is the key to understanding the whole development of enthusiasm.

The following passage from Peter Horrobin's book *Healing through Deliverance* is a good illustration of the process. It concerns a discussion on whether a Christian can have demons or not.

> In the middle of the debate this lady got up, came to the front, took over the microphone and ended the discussion with one of the most profoundly brief statements on the subject I have ever heard. 'Now listen' she said 'I'm your church secretary. I've been born again five years, and I didn't think I had a demon, but I did. And now I don't, so there!' With that she returned to her seat and saved the whole meeting hours of fruitless theological discussion! Christians certainly can, and do, have demons.[45]

The demonic raises many questions, but the point to note here is the basis on which the issue of whether Christians can have demons is resolved. Reasoned reflection is considered to be 'fruitless theological discussion', and the justification of the theology is existential.

> If our theology is inconsistent with the reliable experience of committed Christians who are ministering under the Lordship of Jesus Christ, and whose work is not in conflict with scripture, then we must re-assess the understanding we thought we had in such matters![46]

Horrobin (consistent with this basis) goes to extremes, and develops a complex doctrine of demons and their work, beginning with the Bible, but going well beyond this, based on the authority of experience such as putative conversation with demons during exorcism.

These particular views of demonology are by no means held throughout the whole charismatic movement. Even so Horrobin still gives particular expression to a general tendency, which is to give definitive authority to *experience* in preference to *reason*, and that is quite fundamental to all areas of enthusiasm and the charismatic movement.

The enthusiast has a new status and authority

> Sometimes it (enthusiasm) appears in their imaginary peculiar intimacy with heaven. They are, in their own opinion, the special favourites of God.[47]

A sense of status and authority is expressed in the charismatic movement; the charismatic Christian can consider himself not only a member of the chosen race and the kingdom of God, but that he is also on a different spiritual plane from traditional Christians.

There has been a gradual change in the style of worship as a result of this concept of status. Songs from within the movement express an exalted position. There is an emphasis on sonship, 'Royal sons of a royal king', 'You are a royal priesthood, a holy nation', and so on. In prayer one ought not to 'grovel and beg', but to claim with the authority to which one has a right. Just 'give the word'; '. . . the Lord said "Don't ever beg me for healing again."'[48]

This trait is a particular feature of Wimber's style. One should stand in the presence of the king in prayer, use authority, and expect God to act then and there. This theological emphasis has expressed itself in a curious change in hand movement in worship over the last ten years. Hands used to be raised with palms upwards in charismatic worship as a symbol of receiving from God. However, although they are still raised, increasingly they have turned round to face people, because the believer has come to see himself as a person who stands before God with authority and channels spiritual power. As in all enthusiastic movements, the believer comes to see himself as having a unique status and authority.

One reason for this sense of status and authority is rooted in the way that the relationship between Jesus and the Spirit has come to be understood. The power which was exercised by Jesus is seen as a gift of the Spirit. Because all Christians have also received the same Spirit, then they also are able to be like Jesus, not only in character, but in ability. They are to exercise the same authority that Jesus had over demons and illness, in fact going on to do even greater works. Indeed, this doctrine has been emphasized to such an extent that some charismatic theology has been criticized for devaluing the ontological uniqueness of Jesus, on the grounds that he can come to be seen merely as the prototype charismatic. Wimber has been criticized for this, because his view is that Jesus was only able to do miraculous works after the descent of the Spirit and that he was in some ways as dependent on the Spirit as are his followers.

One difficulty with this line of thought is that it devalues the understanding of the divinity of Jesus by heading towards an adoptionist christology. The other point to note is that it can also have the converse effect on the human side, in that it creates an increased sense of authority and status in the believer, because the believer comes to be, in particular areas, a co-equal with Jesus.

The charismatic movement shares the enthusiastic trait of procuring a new sense of status and authority for the believer.

Always the enthusiast hankers after a theocracy

Forward, forward, strike while the fire is hot! Don't let your sword become cold or blunt! Smite, cling, clang on Nimrod's anvil; cast their towers to the ground! as long as they remain alive you can never rid yourselves of the fear of men. No one can speak to you of God as long as they reign over you. Forward, forward, while it is still day; God is leading you, follow, follow.[49]

The desire for theocracy emerged in the radical house church movement.

> In the Restoration Churches claims are made not only to belong to the Lord's army, but also to be subjects of the King in a theocratic state. Theocracy is not unique in Protestant history, but it is rare in the modern world.[50]

This desire is evidenced in the 'theocracy of apostles', and also in the degree of ordering and control which is exercised over the lives of believers, to the extent of determining their jobs, the upbringing of their children, and even the decoration of the houses of the members. There have also been moves towards establishing schools for the children of the church.

The elders of the house church movement have had extensive control over the lives of the members of their groups (although this has been curtailed over the last few years). In principle, though, it is not the elders who rule. They are considered to have been put in authority by God, and therefore represent divine authority. It is an idea that was given increasing prominence in the house church movement in the late seventies.

At least in some parts, then, the charismatic movement hankers after a theocracy.

A group will sometimes retreat into the wilderness to set up its own society and sub culture

Until recently few charismatic groups had literally gone off in to the wilderness to be a separate society. Doing this, however, is becoming popular, for example within the developing 'Celtic' brand of spirituality, which brings with it a desire for the monastic.

Even without a physical separation from the world a detachment from society can be achieved quite effectively. The members develop their own culture which underlines their distinctive beliefs. This involves a distinctive use of language; and words such as 'teachings' or 'giftings', 'times of sharing'; or use of the 'charismatic subjunctive', 'would have you to know', 'would say to you', and so on; all reveal a distinct charismatic church culture.

The more radical a person's charismatic faith is, the more their lives will be entirely focussed on charismatic Christian music, books, events, language, conversation, and people. One could have holidays at Christian holiday camps and conferences, read charismatic novels, have charismatic decorations in the house, and charismatic car stickers on the back of the car. The desire for life beyond this can vanish before a tide of single-minded enthusiasm, and one would be hard pushed to find much literature from outside the church group in the homes of the more extreme members of a charismatic church.

This trait is also evident in the theological and historical awareness of many groups. The work of contemporary theologians, or the new hermereutic is so far removed from the thinking of most of those within the charismatic movment that it is not even worth considering.

The overall effect of this is to create as effective an isolating 'wilderness', in a cultural sense, as would be achieved by a move to some remote part of the country.

It is fair to conclude that the enthusiastic trait described as 'a separation from general culture' is present in the charismatic movement.

A conviction that the second coming is shortly to be expected

> Whatever you may think of yourself, you have certainly a heated imagination. 'Tis too evident to be denied that you too often take the motions of your own mind, for divine communications. A fragrant instance of this, you gave your hearers not long since, when you told them, it was impressed upon your mind, that the day of judgment was at the door, and you were as sure of it as of some things you then saw with your eyes. A thousand enthusiasts have deluded themselves and others with the same impression, looking upon it as a revelation from God.[51]

This conviction that the second coming is shortly to be expected is a strangely universal trait of enthusiasm. For example, according to Hans Huber in 1527, 'It is twenty-two months before the last day comes.'[52] A similar conviction was also a trait of the New England revival, and Edwards expected that The Awakening would be the start of a 'latter day glory'.[53] The roots of this idea are in an interpretation of the Bible which anticipates that the second coming of Jesus will be preceded by a huge outpouring of the Spirit. Edwards (rather unwisely!), pinned this outpouring down as occurring in America, partly on the questionable grounds of Isa. 60.9: 'Surely the Isles shall wait for me, and the ships of Tarshish first, to bring my sons from far.'

> It is exceeding manifest that this chapter is a prophecy of the prosperity of the Church in its most glorious state on earth, in the latter days.[54] This prophecy therefore seems plainly to point out America, as the first fruits of that glorious day.[55]

Curiously, every movement of enthusiasm throughout the centuries seems convinced that it is itself the last outpouring of the Spirit at the end of time. This expectancy has recently occurred among the 'Kansas City Prophets', who became associated with John Wimber, and have led large conferences in England. They expected an 'end time revival' to begin in England in October 1990, and came over from America to be a part of it. They have been described as 'The Omega Generation'; the last generation before the second coming. People increasingly talk about the 'Toronto Blessing' as being a last outpouring of the Spirit before the end of time.

As we have seen, an imminent expectation of the second coming is also an element of the Restoration movement. It is essentially pre-millenial in character, and sees itself as the 'Latter day rain' of the Spirit.

> The essential thrust of their adventism, however, is the establishment of a mighty kingdom of God prior to the return of Christ.[56]

This eschatological expectation links the current charismatic movement to enthusiastic movements.

The movement is accompanied by a host of abnormal phenomena

I had an opportunity to talk with him (Whitfield) of those signs which have so often accompanied the inward work of God. I found his objections were chiefly grounded on gross misrepresentations of matter of fact. But the next day he had an opportunity of informing himself better: for no sooner had he begun (in the application of his sermon) to incite all sinners to believe in Christ, than four persons sank down close to him, almost at the same moment. One of them lay without either sense or motion. A second trembled exceedingly. The third had strong convulsions all over his body, but made no noise unless by groans. The fourth equally convulsed, called upon God with strong cries and tears. From this time, I trust, we shall all suffer God to carry on His own work in the way that pleaseth Him.[57]

There are many descriptions of such abnormal phenomena from various parts of the current charismatic movement. For example, Dr Philip Seldon described a scene in 1990 where '. . . there were those who fell over, cried, screamed, laughed, appeared hysterical etc'.[58]

Dr David Lewis wrote an extensive report on a Wimber conference held at Harrogate on 3–6 November 1986. This report was published in the form of a book, *Healing: Fiction, Fantasy or Fact*. One chapter in this report is on 'Physical and Spiritual Phenomena'. A questionnaire which Dr Lewis distributed asked the respondents to indicate which of the following phenomena they had experienced.

a) Tingling in your hands
b) Hand or arm shaking
c) Stiffening of your body
d) Weeping
e) Laughing
f) Fluttering of your eyelids
g) Falling over
h) Screaming or shouting
i) Hot areas on your body

j) Changes in your breathing
k) Behaviour resembling 'drunkenness'
l) Other (please specify)[59]

In the returned questionnaires, phenomena noted in the 'other' category included electricity over the head, electricity in legs, a force field running up and down the body, an aura of tremendous power, waves of cold, sensations of weight in parts of the body, head being pushed back, out of the body experiences, visions of angels, experiences that seem demonic, stigmata, and about eighty others.[60]

The most recent outbreak of these phenomena is the 'Toronto Blessing' and the associated phenomena have been reported in the national press on frequent occasions. At Digby Stuart Roman Catholic College, for example:

> People were bouncing, convulsing, trembling, laughing, crying and falling over.[61]

The same events as have occurred in enthusiastic movements are still occurring, and still inspiring the same violent reactions as they have done throughout the generations. What should be noted here is that they are a part of the current charismatic movement, as they have been of all other enthusiastic movements before.

Conclusion

It is acceptable to conclude that some parts of the charismatic movement can be described as 'enthusiastic'. It is important to make this point, as many evangelical writers have such a romantic vision of the perfection and power of past 'revivals', particularly those in the eighteenth century, that they would not equate 'enthusiasm' or present day charismatic experience with them. Granted, they are different in degree, and in the extent of their influence, yet there are notable similarities. They develop in the same way, they are all composed of the same essential elements, inspiring the same opposition from the main-stream churches. There are particular cultural influences which change the apparent shape of the current movement. However the charismatic movement can still be understood properly as a manifestation of 'enthusiasm' in the way that the revivals were understood by their critics.

I have produced enough examples to show that the comparison between the charismatic movement and enthusiasm is not just a superficial resemblance. The differences between them are superficial, while the similarities are in the form of basic traits. 'Resemblance' would be too weak a word to use because what we have is identity.

This in itself opens up exciting possibilities, as it is possible to use the wide body of literature written on enthusiasm as a means of aiding understanding of the current charismatic movement. One bright wintry morning I was working in the Library at Glasgow University looking over the city to the hills around when I realized that I knew what John Locke thought about the charismatic movement! From this point on I knew exactly what the direction of my study was going to be, and it took some restraint not to run around shouting eureka! and hugging people. It is unfortunate that the chapter 'On Enthusiasm' in Locke's *Essay* is omitted from some abridged modern versions, because this implies that enthusiasm is an irrelevant anachronism which does not enter into discussion in modern times. In a church context, 'enthusiasm' is as relevant today as it was in 1690.

I shall be able to define and understand the movement more sharply in the next chapter by exploring the difficulties raised as I attempt to determine how this kind of experience could be assessed.

2

Criticism and Credulity

Practical difficulties in interpretation

Having established that the charismatic movement is in continuity with enthusiastic movements, we can move on to consider
some of the difficulties which need to be overcome if this bundle
of traits called 'charismatic' or 'enthusiastic' experience is to be
assessed. These difficulties will also clarify our understanding of
the nature of charismatic experience. The first two difficulties
under discussion are general problems which are created more by
personalities than by theological or philosophical issues. They are
useful to explore because they reinforce the similarities between
the charismatic movement, revival experience and enthusiasm
and also because these factors have an important impact on the
kind of criticisms that are made of charismatic experience.

Antagonism to enthusiasm

Opposition has accompanied every enthusiastic movement since
the beginning of church history. The opposition comes from two
directions: 'Almost always the opposition is twofold; good
Christian people who do not relish an eccentric spirituality find
themselves in unwelcome alliance with worldlings who do not
relish any spirituality at all.'[1]

Such opposition occurred as far back as the Montanist
movement. The New England Revival also inspired hostility from
its opponents. Charles Chauncey was a minister in the Boston
area during the Great Awakening. He argued in *Seasonable
Thoughts on the State of Religion in New England* that the
revival could not be a work of Grace, because there was no
evidence of love in those who were involved. Rather, Chauncey

considered there to be ungracious fighting between the different factions, and a condescending and judgmental attitude towards those outside.

In a section in which he quotes insults overheard in conversations, and a record of what different ministers had been saying in their sermons, Chauncey cites many examples of this 'uncharitable' attitude. There was certainly friction between those involved in the revival and those who were outside. For example, according to a 'Mr J.D—t'

> most of the clergy of the town of Boston were unconverted, and that if there were a bowl of poison which would destroy their bodies, he would advise any of his dearest Friends to drink it, as soon as go and hear them, or either of them.[2]

Eighteenth-century writers could turn invective into an art, but such attitudes are hardly conducive to fair and constructive assessment. This mutual antagonism is one of the more destructive elements which links the current charismatic movement with other enthusiastic movements through history. For example, in our own century, tongues have been described as 'Satanic gibberish', and Pentecostal Church Services as 'the climax of demon worship'. G. Campbell Morgan described the Pentecostals as 'the last vomit of Satan' and R.A. Torrey accused them of being 'founded by a Sodomite'.[3]

Another contemporary example of this kind of vitriol can be found in the work of Peter Masters. The tone and content of his writing is uncannily similar to that of Chauncey:

> Many in the charismatic fraternity have gone over to ideas and practices which come straight from pagan religions, and large numbers of young and impressionable believers have been spiritually corrupted in the process. Leading healers have arisen who unite the subtle tricks of the theatrical hypnotist with ancient occult techniques in their quest for results, and multitudes follow them.

> This is one of the greatest triumphs of Satan, our malicious enemy, whose aim is to bring into ridicule the Gospel of Christ. Satan is behind charismatic extremists.

Masters continues throughout his book to criticize every aspect of the charismatic movement, and includes personal attacks on people such as John Wimber.

> His conversion (described on a Signs and Wonders cassette tape) does not sound like the experience of a person under conviction, whose heart opens to an awareness of personal sinfulness, and then to glorious Gospel light. He tells of how he became a Christian while bawling hysterically in response to his wife's conversion.[4]

Not true

There is some acceptable criticism in Masters' book, but the problem is that it is written with such apparent venom that whether it contains acceptable criticism or not, it is inconducive to reasonable and persuasive assessment. If readers feel the same antagonism as Masters, then they will be confirmed in this view, not by a balanced appraisal, but by generalizations and parody. If readers disagree, then the ungracious tone is more likely to create a reaction against the criticisms contained in the book, the good along with the bad. All that is achieved is further polarization.

True

If we are to assess charismatic experience, then, we need theological tools more delicate than the sledge-hammer. We also need to understand and overcome this antagonism which the various movements of 'enthusiasm' often arouse, as it is a significant hindrance to a fair assessment.

Why is the mainstream church so hostile towards enthusiastic movements?

One reason for this hostility is that enthusiastic movements usually have a two-tier concept of spirituality, and this is inherently threatening. The focus of enthusiasm is on an experience of individual transformation. The words to describe this transformation may change; in the New England revival it was 'Awakening', for Wesley's followers it was 'Sanctification', and for the Pentecostals, it is 'Baptism in the Spirit'; but the two-tier concept of Christianity remains constant.

The difficulty is that such theology creates a sharp distinction between those who have the particular experience, and those who have not. There are people who are 'in', and people who are 'out', but ought to be 'in'. This is inevitably threatening to those who are outside the specific movement, and threatened reactions do not lend themselves to unbiased assessment.

This division between Christians is one of the awkward implications of the classical Pentecostal doctrine of 'Baptism in the Spirit' which has led 'Neo-Pentecostal' writers to develop doctrines which blur this distinction into a less blatantly two-stage form. This blurring is achieved by talking about the continual 'filling' of a believer by the Spirit throughout his life, rather than an emphasis on a categorical 'second blessing'.

Jonathan Edwards fought against the same difficulty in New England, and wrote a classic section in *Thoughts on the Revival* on the danger of spiritual pride, as this was seen as one of the great dangers of the Revival. However, one must suspect that it was an impossible fight for him, or for anyone else, to win. Even if a person is well motivated and managing to avoid spiritual pride, there is an inherent division between Christians in the notion of distinct second-stage experience. This division is evident in Edwards' description of the New England Revival's effect.

> A sense of the black ingratitude of true saints, as to coldness and deadness in religion, and their setting their hearts on the things of this world, has overcome the bodily frame. There was an experience of great longing that all the children of God might be lively in religion, fervent in their love, and active in the service of God.[5]

Edwards describes a person who has been catapulted into a whole new dimension of spirituality. However, this passage contains an implicit criticism of those who have not had this 'awakening' which is that: 'unless you have experienced the same as me, your faith is not "lively" or "fervent" enough'.

It may be true that the church does need reviving, but the point I want to make here is that, irrespective of the intrinsic value of the experience, a categorical second-stage experience is a notion which can bring out the worst in people.

Mutual antagonism is also aroused because 'enthusiastic' movements are usually formed in reaction to institutional religion. The Montanists reacted in this way, disillusioned with the institutionalized nature of the church. The same was true of the Vaudois, who broke away from the Catholic Church, as well as people such as the Methodists who (reluctantly) broke away from the Church of England. In current times, the house church movement has broken away from denominational structures which it sees as being 'old wineskins', or else made up of people who have chosen rather to 'remain in the wilderness' than to enter 'the promised land'. God is 'moving on', and it is up to those who are 'walking in the Spirit' to follow, or else be left behind. There is a 'restoration' of the true church occurring.

Such thinking contains overt and implicit criticism, and is bound to provoke antagonism. On the 'enthusiastic' side, there is a conviction of having discovered the way that a true church should be, as opposed to the old structures which have putatively grieved the Spirit. Adherents are thankful to have escaped the denominations, and can feel pity, or else smug superiority towards those who remain. On the institutional side, people tend to feel threatened by the new movement with its new leaders and irritated by the attitudes they perceive in the adherents, real or imagined. The reaction frequently is to take delight in the downfalls and problems of the opposite side's churches, and to find as much fault as possible with the new movement. Having been a minister in both traditional and charismatic churches I recognize a glint in the eyes of some people when they talk about how things have gone wrong in the alternative church down the road. Sometimes a person will attempt to feign concern, but underneath it can be detected a sense of smugness or triumph: 'I knew they would soon burn out.'

It is fascinating to find that people haven't changed in this respect. Edwards described this same tendency in 1735. People were:

> abundant in insisting on and setting forth the blemishes of the work; so as to manifest that we rather choose and are more forward to take notice of what is amiss, than what is good and glorious in the work. Not but that the errors committed ought to be observed and lamented, and a proper testimony borne against them, and the most probable means should be used to

have them amended; but insisting much upon them, as though it were a pleasing theme, or speaking of them with more appearance of heat of spirit, or with ridicule, or an air of contempt, than grief for them, has no tendency to correct the errors; but has a tendency to darken the glory of God's power and grace appearing in the substance of the work, and to beget jealousies and ill thoughts in the minds of others concerning the whole of it.[6]

This delight in running down the new movement allows pride to compete with pride. To denigrate the movement creates a degree of self-justification, and enables the institutional to feel superior to the shallow, frothy, emerging movement. The institutional side accuses charismatic people of knowing nothing of church history or theology, and accuses them of parasitism for taking members from the institutional church, which they are so keen to criticize. Enthusiastic pride competes with institutional pride. The results are defensive attitudes, with mutual criticism, suspicion and antagonism.

Edwards considered this to be one of most destructive errors which attend a revival of religion.

The first and worst cause of errors, that prevail in such a state of things is spiritual pride. This is the main door by which the devil comes into the hearts of those who are zealous for the advancement of religion. It is the chief inlet of smoke from the bottomless pit, to darken the mind and mislead the judgment.[7]

Another cause of mutual antagonism is that differences in styles of worship create strong reactions in people. This reaction is predictable because criticism of worship has continued, at least from the time of King David whose wife disliked his dancing before the Ark, and on through Mary who is criticized for pouring perfume on to the feet of Jesus. Criticism of worship continued in the church at Corinth, and on into the Iconoclastic Controversy, and the Reformation. In Edwards' time these same tensions arose, and he himself mentions that he was criticized for the length of services and for 'abounding so much in singing in religious meetings'.[8]

There is a curious reversal in one of today's tensions, in that Edwards faced criticism for 'making use of hymns of human composure', as opposed to exclusive use of the Psalms.[9]

In the present day, the complaint is that simple choruses (which are often drawn directly from the Psalms and Prophets) have a lack of theology in comparison to the 'depth' contained in hymns. There are strong feelings about doing away with the organ as the primary accompaniment to worship, and replacing it with a 'worship group' which will consist of people with a variety of instruments. In Victorian times the reverse situation occurred, and the objection to change was that church orchestras were being replaced by pipe organs.[10]

The issue of change in worship becomes particularly sharp when there is the impact of an enthusiastic movement, because parts of its worship will not only be different, but will be thoroughly disturbing to those who are more used to the order of a traditional church service. This factor created criticism and conflict in New England, and was described by Chauncey:

> Another bad thing, I must not omit to mention, is, the confusion that has been so common, of late, in some of our hours of worship.[11]

This 'confusion' consisted of 'shrieking, screaming, talking and praying, laughing, kissing, singing, jumping up and down, clapping hands, embraces by different sexes'.[12] Chauncey's eighteenth-century sentiment is echoed by Masters in the twentieth century, who describes charismatic worship as being a ploy of the devil 'to destroy all true worship', and 'render the church offensive to Him'. This is achieved through repetitive singing and exciting emotional sensations which are irreverent and irrational.[13]

The point I want to make is that differences over worship create strong feelings, and because enthusiastic movements bring their own distinct forms of worship, this will inevitably create powerful reactions in people and be an area of conflict with institutional religion.

A fourth reason why there is so much antagonism to enthusiastic movements is that they bring with them an experience of unusual power, which forces a reaction in people. This is frequently one of fear. This fearful reaction goes back to the beginnings of the church. The book of Acts describes people who were reluctant to join the disciples because of fear.[14] Fear has been a normal reaction to enthusiasm throughout church history, and been inspired by Montanist prophecy, Camisard child prophecy, Janetist convulsions, Methodist swoonings and Irvingite tongues. Given the dramatic nature of the phenomena which accompany enthusiasm, this reaction is no surprise.

Edwards described these powerful phenomena as follows:

> Extraordinary views of divine things, and the religious affections, were frequently attended with very great effects on the body. Nature often sunk under the weight of divine discoveries, and the strength of the body was taken away. The person was deprived of the ability to stand or speak. Sometimes his hands were clenched, and the flesh cold, but the senses remaining. Animal nature was often in a great emotion and agitation, and the soul so overcome with admiration, and a kind of omnipotent joy, as to cause the person, unavoidably, to leap with all their might, and joy in mighty exultation.[15]

Experience of this kind creates opposition. In Edwards case this came particularly from Chauncey, who described the 'Horrible scene' of these 'strange effects upon the body'

> such as swooning away and falling to the ground, where the persons have lain for a time, speechless and motionless; bitter shriekings and screamings; convulsion like tremblings and agitations, strugglings and tumblings, which, in some instances have been attended with indecencies I shan't mention.[16]

I do wish that Chauncey had told us what these 'indecencies' were! If we compare all of this with John White's descriptions of a 'Wimber' meeting we also see terror, fear, tears, trembling, shaking, laughing and falling to the ground.[17] The same objections to all of this crop up time and again. For instance:

> If he (the devil) can reduce a congregation of born-again people to superficial emotionalism, mystical mutterings, trembling

and weeping, experiencing of physical sensations, clapping and dancing and banal repetitive singing, then he will rob God of worship and render the church offensive to Him.[18]

There is no doubt that unusual phenomena occur. 'We should throw over all belief in human evidence if we denied it.'[19] Whatever the explanation of these phenomena may be, what must be noted here is that this kind of unusual experience is an element of an enthusiastic movement which forces people to react. It is a significant cause of fear, and of opposition to the movement as a whole.

Mutual antagonism is a by-product of enthusiasm, and this is built into the fabric of the situation to such an extent that it can never be fully overcome. Enthusiasm is too different, too dramatic, too much in reaction to the institutional and too sensational in its claims, for it ever to have a smooth relationship with the rest of Christianity, or indeed with the rest of society.

This is significant in our search for an acceptable means of evaluating charismatic experience, because the experience under assessment is set in a loaded context, where both the supporters and the opposition come from extreme, defensive, and biased positions. This is evidenced throughout the history of enthusiastic movements in the harshness of the criticisms made by both sides. It is important to be aware of this, and then to seek means of assessment which can avoid this danger by being as objective as they possibly can be, because the situation itself has inherent difficulties which mitigate against balanced and fair-minded appraisal.

The inherent credulity of enthusiasm

Enthusiasts are characteristically reluctant to engage in a critical analysis of what is occurring and this particular problem is crucial to understanding enthusiasm. This reluctance was noted as a general tendency by Knox.

More generally characteristic of ultraspiritualism is a distrust of our human thought-processes. In matters of abstract theology, the discipline of the intellect is replaced by a blind act of faith. In matters of practical deliberation, some sentiment of inner conviction, or some external 'sign' indicative of divine will, claims priority over all considerations of common prudence.[20]

The word 'enthusiasm' has developed in meaning over the centuries, but this irrational implication remained intact through to the nineteenth century. I would like to take us slightly further than Knox and argue that irrationality in religious beliefs was considered to be what makes an enthusiast by definition. This is suggested by the varied dictionary definitions of enthusiasm. For example, in *A New General English Dictionary* (1744):

the word is generally applied to those persons, who pretend to have divine revelation to support some monstrous, ridiculous, or absurd notions in religious matters, *and thereby takes away both reason and revelation*, and substitutes in the room thereof the groundless fancies and obstinate result of self-willedness, by using extravagant gestures and words, pretending to things not only improbable but also impossible.[21]

The heart of the criticism implicit in the word 'enthusiasm' is that it is a falsely based, unreasonable, and groundless conviction about a religious experience.

Chauncey made the same criticism of the New England Revival, denouncing what he saw as excessively emotional aspects of it, on the grounds that 'God doth work upon us as men, and in a *rational* way'. He objected to the lack of a *reasoned* assessment of experience and check on emotion. To his credit, Edwards accepted the best parts of Chauncey's criticism, and absorbed them into his own writings on the revival.

They looked upon critical enquiries into the difference between true grace and its counterfeits, or at least being very busy in such enquiries and spending time in them, to be impertinent and unreasonable; tending rather to damp the work of the Spirit of God than to promote it; diverting their own minds and the minds of others, as they supposed, from that to which God at such an extraordinary time did loudly call them more specifically to attend. The cry was, 'Oh, there is no danger, if we are but lively in religion and full of God's Spirit and lively of faith, of being misled! If we do but follow God there is no danger of being wrong! Let us press forward and not stay and hinder the good work by spending time in these criticisms and carnal reasonings!' This was the language of many, until they ran on deep into the wilderness, and were caught by the briars and thorns of the wilderness.[22]

That a movement is criticized because it is unchecked by reason is predictable during the age of enlightenment, and it is therefore even more significant that the same criticism was made of the Montanists in AD 220.

> *and they do not judge whatever statements are made by them according to reason*; nor do they give heed unto those who are competent to decide; but they are heedlessly swept onwards, by the faith which they place in these impostors.[23]

The same criticism has continued to be made through the centuries and into the current charismatic movement.

> Most charismatic healing meetings now begin with strenuous efforts to help people to *surrender their rational control* and behave in a completely uninhibited way. The goal is that worshippers should be 'open' to accept anything that happens, no matter how strange, inexplicable or bizarre it may be. *Rational control must at all costs be swept away* because nothing which occurs must be impeded, tested or evaluated by the intelligent mind, versed in the Word of God.[24]

This conflict between enthusiasm and rational criticism of experience has such a continuous line through enthusiastic movements that it is unlikely to be coincidental. It spans the history of the church, and touches such a wide variety of cultures and world views that it is not possible to see this trait as being merely the product of a particular paradigm. It suggests that there is an intrinsic leaning towards credulity within an enthusiastic movement.

What could be the reasons for this suspicion of reason, and the resultant subjugation of rational assessment?

One interesting reason why there is a suspicion of reason within the charismatic movement is that there are some rather distorted definitions of faith in use. One example can be found in the books of Colin Urquhart, where faith is treated as a mental effort to which God must respond if one fulfils the right conditions and tries hard enough to believe.

One of Urquhart's books, *Anything You Ask*, describes a difficult path, where those going along it must ensure that they manage to keep the right level of belief, without being distracted by questions, and making sure that they believe the right things in the right way, while claiming the right promises. In particular it is important to shut the mind to any doubts as these often have their origin in Satan.[25] If a person does this properly, then God is bound by his promises to give whatever is claimed. According to Urquhart, 'Faith is a continuous attitude of believing until the answer is seen', and; 'When you ask, you are to believe that you have already received the answer to your prayer.'[26]

The effect of developing this state of mind is that for 'faith' to be truly effective, it must be as unquestioning as it can possibly manage. 'Faith' is effectively put into opposition to criticism, reason, questioning, and doubt, and the quality of faith becomes inversely proportional to the evidence. To question would be interpreted as 'negative talk and ideas, always grumbling and complaining', which are destructive to faith.[27]

This is a barbed world view, in the sense that when one begins to think in this way, all views which differ from one's own can be put down to 'attacks of Satan' which are intended to undermine faith. This effectively locks a person into a way of thinking which excludes objective checks. Questioning becomes the antithesis of faith, while credulity becomes an integral and essential part of faith. One can ask critical questions or one can have faith, but one cannot do both. This creates a powerful resistance to assessment.

Another reason why there is a suspicion of reason within the charismatic movement is that the movement began partly in reaction to a perceived over-emphasis on doctrine, and is therefore in danger of putting an over-emphasis on experience.

This reaction against doctrine tends to lead to anti-intellectualism. Theological questioning becomes associated with a dead orthodoxy, and with people who are considered to know nothing of the power of the Spirit. Lack of theological background, and preaching without preparation become a virtue, and the emphasis is on the immediate inspiration of the Spirit. A preference for directly inspired knowledge is one of the characteristics of any enthusiastic movement.

> The enthusiast, however, supposes himself in possession of knowledge, the fanatic of directions, immediately (and miraculously) communicated to him from God himself; but neither of them produce any credentials to establish their claim.[28]

> The emphasis lies on a direct personal access to the author of our salvation with little of intellectual background.[29]

> A direct indication of the Divine will is communicated to him at every turn, if only he will consent to abandon the 'arm of flesh' – Man's miserable intellect, fatally obscured by the fall.[30]

In the context of the New England Revival, Chauncey said of those involved that: 'they deny the necessity of human learning, as a qualification for the work of ministry'.[31]

The same trait is currently evident in an attitude to the Bible which emphasizes 'what the Spirit is saying today' rather than exegesis of its precise meaning and application. This results in a wide use of typology, analogy and speculative interpretation, particularly of the Old Testament. Preaching is treated as being *itself* God's word for a particular time, rather than an interpretation of written revelation. It is one example of the claim to be a recipient of direct revelation being given priority over rational understanding.

A further reason for this suspicion of reason is that the way in which some spiritual gifts are practised makes it only possible for them to be tested in a subjective way. For example, if a person 'speaks in tongues', it requires an immediate interpretation. Because there is no cognitive content which can be rationally understood, if one intends to assess the 'tongue' one is forced back to dependence on one's feelings, hoping that they represent 'discernment'. The assessment is subjective, and unverifiable.

This difficulty in assessment is not confined to the charismatic movement, as it is a particular and rather sharp example of an issue which is raised by the whole doctrine of revelation. How does God reveal himself? How could one distinguish genuine revelation from non-genuine?

In a charismatic context, however, such a question becomes an immediate issue, often demanding an instant response. If a person believes that God is guiding by an internal impulse in some way, then he or she is forced into a quick judgment on whether some putative revelation is in reality from God, and this must be done without much in the way of objective testing.

> We may talk in rather exalted terms about the guidance of the Holy Spirit and the way he prompts our actions; but we need to remember that quite often obedience to the Holy Spirit's promptings is really a question of 'playing our hunches'.[32]

The same tendency was apparent in the New England revival, and was heavily criticized by Chauncey.

> Impulses and impressions, which have prevail'd among too many; their aptness to take the motion of their own minds for something divinely extraordinary, or to put those constructions upon common occurrences, which there is no ground for but in their own imaginations.[33]

Whether these impulses are nothing but imagination is the question which needs to be answered. The point here is that by its very nature, reliance on claimed revelation as a source of authority has such inbuilt problems in assessment that it would seem to demand a degree of credulity.

A more fundamental reason why rationality is subjugated within the charismatic movement is that the central focus is on experience, rather than theology. In this sense, it is an existential movement, with theology following in the wake of experience. It appears that we have the all-too-common situation of experience in search of a theology. This is put with more precision by Tom Smail:

> Dr James Packer once described the charismatic renewal as being a movement looking for a theology. If he had said that it was a movement desperately in need of a theology, I would have agreed with him straight away – but, looking for a theology, how I wish it were true![34]

There have been some theologians who have written about charismatic experience, particularly in a Roman Catholic context Muhlen is one of the best. In England however, apart from J. D. Dunn, few theologians have concerned themselves much with the charismatic movement, and the charismatic movement has not been widely involved with the theologians. Again, Tom Smail:

> I can remember in the mid-1970s, in my early days with the Fountain Trust, if you said the word 'theology' in a gathering of charismatic clergy, the chief reaction would be a scornful titter, as if they were saying, 'Now that we have been renewed in the Spirit, we do not need to bother with that sort of thing any more'.[35]

The same is true of the relationship between the charismatic movement and philosophy. While Locke and Leibniz were concerned about enthusiasm, writers such as Ayer, Quine and Chisholm have had no interest in such issues. As for those who make such dogmatic claims to knowledge within the charismatic movement, there is little evidence of a concern for philosophical epistemology.

Within the charismatic movement reason and theology may be used in defence of an interpretation of experience, but essentially the experience has priority, and is justification in itself. It would be unfair not to point out that this can also be a common trait of evangelicalism generally. 'You ask me how I know He lives, He lives within my heart.' However we should expect a focus on experience to have particular emphasis within the charismatic movement, because it is a trait which has always been a strong aspect of enthusiasm. This kind of experience tends to make people feel certain:

> It is found by abundant experience that those who are led away by impulses and imagined revelations are extremely confident; they suppose that the great Jehovah has declared these and those things to them; and having his immediate testimony, a strong confidence is the highest virtue. Hence they are bold to say, I know this or that – I know certainly – I am as sure as that I have a being, and the like; and they despite all argument and inquiry in the case.[36]

This existential basis of certainty is the issue here because it is a basis for knowing which relegates critical reflection to a secondary place.

Edwards was so disturbed by this trait that he argued that it is essential to lose this confidence in experience to avoid running into heresy and unbridled enthusiasm. This abandonment of confidence in one's own experience:

> is what all the most glorious hypocrites, who make the most splendid show of mortification to the world, and high religious affection, do grossly fail in.[37]

What I want to point out is the fact that today, an exactly opposite path is advocated by Wimber. Because experience is so convincing, his suggestion is that experience (of healing) should be the primary basis of evangelism, and so 'programme' evangelism is rejected in favour of 'power' evangelism. Rational checks are deliberately subdued, because they are seen as being inhibitive to the experience of God. The essence of his argument is that one must escape from the limited, rational, Western world-view by making a 'paradigm shift', because doing this will free one to experience supernatural power. His justification for this subjugation of reason is partly biblical, but also pragmatic, in that he argues that evangelism is considerably more effective when it is used in third-world cultures. Wimber argues that the reason for this evangelistic success is that non-Westerners are uninhibited by rational restrictions, and are therefore open to supernatural experience such as healing.[38]

Now this provides us with two quite contrary positions on the relationship between experience and reason. Experience is so convincing that, according to Wimber, *reason* should be subdued, so that experience is enabled to persuade. According to Edwards, *experience* should be subdued as a basis of confidence, because it will mislead with a falsely grounded sense of certainty. Edwards describes the effect that this trust in experience has on believers:

> they have looked upon it (supposed revelations) as a sure promise from the most high, which has made them most ridiculously confident, against all manner of reason to convince them to the contrary, and all events working against them.[39]

It does seem that Edwards has the more persuasive arguments on this issue. If experience is unchecked by reason, it could lead one to be more open to God, at least if a person were to happen on to a 'genuine' experience, even though their understanding of it was misguided. This would simply be a lucky shot in the dark. However, it also leaves one open to any form of experience whatever its source, as well as being unprotected from heresy, or nonsense, or able to test by objective truth. It is consequently a short step from here to a superstitious and pre-enlightenment world view, with no measured distinction between faith and stupidity, and nothing to distinguish between good or bad experience, nor to prevent the good from being driven out by the bad. The subjugation of reason in favour of experience by Wimber inevitably leads to a situation where there are inadequate objective checks on the way that experience is understood.

Conclusions

Charismatic experience has diverse forms, and is difficult to define, but it is crucial that this mix should be properly understood and assessed. If it is not, then there are strong historical grounds to suppose that the good will be driven out by the bad, with consequent confusion and disillusionment. This is bad for the whole church, charismatic or not. Failure to distinguish between what should be kept and what should be rejected is the primary cause of the eventual disintegration of an enthusiastic movement

The task is especially difficult because there are particular factors which mitigate against fair assessment in this context. The strength of opposition which arises in response to an enthusiastic movement leads to polarized positions and vicious criticism. This means that assessment is frequently offensive, or defensive, but almost always biased.

Another difficulty in assessment is that the focus on experience, if left unchecked, will naturally lead towards a subjective concept of truth. This in turn gives critical reflection a secondary role, and an uphill struggle in the face of overwhelmingly convincing experience. Enthusiastic movements are therefore instinctively credulous, and in constant need of rational assessment. The task is difficult, but it is crucial to develop criteria which are capable of providing fair criticism.

Agree with lots of this argument

3

Theological Surf-Boarding

Conceptual difficulties in interpretation

Criticism and credulity are interesting features of enthusiasm, but the three I shall be looking at in this chapter are even more so. We are approaching closer to the heart of the issue which needs resolution: if someone claims that he has had an experience of God, how can one tell if he really has or has not?

It is difficult to assess charismatic experience because experience is almost invariably equivocal

> In all my life I have met only one person who claims to have seen a ghost. And the interesting thing about the story is that that person disbelieved in the immortal soul before she saw the ghost and still disbelieves after seeing it. She says that what she saw must have been an illusion or a trick of the nerves. And obviously she may be right. Seeing is not believing. [1]

This is a useful example of what occurs when people are confronted with an unusual experience. They interpret what they see in the light of what they believe, and rarely do they interpret what they believe in the light of what they see. This form of hypothesizing is essential if we are to retain any form of coherent understanding of what we experience. If we did not think in this way, then the whole framework with which we interpret the world could be upset by every unusual occurrence, say, for example, when a magician brings a rabbit out of thin air. It would be insane to be so easily persuaded; it would wreak havoc with our web of belief. This process implies that seeing is not believing. What we see and what we believe are different.

The same process operates with enthusiastic experience. Say, for example, one heard that a person had suddenly got out of a wheelchair and started walking, claiming that he had been healed miraculously. There are many possible interpretations of this experience. If one has a strong charismatic belief, then the inclination will be to say that this was caused directly by God. If one were opposed to the use of charismatic gifts, but still within a Christian paradigm, then one might attribute the 'healing' to Satan's deception. If one were unsure of the nature of what occurred (either believing, or with no belief in God), then what has occurred could be described as false diagnosis, spontaneous remission, exaggerated reporting, my eyes deceived me, a con trick, and so on. A person with Humean persuasions would dismiss the 'miracle' on the grounds that there is always far more evidence to disbelieve a reported miracle than to believe. Even if one could not find any alternative rational explanation, then this failure to explain could be attributed to limited human understanding of the working of the mind and body. One day we will have a proper scientific explanation. The meaning and cause of the experience are equivocal.

St Paul suffered the effects of this ambiguity in his unsuccessful attempts to preach at Lystra (Acts 14.1–20). He and Barnabas healed a 'cripple', but the response from the locals was not to see this as a sign which pointed to Jesus. Instead they incorporated what they saw into their own world view and concluded that Paul and Barnabas must be Hermes and Zeus. The next stage, when the onlookers had been persuaded of an alternative interpretation by some Jews from Iconium and Antioch, was to stone Paul and Barnabas. This was hardly the effect that the miracle was intended to create!

This illustrates again that one's interpretation and understanding of experience is not only influenced, but is frequently determined by one's presuppositions. Experience therefore cannot be understood properly in isolation from theology or philosophy. What one believes before an experience will, in most circumstances, determine what one believes afterwards. The experience itself is equivocal.

A charismatic example of this process would be a sick person

who claims that the mental torment he is suffering is being caused by demonic oppression. One way to assess this claim would be to start with the belief that there are no such things as demons. One must therefore dismiss the sick person's diagnosis as, say, the product of a superstitious world view; an expression of his unbalanced mind and an unhealthy psychological state. The charismatic viewpoint is ruled out from the start. On the other hand, if one does believe in demons who do directly inflict such oppressive mental states on individuals, then the disturbed person could possibly be correct in his understanding.

Which of these two interpretations of the evidence is correct will depend firstly on whether there are, in reality, demons who afflict people, or not. The possibility that the cause was demonic would be ruled out if one has atheistic presuppositions. The charismatic believer, however, considers that demonic activity is a possibility, and is confirmed in this view by the evidence of his own mental anguish. Which of the two options a particular person chooses as the explanation will be determined by which beliefs he brings to the experience.

This implies that there is a whole context of understanding which needs assessment along with the particular experience. In the case of charismatic experience the complexity of the task is compounded by the fact that the varying interpretations of events are not straightforwardly different theories, but can be situated in contradictory paradigms, theistic or atheistic. As one attempts assessment, one therefore is forced away from what seemed like a straightforward experience into an assessment of a person's whole view of reality. A materialistic or theistic view of existence? Are there supernatural beings called demons, or are there not? To choose the correct explanation of the experience also means choosing the correct paradigm.

This is a crucial issue with many implications which we must attempt to resolve. There are many ways to interpret experience, and the sheer complexity of the problem makes assessment difficult, because it is so easy to evaluate on the basis of equivocal evidence, and in a way which is dominated by one's own assumptions.

This needs to be pointed out because the intricacies of this issue do not seem to be widely appreciated in much of the literature which is concerned with the charismatic movement. This lack of understanding is shown by the kind of arguments which are used in support of and in opposition to charismatic experience. A charismatic interpretation of events claims support on grounds such as the success of physical healing, experience of psychological well-being, physical manifestations in worship, material prosperity, gifts of the Spirit, etc. etc. However, although they are being used in some contexts as though they are individually reliable indicators of a work of the Spirit, they are all ambiguous 'signs' which point in at least two directions at once, and often in many more. The same events may be reinterpreted in reductionist terms as being hysterical behaviour, the product of sexual frustration, caused by brain washing techniques, self delusion, hypersuggestibility, or mental instability. Experience alone is an equivocal criterion which provides an unreliable indication of an encounter with God.

Charismatic experience is consequently being both opposed and supported on the basis of unjustified, superficial and misleading criteria. It is therefore important, first, that these simplistic mistakes should be pointed out, and then secondly if possible, that something more reliable should be put in their place which can do justice to the complexity of the issues involved. An experience in isolation from an interpretive framework is equivocal, and how an experience is understood is related to a whole view of reality.

How can one distinguish between genuine and false 'revelation'?

If an enthusiast has a revelation from God then he clearly ought to submit to it. This is reasonable, as it would be foolish or ridiculously arrogant to prefer limited human understanding over something which has been revealed by an omniscient and infallible God. This is why the enthusiast is so certain in his faith; he believes what he says because he is sure that his beliefs have been revealed to him by God.

In practice, though, there is a big problem. 'How do you know which "revelations" are given directly by God and which are not?' John Locke pin-pointed this as the crucial issue facing enthusiasm:

> The question then here is: how do I know that God is the revealer of this to me, that the impression is made on my mind by his Holy Spirit, and that therefore I ought to obey it? If I know not this, how great soever the assurance is that I am possessed with, it is groundless, whatever light I pretend to, it is but enthusiasm.[2]

Since we need to test and sift experience/claims to revelation, it would seem that we need some standard which must be applied to experience/revelation from another authority, and to which that experience/revelation must submit. According to Locke, experience and revelation have to be interpreted by reason, because reason is a God-given faculty which ought always to be used in this context.[3]

However, if the enthusiast is a conveyer of divine revelation then his words represent absolute authority. The problem is that if this *is* ultimate authority, then how could it be verified except with reference to itself? According to Karl Barth:

> God's revelation has its reality and truth wholly and in every respect . . . within itself. Only by denying it can we wish to ascribe to it a higher or deeper ground. Obviously the adoption of revelation from the vantage of such a ground, different from it and presumably superior to it, eg. an affirmation of revelation in which a man previously set up his conscience to be a judge of it; can only be achieved by denying revelation.[4]

This was written as a defence of revelation which came through Jesus, but the principle of Barth's argument is still applicable to our discussion in this context. If Barth is right, then there is little that can be said to the enthusiast who claims revelation, except perhaps to see if his words are contradicted by the words of Jesus, or by biblical revelation. There is no way that it could be externally assessed on other grounds such as reason, and therefore our present attempt to sift rationally claims to be the recipient of revelation are a denial of revelation as a source of truth, and a blasphemous waste of time.

If this attitude were adopted, however, it would leave no external means of assessing conflicting claims to revelation. One simply has to believe that such and such *is* revelation from God, and no objective verification can be provided. This presents extreme difficulties in practice, because it effectively provides intellectual support for the contradictory claims of every belief system.

> Every conceit that thoroughly warms our fancies must pass for an inspiration, if there be nothing but the strength of our perswasions, whereby to judge of our perswasions; if reason must not examine their truth by something extrinsical to the perswasions themselves, inspirations and delusions, truth and falsehood, will have the same measure, and will not be possible to be distinguished.[5]

The difficulty which consequently needs to be overcome if we are to assess charismatic experience, is (a) to contradict Barth, and much twentieth-century theology, by attempting to justify the *assessment* of claims to absolute authority, and (b) if this can be done consistently, to find some extrinsic criteria on which the assessment could be based.

The problem of the criterion

On top of this theological problem, there is a significant philosophical difficulty to be faced. Attempting to justify one's beliefs using some extrinsic criteria may sound simple, but in practice it leads us into a basic problem in the branch of philosophy concerned with the theory of knowledge.

The traditional approach to the issue of determining what can be known has taken the form of a 'foundational' structure. What I mean by this is, if you want to construct a foundational argument, then you have to begin by looking for something about which you can be sure ('I think therefore I am' was Descartes' suggestion), and then build up your tower of knowledge on this basis. As long as the foundation is sure then you can end up with all kinds of other knowledge which is true by implication. This epistemic model has been dominant in Western philosophy, from Descartes and Locke and on through the work of Hume. It also underlies the work of Russell and Ayer in the twentieth century.

In recent years, however, it is an approach which has been increasingly rejected, (a) because these foundational truths have turned out to be rather less self-evident or incorrigible than they seemed to be and (b) because many apparently quite justifiable beliefs (such as cause and effect) fail to reach this standard.

This has led to considerable turmoil within philosophy, because there is no consensus on which models could provide a satisfactory belief system, or agreement on where the starting point could be to provide a structure for knowledge, nor agreed criteria which could resolve this problem. There is effectively an impasse throughout the field. We do not know how to know.

Interestingly, this difficulty is parallelled in the theological stream of thought which sought to argue from supposedly incorrigible foundations that it is reasonable to believe in God. This attempt to justify Christian belief goes back at least as far as Aquinas and the 'five proofs' of God's existence, and continued to dominate scholastic thought in the Middle Ages.

Demonstrating that belief in God has rational foundations, however, has not been a priority of theology since those pre-Reformation times, because of the Reformers' antipathy to this approach, and also in the wake of Immanuel Kant's work. Indeed, in the twentieth century, foundationalism in the form of natural theology has been rejected outright, even aggressively by theologians such as Bultmann, Barth and Niebuhr.

> If you really reject natural theology you do not stare at the serpent with the result that it stares back at you, hypnotizes you, and is ultimately certain to bite you, but you hit it and kill it as soon as you see it.[6]

These theological issues mirror the current problems in philosophy because it is an argument about how to justify a claim to knowledge. The scholastic approach was determined by a particular method which was used to determine what ought to be counted as knowledge; claims to know (about God) were built on a rational *foundation*. The approach of Barth (and the Reformers) was quite the reverse, as he began with knowledge that he was certain had been revealed by God, and submitted rational methods to what was 'known' to be true. A method which did not reach the required conclusion would for this reason be considered to be unreliable. The issue is the same as the philosophical problem, in that it hinges around the same question. Should you begin with what you 'know' or with a method which can determine what counts as knowledge?

The nature of the philosophical issues which underlie this debate are focussed rather succinctly into two questions by the philosopher R.M. Chisholm.

> We may distinguish two very general questions. These are, 'What do we know?' and 'How are we to decide, in any particular case whether we know?' The first of these may also be put by asking 'What is the extent of our knowledge?' and the second by asking, 'What are the criteria of knowing?'[7]

If one knew the answer to either one of these questions, then it would seem quite possible to go about finding an answer to the other. The difficulty, however, is that if we have no answer to the first question, then there would seem no way of answering the second. And if we have no answer to the second question, then there would seem no way of answering the first.

It is such an intransigent problem that Chisholm states:

> 'The problem of the Criterion' seems to me one of the most important and one of the most difficult of all the problems of philosophy. I am tempted to say that one has not begun to philosophize until one has recognized how unappealing, in the end, each of the possible solutions is.[8]

In the context of this book, this implies that there are no generally-accepted criteria in philosophy or theology which can be applied specifically to the kind of religious experience we are discussing, and used to assess a cognitive claim which is made on the basis of that experience. Consequently, if we intend to use some external criteria as a means of assessing charismatic experience, then we will need to discover and justify our own approach to what constitutes warranted belief in the context of charismatic experience.

Some implications of chapters 1 and 2

(i) The first point is that the charismatic movement can be described as an enthusiastic movement. The word 'enthusiast' has become ambiguous in terms of approval or disapproval. However, this eighteenth-century label 'enthusiasm' is a useful description of these many movements, as it implies a subjugation of reason as a source of knowledge, in favour of a supposedly self-evident experience. This is also a tendency throughout the charismatic movement. When a group of people consider that claimed experience of God is the source of authority rather than reason then that group can be called 'enthusiastic'.

Because of restrictions of space, our survey of such movements must be limited. There are doubtless differences between these varied movements: in the historical settings, in the experience of the people involved, difference of emphases, difference in impact, and so on. This does not undermine the comparison, however, as there are still striking areas of similarity. Indeed, the fact that the traits discussed above do recur in such differing settings, cultures, and eras of history makes the evident similarities between them even more curious and in need of explanation. The onus is on the reader if it is to be demonstrated that the differences are of such significance that the comparison is meaningless.

Even if it were to be conceded that these movements are so different that they were unconnected to the charismatic movement, it would not destroy the main thrust of this book. This is because the aim is to establish how *in principle* amorphous enthusiastic or charismatic experience of *any* sort could be assessed. However, it is helpful to see that such experience has been and still is a significant part of church history, and that it is important to assess it with care. The context provides useful insights into how charismatic experience may be appraised, and also indicates the kind of dangers to be aware of in an attempt at assessment.

(ii) The next thing that I would like to point out is that the charismatic movement is in reality a series of movements. This would be a more accurate understanding of what is occurring at present. There are numerous forms of 'teachings', which come and go, often associated with strong 'charismatic' figures. Initially charismatic experience took the form of Pentecostalism. This moved on to 'Neo-Pentecostalism' and developed from there, with leaders coming into fashion for a few years and then fading in influence. The idea of 'authority' with elders and apostles became an issue for a while as a result of the modern house church movement. Healing remains central, and yet takes on differing approaches. Initially there were Pentecostal healing crusades, then Neo-Pentecostal crusades. 'Praising God for all things' was a subsequent idea, then 'healing of memories' came along, to be swamped by the popularity of Wimber's theology. Leanne Payne's style is a current model which has had some prominence.[9] The 'Toronto Blessing' provides dramatic current instances of the phenomena of enthusiasm.

The music of the movement develops just as quickly, with songs becoming soon too dated to use in worship. It has to move fast to keep up with changes in theology.

What are the reasons for this rapid change? There could be a cultural influence at work which mirrors a society that is used to rapidly changing fashions and styles in every area of life. An unchanging form of worship and understanding would be an anomaly in the twentieth century. Rapid change could therefore reflect a degree of conformity to the spirit of the age.

Communications are more developed than in the past, with an explosion of Christian books, magazines and conferences. As a result, one is aware of charismatic claims from all parts of the world, and one wonders why all these exciting reports of the miraculous are not occurring in one's own church. The effect of this is to create a sense of dissatisfaction about, or at least a longing for, what can seem to be a form of Christianity that has got it right, in some part of the world. This awareness helps create a desire for something different and new.

There is also a theological impetus to this rapid change, particularly in the doctrine of revelation, since effectively the Bible is not the entire source of authority where charismatic gifts are used. While the Bible is generally seen as being the basic standard, more than this is needed because the question is often asked, 'What is God saying to this generation?' The story of the Exodus is given prominence, and since God is 'moving on', it is up to his people to follow where he is leading. Consequently, there are books which develop an elaborate system of 'ministry', in the form of healing, dealing with demons, evangelism, and so on. These start with the Bible, but go beyond this into new ideas. The Bible is a base for, but is not seen as an exhaustive revelation, and so there are few theological limits to the shape or doctrines of the movement.

The most fundamental cause of this rapid change, however, is philosophical, as the existential nature of the charismatic movement means that its theology is continuously developing in the light of experience. As I have argued, experience is equivocal or ambiguous, and consequently, it can point in numerous directions, effectively leaving scope for endless reinterpretation. There is no limit to the experiences on which one can focus, and on the interpretations of them which can be incorporated into the theology of the charismatic movement. This allows for the retention of the basic enthusiastic qualities, while offering the chameleon-like ability to adapt to different backgrounds. This is why we can observe distinct parallels in the basic traits of different historical movements.

The effect of all this is to create a rapidly-developing series of movements. The particular churches which have managed to keep the impetus of charismatic experience going over an extended period of time have been able to surf on the top of each new wave of ideas, but have also managed to mount the next wave before the former one hit the rocks and died. Consequently, the basic elements of enthusiasm remain, but are given fresh and recurrent impetus, from a variety of new experiences, personalities, and doctrines. These also alter the superficial structure of the movement.

(iii) The next point I would like to argue is that enthusiasm has a single fundamental cause. The impression these movements give at first sight is of a jig-saw which seems to assemble itself repeatedly, using the same essential pieces. This pattern may vary in size, and be assembled in differing locations and times, but it is essentially the same picture. To see it like this, however, would be somewhat bizarre; jig-saws do not generally assemble without a cause, and so we are led to questioning what it is that creates this pattern.

Perhaps there is a clue to the reasons for this repeated pattern in that the majority of enthusiastic movements were cradled in Reformation Protestantism. Could it be that 'enthusiasm' is simply the result of returning to the Bible as sole authority, subjugating reason and tradition to it, and attempting to build a spirituality which is as it was in the beginning? This is certainly the claim of many 'enthusiasts'.

This is attractive, as all of the elements we have discussed could be explained as originating in an attempt to be true to the New Testament, in all its vigour and supernatural power. However, while this offers a partial explanation for some enthusiastic movements, it is not enough in itself.

Firstly, since numerous movements aim to live according to the Bible, but do not take on the character of enthusiasm, there must be other element(s) at work. Indeed, those who oppose enthusiastic movements from within the church do so primarily on the basis of biblical authority. One can reasonably conclude that something else distinguishes the non-enthusiast from the enthusiast, at least in the way the Bible is interpreted. Secondly, there are enthusiastic movements which do not maintain a 'fundamentalist' attitude to the Bible (such as Quietists, or Manicheans). A particular approach to the Bible is therefore not inherent in enthusiasm.

Knox gives us a hint that the primary cause of enthusiasm is rooted in a distinctive epistemology. Enthusiasts claim that knowledge is directly revealed by God, rather than achieved by rational argument.

Basically it is the revolt of Platonism against the Aristotelian mise en scène of traditional Christianity. The issue hangs on the question whether the divine fact is something given, or something to be inferred. Your Platonist, satisfied that he has formed his notion of God without the aid of syllogisms or analogies, will divorce reason from religion; it is a faculty concerned with the life of the senses, and nothing assures us that it can penetrate upwards; he is loth to theologize.[10]

To typify Platonism as being anti-rational is rather a caricature; however, if this is taken to refer to an *intuitive* insight into truth, then we can see what Knox means by this statement. One can forgive Knox's use of words here, and retain the sense of his analyses without his particular way of expressing it. This provides a valuable insight into enthusiasm. Existentialism v. rationalism may be a better description, or experience v. theology; subjective truth v. objective; knowing a person rather than knowing about a person; I thou or I it.

In other words, we are back into this basic tenet of enthusiasm discussed earlier; in essence, it is a reaction against a logical, rational approach to God. The ultimate is discovered in experience rather than in rational thought. This enthusiastic response to reason was at work throughout the 'revivals' of the eighteenth century, echoing the contrast between Plato and Aristotle, and it anticipates Kierkegaard's reaction against enlightenment rationalism in favour of personal truth.

This concept of knowledge is enough of a starting point to generate all the other elements of enthusiasm. It is the key to understanding the recurrence of this mix. There is a reaction against the institutional church with its 'dead' doctrine and rationalism. Reason is limited, even mistrusted, and essentially subjugated in favour of claims to have revealed truth which is the product of an immediate experience of God. The enthusiast is experiencing direct revelation in the form of an 'inner light', or the 'gift of prophecy', or 'words of knowledge'. Such people prove difficult to argue with, because their views are held with the conviction that they have divine authority.

Those (such as Locke) who oppose enthusiastic beliefs do so on

the basis of biblical authority and reason. However, the enthusiast is unimpressed by such argumentation because he uses a
different, and existential means of justifying his beliefs. The
enthusiast answers rational objections to his belief by saying 'but
I *know* this is true, I experienced it'. In other words, there is a
basic difference in authority. The traditional Christian wishes to
assent to a rationally-argued objective proposition in the form of
doctrine, the enthusiast prefers to have a putatively direct
experience of revelation.

With this focus on experience as a source of certainty and
authority, there is a stress on internal feelings, and on the
transformation of the personality. The traditional Christian
writes books on doctrine which seek to understand God through
reasoned analysis of the Bible (systematic theology and objective
truth). The enthusiast, however, writes numerous books of
'testimonies' about experience, and then seeks to justify these
claims so that others can share the same experience. The former
emphasizes doctrinal truth, the latter focusses on transformation
of the personality.

This leads to distinct change in forms of worship as they
become more and more subjective. Consequently the criticism is
made that charismatic hymns do not have the depth of theological truth that traditional hymns have (an objective concept of
truth, with God revealed in rational propositions, analogies, and
doctrines). The enthusiast replies that these new songs express
how he feels about God, and that he experiences God in worship
(subjectivity in reaction). The former wants to sing about truth,
the latter wants to experience truth as he sings.

If my hypothesis is correct, we ought to suspect that this subjugation of reason in favour of experience could also be the cause
of the host of abnormal phenomena which accompany enthusiasm. It is quite possible to argue that the phenomena
associated with enthusiasm are the product of hypnotic techniques which depend for their effect on by-passing the rational,
critical faculty of the mind.[11]

All of this apparent power and direct experience of God creates
a sense of separation and authority. The enthusiast knows God,
has direct communication with him, and even speaks with divine

authority. This may lead to theocracy. Why should one submit to the will of a 'fallen' government when one has direct access to God?

When it comes to exegesis, the traditional approach is to understand the literal meaning of the text, find out what it meant in its day, and explain what it means to today's society. So a revealed truth is discussed rationally. This, however, is not enough for the enthusiast, who wants to know what God is saying today through a particular passage, regardless of what it might have meant originally. This leads to speculative and subjective interpretations of the Bible, and also to a preference for speaking without notes, a method generally considered to be more directly 'inspired'. The traditionalist does an exegesis and understands rational truth derived from past revelation, but the enthusiast wants an immediate experience of revelation. This is Platonism in preference to Aristotelianism, if we use Knox's terms.

The overall effect of these differences is so dramatic, disturbing and threatening to the institution that it invariably leads to opposition and distrust.

Problems usually arise because such a subjective basis of authority is uncontrollable, and any objective authority which could be appealed to has been devalued. One person feels that God is saying 'do this', and the other feels he is being told to 'do that'; but the problem is that there is no higher authority than divine authority, and both are convinced that this is what their own views represent. This creates a need for strong leaders (Apostles and Elders in the case of the current movement), but even these will not hold things together. There will eventually be schism within the groups under their own 'charismatic' leaders, who have their own particular styles and doctrines. Each considers his own view to be justified by the experience it represents.

As usual, when it comes to experience, what one believed before usually determines what one believes afterwards, and the direction from there on. Consequently, enthusiasm can take a wide variety of different forms; evangelical, mystical, monastic, antinomian, or rigorist. Someone who begins with a 'fundamentalist' attitude to the Bible will end up as an evangelical charismatic; a Catholic may find that his charismatic experiences leads to a deeper reverence for Mary; a mystic will find inner light as a guide. In a former generation Wesley thought that his Arminianism was validated by the effect of his preaching, and Whitfield thought that his Calvinism was justified by the phenomena that accompanied his preaching.

The outer shape and colour of the movement is therefore moulded by the enthusiasts' varying preconceptions, but the essential traits of enthusiasm begin to develop when Platonism reacts against Aristotelianism; the subjective reacts against the objective.

Enthusiasm is therefore better thought of as a plant which can grow given the right conditions, rather than as a jig-saw. An existential approach to truth, in reaction to a cerebral, institutional religion, is the starting point. When this is combined with a desire to return to the primitive spirituality of the church and with a 'charismatic' leader who is strong enough to lead people through the process, it is enough to set the process in motion, which leads to evangelical enthusiasm.

If we test this against a modern enthusiastic movement, we can see this process at work. In the 'Wimber' movement, we have a strong leader whose starting point is a rejection of what is described as a rational Western world view, on the grounds that it is unChristian and inhibiting to spiritual life and power. Subjective truth reacts against the objective:

> The conception of truth proper to the Christian mind is determined by the supernatural orientation of the Christian mind . . . truth is supernaturally grounded: it is not manufactured within nature.[12]

This is added to a desire to return to the life of the early church by taking the Bible literally without filtering out supernatural events which would reinterpret them on non-supernatural ways. The modern church ought to be performing the same kind of miracles as did Jesus and the disciples.

> Even as a successful pastor, I remained uneasy, always sensing

the gap between the early disciples' experience as they spread the gospel of the kingdom of God, and what my congregation experienced.[13]

From this starting point, Wimber emphasized a message that one ought to see the same healing in the present-day church as at the beginning, and stuck with it until dramatic things began to happen. All of the other enthusiastic traits look after themselves from this point forwards.

(iv) What is the relationship between these two ways of knowing? This connection between objective and subjective knowledge is a massive issue which impinges on many significant areas of thought, the nature of truth, existential or objective, along with all the theological implications of this, such as the place of propositional revelation, and the experience of God.

As we have argued, the essence of the difference between traditional Christianity and enthusiastic belief lies in their varying ways of knowing. The former puts the stress on rational, propositional, doctrinal truth, and the latter puts the stress on experience.

It should be noted that it is a stress, rather than an absolute difference, because both sides have aspects of the other's focal emphasis in them. The traditional church has the experience of conversion, worship, joy, prayer, and so on. The charismatic movement develops doctrines on the basis of the Bible which are used in support of its experience. The situation resulting from this is consequently not one of two wholly separate systems of thought, but rather one of two poles with a gradation of attitudes between. Neither side attains the (normally impossible) state of being purely objective, nor purely subjective; and both sides are weakened if they neglect what is helpful in the other.

The difference is therefore not absolute, but there is a difference of priority. For traditional evangelicalism, it is biblical revelation reasonably assessed which is the arbiter of claims to know, and the basis for determining which experiences should be expected. For the enthusiast this is reversed. Experience is subsequently justified, and theology modified in its light.

The significance of this order is that there comes a point where experience becomes authoritative, and it is at this point that we have the beginning of enthusiasm. It runs parallel in this respect with liberal approaches to theology, which will allow doctrine to be altered if it seems unreasonable. For the enthusiast, experience performs the same function, as it becomes the primary basis of the knowledge of God. The Bible is filtered through experience; and reason, where it is used, is used in justification of a view which begins existentially. Therefore it could be justly described as an 'existential liberalism', as opposed to a 'rational liberalism', because in both cases something other than biblical revelation is given primary authority.

This does, however, imply that it is unjust to dismiss the charismatic movement as being dualist in its concept of truth. First, because there is a gradation of attitude rather than an absolute distinction between objective and subjective truth; but secondly, because each of these views do have their own internal consistency. If one assumes that the Bible is inherent revelation, then one is forced to submit one's limited understanding to words which come from God. This is not dualism, it is a distinction between what is considered to be absolute revealed truth, and human ability to know the truth. Enthusiastic epistemology has its own admittedly circular, but nevertheless consistent, structure. The question it must answer is how the initial claim to be the recipient of direct revelation could be justified.

Conclusion

Enthusiasm, then, has as its character a mix of elements, but it is a mix which is explicable, because it is created from a single starting point. By definition, enthusiasm begins when experience is given priority over reason as the basis of truth. Revelation and truth are consequently considered to be primarily subjective. This is the fundamental characteristic of enthusiasm, and is a trait which is evident enough in the charismatic movement for it to be classed as enthusiastic.

This starting point is, ironically, the beginning of its own destruction, because the lack of objective control on its development means that it is generally unable to resist the pull into the

dominance of subjectivity. Its theology and experience consequently have the capacity to grow and mutate malignantly,
eventually destroying the movement itself.

If we are to assess charismatic experience, then it is this central
epistemology which ought to be our focus. The other traits of
enthusiasm are comparatively superficial in that they are
symptoms of a way of knowing. It is a distinctive epistemology
which is the essence of enthusiastic belief.

4

I Dreamed God Spoke to Me?

Sifting through the options

The term 'religious experience' is applied to an extraordinarily wide jumble of experience. It is used to describe 'enthusiastic' visions, emotional upheaval, feelings of awe, a 'sense' of God's presence, physical sensations, deep convictions and beliefs, mysticism, or a sense of the numinous. Inner consciousness of guilt or forgiveness are each described as 'religious experience', as is physical healing, a sense of moral duty, near death experiences or simply a response to music, or attendance at church. Indeed any experience seems to be capable of a religious interpretation. What is seen by one woman simply as a rainy day is seen by another as God's bounty in constantly providing us with food by means of watering plants. What is seen by one person as just a headache is seen by another as the devil's attempt to keep him away from church that day. What is seen by one person as bumping into another fellow he knows in the street is seen by another as God's 'trying to tell him' that he ought to 'deal with' his dislike of that person.

Some people claim to have an experience of God which is directly communicated to the mind or emotions, and others have a religious encounter through the senses; touch, smell, sight, taste and hearing. Sometimes it is a purely emotional phenomenon, and at other times there is a didactic content.

'Enthusiasm' is one collection of religious experiences which form a part of this wide Christian history. The experience of the enthusiast is characteristically that of being confronted by something of overwhelming significance and power, something which seems to have come from outside the natural world. It presents itself to the subject as being self-authenticating, and with such force that the individual is unable to doubt either the reality of what has occurred, or his own interpretation of it. He simply 'knows', and what's more, is often certain.

Thus far we have been able to link the experiences of the enthusiast with the current charismatic movement. The similarity between the two is not just a superficial resemblance, because both are shaped by the same deep-rooted and determining feature, which is a distinctive epistemology. To paraphrase Locke, there is a substitution of reason by claims to revelation. This is the heart of enthusiastic belief, and this is also what must be assessed if charismatic experience is to be interpreted properly.

There are parts of the charismatic movement which differ from 'enthusiasm' in that they give experience less over-riding authority. However, the kind of assertions which are to be appraised here are the true enthusiastic ones which begin with a claim to experience revelation from God, and on the basis of that, subjugate all other claims to knowledge in favour of this putative revelation.

This varied mixture of phenomena and interpretation creates an almost endless stream of questions. Is it possible for a person to experience an infinite God? How could God be confined to an experience? How could one be aware of an 'object' so vast and transcendent? Or, conversely, how could one *not* be aware of an 'object' so vast and transcendent? How could one be aware of an experience apart from through sensory input? How does God make himself 'felt'? How can information about him be picked up and processed? How should such experience be understood? What is the relationship between experience and interpretation? Should religious experiences be classed as basic perceptions? Could any experience not have been caused by an omnipotent God? How should belief relate to experience?

It is quite impossible to answer all of these questions in the space of a short book, and so I am focussing on one crucial question. Suppose people claim to be encountering God in their experience, how could it be known whether they really are?

This question contains an implicit assumption that there are two distinct aspects of a religious experience which need to be examined, and these also need to be related to each other in a satisfactory way.

(a) The first distinct aspect is the uninterpreted, raw, or basic subjective emotional/physical experience of the person.

(b) The second aspect is the implication or conviction that there is some actual object involved with this in the outside world. What does this experience imply? How should it be understood?

The crucial nature of this distinction between the objective and the subjective and the difficulty of distinguishing between the two aspects was illustrated rather elegantly by Thomas Hobbes.

> For if a man pretend to me, that God hath spoken to him supernaturally and immediately, and I make a doubt of it, I cannot easily perceive what argument he can produce, to oblige me to believe it . . .
>
> *To say he hath spoken to him in a dream, is no more than to say he dreamed God spake to him; which is not of force to win belief from any man*, that knows dreams are for the most part natural, and may proceed from former thoughts; . . . So that though God Almighty can speak to a man by dreams, visions, voice, and inspiration; yet he obliges no man to believe he hath so done to him that pretends if; who, being a man, may err, and, which is more, may lie.[1]

There is a distinct difference between the statements 'God spoke to me in a dream,' and 'I dreamt God spoke to me.' The former assumes the intervention of an objective God in the dream, the latter implies a purely subjective experience which does not entail the existence or intervention of any external being. The problem we are facing is how to decide which of these two possibilities is occurring in a specific instance: suppose a person claims to be encountering God in his or her experience, how could it be known whether he really is?

In the next three chapters I will be sifting through the possible epistemological options which could be used to resolve this question. This claim to knowledge is central to enthusiasm, and this is what must be assessed if it is to be appraised properly.

Enthusiasm and strict rational proof

It ought to go without saying that one should not claim rational proof in a strict sense for one's interpretation of a religious experience. In practice, however, it does need to be said because we are examining a context where people talk of 'unassailable proof' and claim to know with certainty.

There are a number of reasons why it is not possible to provide strict rational proof for one's interpretation of a charismatic experience.

(i) When you want to understand charismatic experience, there are always alternative explanations to choose from, often dependent on fundamentally different ways of looking at the world. This creates the particular problem of attempting to talk across a gulf created by differing presuppositions. In such a setting, it is not even possible to agree on what all the facts are, even before these 'facts' are interpreted in a specific way.

(ii) On top of this, if one is attempting to examine a subjective experience, such as a claim that God has spoken inaudibly, it is practically impossible to demonstrate, in anything approximating to a conclusive manner, what is the precise cause of such experience. We do not have perfect access to the mind, nor is there anything but a very incomplete understanding of what it is or how it functions. The nature and the cause(s) of such experience are therefore uncertain and inaccessible.

(iii) By the time one comes to understand an experience, the experience is a historical event, and history can only yield results which are, at best, tentative and open to revision. In so far, therefore, as an understanding of an experience is based on a historical event, it can never achieve certainty.

(iv) One is also dealing with the evidence of a witness, as the observer, or the subject of an experience. A witness can always be questioned and doubted, and therefore such evidence could never be in principle beyond question.

(v) An attempt to argue that God was the cause of an experience presupposes that the existence of God has been *proved*, in the strictest sense of the word. This in itself has not been done. Certainly the traditional arguments for the existence of God are all questionable in a variety of ways.

Even though these objections could be met to some extent, they are enough to show that a claim to divine inspiration of an enthusiastic experience could not be proved in any strict sense. The result of this is that if an enthusiast claims to 'know' with certainty, then in the generally accepted sense of the word, he is deluded. Even if he is right in what he believes, he has no grounds to claim rational certainty for his claims to knowledge on the basis of strict rational proof.

To be fair, however, points (i) – (iv) are not just applicable to theistic understandings of events, as they would also be applicable to any other definite interpretation of experience (such as a psychological or sociological understanding of an occurrence). No one could justifiably claim to have rational proof for their particular interpretation.

It is also true that each of these five reasons why rational proof could not be provided would also imply that a specific interpretation of charismatic experience would be equally difficult to disprove rationally. One could argue against a claim to certainty *per se*, but given the nature and inaccessibility of the data, it would be equally difficult to prove that a specific understanding was false (at least, excluding hopeless internal inconsistency).

There is a need for some other approach than an attempt to 'prove' a particular interpretation of a charismatic experience. Are there some other methods available? I am now going to explore three possibilities which could be described as 'methodist'. I do not refer to the followers of John Wesley, but I am using the word in the way in which it was used by Chisholm in *The Problem of the Criterion*. This is with the sense of an epistemology which gives priority to some *system* or criteria which determine what can and cannot be known. The opposite of this is a 'particularist' method which begins with a claim to know *already* and then develops criteria which fit in with the way that reality is putatively known to be. Empiricism and rationalism are both fitted into the 'methodist' category by Chisholm because he maintains that they begin with criteria, and these are used to assess the epistemic status of particular beliefs. What can be known is determined by a method.

Enthusiasm and empiricism

One example of an empiricist approach is in the work of John Locke. His 'method' was to see the way in which a claimed case of knowledge is derived from sensations, and if it is to be considered credible, then it must be in a proper relationship with sense experience.

It must be mentioned that there is far more to Locke's epistemology than pure empiricism and 'methodism'. Along with the empiricist presuppositions, Locke also has strong rationalist elements in his writing. The development of his case in *The Essay* was also intended to gain credibility by fitting in with seventeenth-century views about what is knowledge. This is a 'particularist' approach working along with 'methodism'. Locke's epistemology is therefore rather more complex than these two simply polarized categories may imply. However, the main point still holds good, and it is fair to say that Locke does make progress towards knowledge by beginning with a criterion, and this criterion is used to assess a claimed case of knowledge. This is his method.

Happily for us Locke applied his epistemological tests specifically to enthusiastic claims; they failed to meet his standards for knowledge. The thrust of Locke's argument is that the enthusiasts' claims to be recipients of prophecy and to encounter God in their experience should not be accepted, because there is not sufficient evidence to justify the belief that this is what has really occurred. In the absence of supporting evidence, whatever the content of such experience and 'revelations' may be, there are no grounds for believing that they do have divine origin. This is the reason enthusiastic propositions were dismissed by Locke: 'Enthusiasm fails of evidence, that the Proposition is from God.'[2]

Locke allows for the possibility of divine revelation in principle, but contends that such revelation will be accredited by other features. So, for example, we are entitled to believe that Jesus gave genuine revelation because his words were attested by real miracles.

> But the truth and obligation of its [the New Testament's] precepts have their force, and are put past doubt to us, by the evidence of his mission. He was sent by God: and his miracles show it; and the authority of God in his precepts cannot be questioned. Here morality has a sure standard, that revelation vouches, and reason cannot gainsay, nor question; but both together witness to come from God, the great law-maker.[3]

Here Locke argues that what has been revealed by Jesus is genuine revelation on the grounds that it has been attested by the miraculous acts of Jesus. The evidence for this is so strong that its verity is 'put past doubt'.

This is just one application of Locke's main point, however, because the final decision on whether any particular claim should be considered as true revelation can only be made in the end by reason. It is *reason* that requires adequate evidence if it is to give assent.

> Revelation must be judged of by reason. He, therefore, that will not give himself up to all the extravagances of delusion and error must bring this guide of his light within to the trial. God when he makes the prophet does not unmake the man. He leaves all his faculties in their natural state, to enable him to judge of his inspirations, whether they be of divine origin or no. When he illuminates the mind with supernatural light, he does not extinguish that which is natural. If he would have us assent to the truth of any proposition, he either evidences that truth by the usual methods of natural reason, or else makes it known to be a truth which he would have us assent to by his authority, and convinces us that it is from him, by some marks which reason cannot be mistaken in. Reason must be our last judge and guide in everything.[4]

This priority which Locke gives to reason is also evident in Book IV in the chapter on 'Faith and Reason'.

... no Proposition can be received for divine revelation, or obtain the Assent due to all such, *if it be contradictory to our clear intuitive knowledge.* Because this would be to subvert the Principles, and Foundations of all knowledge, Evidence and Assent whatsoever: And there would be left no difference between Truth and Falsehood, no measures of Credible and Incredible in the World, if doubtful Propositions shall take place before self-evident; and what we certainly know, give way to what we may possibly be mistaken in.[5]

The section following this argument in the *Essay* is the chapter 'On Enthusiasm', and it applies this theory of revelation attested by 'marks which *reason* cannot be mistaken in', to enthusiastic belief. Consistent with what has preceded this chapter, Locke's main criticism of the enthusiastic method of knowing is that it is a *substitution* of reason in favour of revelation. If Locke is right to argue that reason is the main test of revelation, then in rejecting the primacy of reason the enthusiast has been left with no means of establishing the truth of *any* revelation, and no means of distinguishing the true from the false.

It is not the principle of claiming to know on the basis of revelation from God that is questioned by Locke at this point. Rather the inquiry is centred on the same question at issue here, i.e. if someone claims that his or her words have been revealed by God, how could one know whether they were from God or not?

In theory revelation is capable of supplying 'Assurance beyond Doubt, Evidence beyond Exception'.[6]

The reason whereof is, because the Testimony is of such an one, as cannot deceive, nor be deceived, and that is of God himself. This carries with it Assurance beyond Doubt, Evidence beyond Exception. This is called by a peculiar Name, Revelation, and our Assent to it, Faith: which as absolutely determines our minds, and as perfectly excludes all wavering as our Knowledge it self; and we may as well doubt of our own Being, as we can, whether any Revelation from GOD be true. So that Faith is a settled and sure Principle of Assent and

Assurance, and leaves no manner of room for Doubt or Hesitation.[7]

There is, however a significant proviso on this certainty, and it is this proviso which distinguishes Locke's 'certainty' at this point from enthusiastic certainty:

> Only we must be sure, that it be a divine Revelation, and that we understand it right: else we shall expose our selves to all the Extravagancy of Enthusiasm, and all the Error of wrong Principles, if we have Faith and Assurance in what is not divine Revelation. And therefore in those Cases, *our Assent can be rationally no higher than the Evidence of its being a Revelation*, and that this is the meaning of the Expressions it is delivered in.[8]

To summarize Locke's main criticism of enthusiasm: the enthusiast *substitutes* a claim to revelation in the place of reason. However, because reason is the primary test of what should be considered as revelation, the enthusiast thereby loses both reason and the capacity to recognize true revelation. Because of this substitution, he has failed to meet the standards of 'empiricism' as developed by Locke.

This is not the last word on the issue, however, because there are significant difficulties with empiricist criteria for determining what counts as even a reputable claim to knowledge. These criteria were given such dogmatic authority that according to Hume, if one were to find a book in the library that did not conform to the empirical criteria, then it should be discarded:

> If we take in our hand any volume; of divinity or school metaphysics, for instance; let us ask, Does it contain any abstract reasoning concerning quantity or number? No. Does it contain any experimental reasoning concerning matter of fact and existence? No. Commit it then to the flames: for it can contain nothing but sophistry and illusion.[9]

The epistemological difficulties inherent in this attitude are already well documented, and so we will simply mention two which are especially significant, and of particular relevance to our current quest.

The first is a problem with the empiricist criteria themselves, as they are very broad and far reaching, yet at the same time could be accused of being arbitrary because of the problem in defining how they are generated. The difficulty is that Locke never did explain precisely how he arrived at these criteria. Exactly what their relationship to the sensations should be is consequently open to question.

This is a strange starting point for a method which proceeds so cautiously and meticulously from there on, as it is difficult to see what reasons could be given to justify the use of these particular criteria rather than some others. The criteria do not meet their own standards.

The second is a problem in the application to reality, because so much is excluded from the system that there is little of any value left. It becomes impossible to be sure whether sensations even represent any external reality. All that one can know is that one has certain sensations here and now.

For example, as I write this page I believe I am in a small cottage on the moors at the far northern tip of the Outer Hebrides overlooking the Atlantic. There is nothing but sea between me and the arctic. The sky is wild and huge. The whole place is hopelessly romantic. However let's assume that I have just accepted these empiricist criteria. Now when I look out of my window I am not entitled to say any of these things, I can't even be sure that what I am looking at is 'sky'. The most definite statement I could manage would be 'I am being appeared to bluely'. This much would be fairly sure, but on a bad day I could even question this!

The empiricist criteria were pushed to extremes by Hume, and when this was done it became obvious that when treated as the sole arbiters of what can be known, they provide no basis for believing much that would seem to be evidently acceptable. They would exclude, for example, belief in the existence of your own body, or any other physical things such as houses or trees even less atoms and sub atomic particles or other minds. If one is ruthlessly consistent with the empiricist criteria, it even becomes inconsistent to believe in cause and effect.

Constructionist theory

It is consequently not just enthusiasm that fails to reach empiricist standards because the same is true of many other beliefs which would seem to be quite justifiable under normal circumstances. Hence, to say that enthusiastic belief does not live up to such criteria is not enough to determine conclusively the epistemic status of enthusiasm. The empiricist criteria themselves would seem to be inadequate as a means of establishing what can be known.

Amen

Enthusiasm and Rationalism

If Rationalism is considered to be another form of 'methodism', then one finds that there are analogous problems here too. At this point I am using 'Rationalism' in the narrower sense of the word as referring to a group of seventeenth and eighteenth century philosophers who are typically represented by Descartes, Spinoza and Leibniz. One could characterize this kind of Rationalism as the belief that it is possible to obtain an understanding of the nature of what exists by reason alone. One has a faculty of intuition which enables one to 'see with the eye of the mind'. This faculty provides 'clear and distinct perceptions' which can supply knowledge which is beyond doubt (at least if God exists in perfection and is of 'being no deceiver').[10] Rationalism has a concept of knowledge which forms a single system, deductive in character and all inclusive. Everything is in principle explicable.

Descartes is considered to be the first modern Rationalist. As a mathematician his ambition was to introduce into philosophy the rigour and clarity of mathematical thought. In order to do this he set out to doubt everything in the hope of arriving at something indubitable on which his philosophy could be built. This was what he claimed to have achieved in his famous *cogito ergo sum* because to doubt one's own doubting would be absurd. This was the foundation from which he aimed to deduce other propositions, each following with the same self-evidence. For the most part Descartes argued for the view that 'ideas' are innate, and that they could not be derived from experience or 'sensation'. This is why Rationalism is normally seen as being in opposition to empiricism. Descartes' views would also be a denial of enthusiasm with its claims to know based on experience.

Spinoza and Leibniz adopted the same method of knowing as Descartes, although they started in different places. Rather than beginning with the existence of self, Spinoza began with the existence of the universe, or 'substance' as he called it.[11] Leibniz began by distinguishing those truths which are 'necessary' from those which are 'contingent', and built from there.[12]

Leibniz specifically addressed enthusiasm in *New Essays on Human Understanding*. In it he begins with a summary of Locke's views on this issue by putting Locke's words into the mouth of a character called 'Philalethes'. 'Theophilus' replies to him with the views of Leibniz. Consequently we are in the delightful position of being able to discover what Leibniz's views on charismatic experience would be.[13]

> Todays 'enthusiasts' believe that they also receive doctrinal instruction from God. The Quakers are convinced of this, and their first systematic writer, Barklay, claims that they find within themselves a certain light which itself announces what it is . . . but this image of corporeal light, aroused when their minds become overheated, brings no light to the mind.[14]

Leibniz outlined some of the phenomena which are interpreted by enthusiasts as indications that their experience is a real encounter with the divine. Interestingly, all of these criteria were also mentioned by Chauncey and Jonathan Edwards who wrote in the context of American Enthusiasm within twenty years of Leibniz's comments.

> Some half-wits, when their minds become over-heated, become worked up, form conceptions which they did not previously have; they become capable of saying things which strike them as very fine, or at least lively; they astonish themselves and others with this fecundity which is taken to be inspired. They possess this ability mainly in virtue of a powerful imagination aroused by passion, and a fortunate memory which has copiously stored the turns of phrase of prophetic books which they are familiar with through reading or through

hearing them talked about . . . And I know a visionary who rests his claim on his capacity to speak and pray aloud almost all day long without tiring or running out of words. There are people who, after practicing austerities or after a period of sorrow, experience a peace and consolation in the soul; this delights them, and they find such sweetness in it that they believe it to be the work of the Holy Spirit.[15]

Leibniz points out the ambiguity of such means of assessment. He also outlines some examples of enthusiastic conviction; a woman who claimed to be able to dictate words which came from Jesus, a man who was convinced he was immortal, a variety of prophecies that turned out to be erroneous, and so on. Interspersed between these anecdotes one can gather the means of assessment that Leibniz was suggesting.

Sometimes Leibniz proposes that an alternative interpretation may be preferable:

It is certainly true that the contentment we find in contemplating God's greatness and goodness, and in carrying out his will and practicing the virtues, is a blessing from God, and one of the greatest. *But it is not always a blessing which needs renewed supernatural assistance*, as many of these good people claim.[16]

Leibniz gives some examples of prophecies which have turned out to be false. If this falsehood can be demonstrated then one has effectively provided a means of external assessment:

When these people are sincere in their behaviour they are hard to bring around; sometimes having all their schemes go to ruin sets them straight, but often this comes too late.[17]

Pointing out a contradiction with other enthusiastic claims to revelation is also suggested by Leibniz as a means of persuading the enthusiast to abandon his views.[18] Leibniz accepted Locke's central argument that revelation can only be accepted as being true if it is accompanied by marks which reason cannot be mistaken in, such as miracles.

The way these people clash with one another should further convince them that their alleged 'inner witness' is not divine, and that other signs are required to confirm it ... Their disputes show, at the least, that their inner witness needs outer verification if it is to be believed, and they should have to work miracles before they would deserve to be accepted as inspired prophets. Still, such inspired utterances could bring their proofs with them; this would be the case if they truly enlightened the mind through the important revelation of some surprising truth which was beyond the powers of the person who had discovered it, unless he had help from outside.[19]

Leibniz has written his own (rather loosely constructed) comments on Locke's *Essay*, and added some examples of enthusiastic experience. He seems to agree with all points of Locke's analysis and criticism of enthusiasm.[20] Locke has such strong Rationalist elements in his work that on this issue he has written the strongest available Rationalist approach to enthusiastic belief.

In the case of both Rationalism and empiricism, the status of a claim to knowledge is determined by a particular method, and they both make similar criticisms of enthusiasm.

The confidence that Rationalist principles had in reason and proof tended to be exclusive, because claims not based on Rationalist principles would be considered as being based on false premises, and so could not constitute knowledge. Consequently Rationalism excludes other claimed ways of knowing, such as empiricism would allow. It would also be a denial of 'knowledge' based on mystical or charismatic experience, claims to revelation, intuition and so on. Each of these ways of 'knowing' would be ruled out because they were not built on incorrigible foundations, and they did not conform to the Rationalist methods. According to Rationalism, none of these alternatives should claim to provide knowledge because this 'knowledge' would be based on sense experience, which would rule out the claim in principle. Enthusiastic belief which was rooted in experience, and substituted reason in favour of claims to revelation, would be nonsensical as far as Rationalism was concerned.

As with empiricism, however, this is not the last word on the issue because there are also significant problems with rationalist epistemology. There is a long history of challenges to Rationalism from empiricists such as John Stuart Mill, and from logical positivists such as A.J. Ayer and Rudolph Carnap. Rationalism is criticized through linguistic analysis. The possibility of being certain of any 'truths' has been widely attacked. The Rationalist rejection of knowledge which comes from experience seems to be out of touch with reality. The concept that ideas are innate has been questioned by Leibniz on the grounds that 'innate' ideas do not manifest themselves before experience. So much apparent 'knowledge' is excluded that a question is raised about the acceptability of rationalist methods.

Consequently it is not just enthusiasm which fails to meet Rationalist criteria for determining what can be known, and failure to satisfy Rationalist requirements is not enough to determine whether enthusiastic claims to know make any sense or not.

Enthusiasm and rationalism

There is another use of the term 'rationalism' which is relevant to our search. This is not meant in the specific sense that Descartes, Spinoza, or Leibniz were Rationalists, but in a broader sense in which superstition, prejudice, habit or other unreliable methods of belief formation are rejected in favour of subjecting ideas to a reasonable appraisal. If one were to take such a rationalist approach to religious experience, then the onus is on the philosopher or theologian to determine, as far as he can, whether there is adequate evidence to justify a religious claim.

For example, if a rationalist were to hold justifiably a belief in God, then he would need to answer many questions satisfactorily. Is the concept of God coherent? What reasons are there for such belief? What are the arguments against theistic belief? After sifting through the evidence he comes to a decision whether, on balance, the case for God's existence is strong enough to warrant its acceptance.

A good recent example of this kind of approach can be found in Richard Swinburne's three books, *The Coherence of Theism*, *The Existence of God* and *Faith and Reason*. He briefly summarizes his method of approach in the introduction to *The Existence of God*: 'The book is written in deep conviction of the possibility of reaching fairly well justified conclusions by *rational argument*.'[21] According to Swinburne the existence of God can be supported through rational argument, but only up to a limited point. 'I shall, however, argue that although reason can reach a fairly well justified conclusion about the existence of God, it can only reach a probable conclusion, not an indubitable one.'[22] The implications of this with regard to Christian faith are explored by Swinburne in his later book *Faith and Reason*.

Although Swinburne is discussing the rationality of believing in the existence of God, the methods used to explore this issue are still applicable to a search for ways to assess charismatic belief, because in both situations one is making a choice to interpret reality in a theistic or non-theistic way. In choosing theism over atheism a person is attributing a specific cause to the existence of all that is, and in choosing enthusiastic belief over any of the alternatives, one is attributing the cause of a particular experience directly to God. The question raised in both situations is how such a claim can be justified, and the epistemology of each choice is analogous to the other.

Such rationalist approaches to religious belief have been criticized recently because of their 'classical foundationalist' epistemology. The same criticism is also applicable to the empiricism of Aquinas and Locke, because both rationalism and empiricism have a 'foundationalist' structure. The way to think of this epistemology is to imagine a foundation with stones built one on top of each other into a tower. 'Foundationalism' is the conceptual version of such a tower. It commits a person to the thesis that it is unreasonable to believe in God unless the hypothesis that there is a God is supported by evidence in the form of facts which are less open to question than theistic belief itself. These facts must be supported by other facts which in turn justify their acceptance. This process continues until one reaches a layer of facts which require no other support, because they are considered to be inherently incorrigible or self-authenticating. This is a layer of basic belief.

Those who oppose such an approach, however, have no difficulty in demonstrating (a) how problematic the concept of incorrigible data is, and (b) how difficult it is to define what should constitute a basic belief. This seriously undermines the basis of foundationalist epistemology.[23]

Rationalism is also criticized by writers such as Nicholas Wolterstorff on the grounds that it gives an unrealistic description of the way in which people develop and maintain their religious beliefs.[24] Ideas do not march before totally detached and neutral thinkers, who determine the value of the evidence for and against each proposition, giving their assent to them with a strength which is proportional to the evidence. As a rule, the believer is brought up in a system which believes in God, and accepts this in the way in which he accepts many other beliefs which have been nurtured by his home and culture. For a person to assess all his or her beliefs in a thoroughly rationalist way would take many lifetimes, and is simply not possible for the individual to achieve.

There are significant problems with each of these forms of 'methodism'. Rationalism and empiricism both begin with criteria to determine what can be known, and then run into apparent difficulties in the application of their criteria to reality. We will need more than these methods if we are to be able to assess the claims to religious experience made by the enthusiast.

5

Do We Know Already?

Sifting through particularism

Rationalism and empiricism have led to conclusions such that no one accepting them will behave in a way which is consistent with that acceptance. Dissatisfaction with this situation has led to attempts to resolve the problem by beginning at the opposite end of the quandary. Rather than using a particular *method* as the arbiter of what is known, one could begin with what is putatively known, then develop a method which will provide conclusions that fit in with the way we 'know' reality is. It is an approach taken by Thomas Reid in the eighteenth century, also by G.E. Moore, and more recently by Chisholm. 'Particularism' is a way forward that is also accepted and applied to theological issues by writers such as Farrer and Plantinga.

> There is no reason why we should not, in this respect, make our philosophical opinions agree with what we necessarily believe at other times. There is no reason why I should not confidently assert that I do really know some external facts, although I cannot prove the assertion by simply assuming that I do. I am, in fact, as certain of this as of anything and as reasonably certain of it. [1]

This is a promising approach which attempts to derive criteria of knowing by accommodating criteria to prior assumptions about what one does 'know'. This also involves a rejection of scepticism, because in this way one can assume that one's knowledge goes beyond that which is directly evident or *a priori*.

One group of modern theological and philosophical writers who fall into this 'particularist' category are especially interesting in our examination of enthusiastic epistemology; Plantinga,

Wolterstorff, Alston, Farrer, and others. Their thought is linked firstly by a rejection of 'classical foundationalism'. A second connection between them is a refutation of the 'evidentialist challenge' to religious belief. This means a rejection of the notion that religious belief is not acceptable unless it is justified by 'adequate evidence'. A third link is (what is described by Plantinga and Wolterstorff as) 'Calvinist epistemology' or 'Reformed epistemology', which is the view that theistic belief can be justified in the absence of any evidence whatsoever.[2]

In order to clarify the direction of this chapter, briefly, the core of this 'particularist' argument is as follows. Belief in God is properly 'basic', and therefore needs no support from other evidence. The same is true of a statement such as 'I feel pain', which can *justifiably* be accepted without external support from evidence or rational argument; you just *know* that it hurts. The person who claims to have had an experience of God is in a similar epistemic position to the person who feels pain, and should normally be believed because: (a) the experience of God can be considered as a basic perceptual practice, and (b) beliefs based on such perception ought to be treated as being innocent until proved guilty.

What makes such argument so important in this book is that it has a striking similarity to the way in which enthusiastic claims to knowledge are justified. It is important that we consider it because if such an argument does provide an acceptable means of determining which beliefs are justifiable, it would also seem to offer a support for enthusiastic claims to knowledge. When using this 'particularist' criterion, enthusiasm certainly fares rather better than it does when tested against empiricism or rationalism. Indeed, this way of justifying belief is essentially the same as the methods of the enthusiastis, in that it begins with 'knowledge', and then adjusts its criteria in a variety of ways by testing them against what is 'known', and adjusting these criteria accordingly. In the case of the enthusiast it is a rather crude adjustment, normally involving ignoring reasonable argument on the grounds that it must be submitted to 'revelation'. It is similar, however, in that the enthusiast's theistic beliefs are considered to be basic. An enthusiastic context also creates an unusual degree of certainty, but essentially it has the same epistemic framework. If we apply the phraseology of Chisholm to it, it is 'particularist'.[3]

This would help us to understand the debate between Locke and the enthusiasts, as they represent two systems of thought which have fundamentally different starting points. They inevitably reach contradictory conclusions because they begin with opposite presuppositions. An enthusiast would have no reason even to listen to Locke's arguments, because he already 'knew' what was true. Locke would find enthusiasm wholly unacceptable because its claims to knowledge were not supported by adequate evidence. The enthusiast begins with a definition of the extent of his knowledge, and the empiricist begins by asking the question 'How can we decide whether we do know?'

Nicholas Wolterstorff is an example of a modern writer who has written in support of this 'particularist' epistemic structure. Interestingly for this book, he also makes a direct link between this system of thought and enthusiasm. He has a section on enthusiasm in one of his essays, in which he contradicts enthusiastic claims. Wolterstorff says that his epistemology would not leave one 'speechless in the face of crackpots', but: 'Rather than demanding evidence from the enthusiast, one offers him adequate reasons for the falsehood of his belief.'[4] In spite of this contention, a contradiction of enthusiastic claims does not follow on naturally from Wolterstorff's argument. In fact an epistemology of the sort he (or Plantinga) constructed would be attractive to enthusiastic belief because it has such a similar structure. The enthusiast claims that God has spoken directly to him, and that he knows 'as sure as he has being'. He could claim that his experience was a direct perception of God, and therefore a justifiable belief even in the absence of any external supporting evidence.

Enthusiasm – innocent until proved guilty?

Wolterstorff starts in a very different place from Locke and presupposes a set of beliefs which are already held by a person. The search is for criteria which could separate those beliefs which are rational from the non-rational. In order to do this Wolter-storff's approach is to look for adequate evidence to cease believing, and to work on the assumption that beliefs are 'innocent until proved guilty, not guilty until proved innocent'.[5] This implies a 'credulity disposition'.[6] One is rational in belief, only if one does not have good reasons to *cease* from believing.

Wolterstorff applies this criterion to orthodox religious belief, as well as to enthusiasm. The believer is often brought up in a home and culture which teaches belief in God, and so he grows up accepting this along with many other beliefs. It is unreasonable to expect a person to rebuild all his beliefs from scratch in the manner of Descartes, and so if his system continues to 'nourish' him, then he has the best of reasons for continuing to adhere to it. 'If a person lacks adequate reason to cease from some one of his beliefs, then he is rationally justified in holding it even if it was produced in him by an unreliable process.'[7] A reasonable belief is, therefore one which is held because it has *not* been shown to be false, rather than one which has been positively demonstrated to be true.

Some examples will clarify the problems of this epistemology. Bertrand Russell once gave the nice example of belief in a tea pot flying around Mars, as a belief which would be practically beyond disconfirmation. However, this would be rather too easy a target, as well as being unfair. One would be hard pushed to find someone who really did hold such a belief. Better examples than this are needed because it is important to see that the capacity to include potentially unreliable beliefs is not simply an abstract theoretical objection to a presumption of innocence, but one which is evident in the real world and especially in the charismatic movement. Different people *do* hold logically contradictory beliefs which are unable to be disconfirmed.

A more useful example would be to apply this 'innocent until proved guilty' criterion to differing religious beliefs and see how it fares. When we do this it becomes apparent that such a method of belief formation could just as well be used to support the existence of Zeus as it can the Christian God. How *could* you demonstate that Zeus did not exist? Or take the example of a Hindu who believed in reincarnation of the soul, a belief which would be virtually impossible to disconfirm. What evidence could be given which would demonstrate that this belief was unsound? On the other hand, a fundamentalist Christian would believe the antithesis of the Hindu's belief that 'it is given to men once to die, and after that comes judgment' (Heb. 9.27). He believes that there is no reincarnation.

This leaves us in the position where two groups of people hold their beliefs with sincere conviction, and neither set of beliefs are capable of disconfirmation. These beliefs are logically contradictory; but if we use the criterion suggested by Wolterstorff, both are justifiable epistemological positions. A criterion which leads to such contradiction must be suspect because it is unable to make a decision between the two opposing views. If one intends to avoid accepting logical contradiction, then one needs a criterion which is more selective in what it will include, than beliefs being 'innocent until proved guilty' can produce. It may provide a realistic starting point, but some other means of refining the beliefs included by this definition will be needed if one is to sift out that which should not be there.

All one can do with such an epistemology is to examine empirically what basic beliefs different groups have, and then work out what criteria these people use for judging whether a belief is basic or not. It leaves basic beliefs as an assumption, relative to a variety of communities. Justifiable belief means accepting the basic beliefs of the community to which one belongs. This is more akin to sociology than to epistemology.

If we apply Wolterstorff's re-definition of reasonable belief to a current charismatic example, then we find the same inability to sift out varied beliefs.

For example, the use of 'tongues' would illustrate the problem. If we assume that there is such a gift, and that there will be both genuine and non-genuine instances of its use, how could it be assessed by this epistemology? The people speaking quite sincerely believe that they are having a direct communication from God to their minds. There is, however, no rational content in the words which one could analyse and then demonstrate to be true or false. In the absence of a rational content which could have been assessed in the way that Wolterstorff recommends, one has considerable problems if one is *not* going to interpret this experience as being an encounter with God or a case of direct revelation through tongues and interpretation. In order to reject the words of the speaker, one would have to demonstrate conclusively that a past, and subjective experience that the person believed to be a revelation from God, was not in fact caused by God.

This will be impossible:

(a) In principle, because if one is claiming that the God who is involved in these events is the omnipotent initiator and sustainer of every event in the universe, then how could one possibly prove that at some stage he was not the original cause of the happening?

(b) On top of this, it is also quite impractical to delve into the origins of a subjective experience (even with lengthy psycho-analysis!) and if it is not possible to do this, then these convictions are all (using Wolterstorff's definition of rationality), rationally held beliefs because they cannot be disconfirmed.

The person 'speaking in tongues' has done what can rightly be expected of him if he is submitting himself to the contents of this 'revelation from God', because there is no way to demonstrate that his belief in the origin of this 'tongue' is false. Both the observer and the speaker would have an obligation to treat the words as being of divine inspiration.

The effect of all this is that if forming beliefs on the basis of 'speaking in tongues' cannot be demonstrated to be unreliable, then believing the 'tongue' to be divine communication would have to be classed as an acceptable belief because in the absence of demonstrating that the belief is false, it should be assumed to be true, even if it had been produced by an unreliable method of belief formation.

Unfortunately, this epistemology would force one to the uncomfortable conclusion that chatter created by nothing but a person's own mind should be classed as divine revelation. It has the same epistemic justification as the genuine article would have, because in both cases the person believes it to be a revelation, and in neither case is the content of the 'revelation' demonstrably false.

If we take some older examples of enthusiastic conviction, we can see similar difficulties. The following extracts are from *Seasonable Thoughts*, by Charles Chauncey.

> They imagined Devils were about them, and ready to lay hold on them and draw them away into Hell. Impulses and impressions, which have prevail'd among too many; their aptness to take the motion of their own minds for something divinely extraordinary, or to put those constructions upon common occurrences, which there is no ground for but in their own imaginations.[8]

Chauncey is careless in his criticism; how could it be demonstrated that these experiences were just the product of an 'overheated imagination' rather than a real encounter with the supernatural? Chauncey has begun with a set of assumptions about what kind of experiences are genuinely religious or not. These assumptions are not stated, but they determine what he selects from the Bible in support of his argument, and his whole criticism of enthusiasm.

In what ways would Wolterstorff's definition of reasonable belief improve on Chauncey in an attempt to determine whether enthusiastic 'impulses and impressions' such as these were revelations from God or not?

Consistent with an 'innocent until proved guilty' view of knowledge, Wolterstorff suggests that the way to approach the enthusiast is not to use Locke's method, which was to argue whether or not there was adequate evidence *to support* a particular belief. What should be done is to 'offer him adequate reasons for the *falsehood* of his beliefs', and show in this way that these beliefs are not acceptable.[9]

This 'innocent until proved guilty' approach to the formulation of justifiable belief leaves a number of potential ways in which the enthusiast could be approached. We will apply this criterion in differing ways to explore its results.

(i) Would it be possible to point out that every sane person knows that it is unwise to take up irrational belief? The possibility of simply taking up irrational belief is mentioned in section XI of Wolterstorff's essay.

Frequently an objection of the following sort is lodged against the criterion I have proposed. Suppose a person takes a fancy to a proposition and just up and believes it. Suppose, further, that he neither has nor ought to have any adequate reason to give up that proposition. Then by our criterion he is rational in his belief. But surely he is not.

The truth is that by our criterion he most assuredly is not rational in his belief. The 'mechanism' operative in this imaginary case – *one may well doubt whether there really is any such 'mechanism' and whether anybody really can believe in this fashion*, but let that pass – the 'mechanism' operative is that of believing what one takes a fancy to. But certainly any normal adult human being not only ought to know but also *does* know that this is a most unreliable 'mechanism' of belief formation. Knowing this, he has a very good reason indeed for giving up that belief.[10]

Wolterstorff's dismissal of this 'mechanism' is not developed, and is unjustified. People *are* capable of taking up irrational belief, and they *do* use 'unreliable' methods of belief formation, and *do* hold contradictory beliefs on such a basis.

It is precisely such a belief-forming mechanism which is at the root of enthusiasm. The essence of enthusiasm is the ability to react against rational thought, dismissing it as 'carnal reasoning', or 'the arm of the flesh', or 'Saul's armour'; and to put in its place an experience of direct revelation from God which becomes the foundation of belief.

There is consequently a 'mechanism' at work in enthusiasm which does enable a person to 'take a fancy to' virtually any belief, i.e. the conviction that some message is a revelation from God requires belief in the content of that 'revelation', whether that content seems rational or not. This process is therefore capable of allowing irrational belief to be simply accepted. If such a mechanism does exist then Wolterstorff's notion of justifiable belief is unable to refute it. This would leave Wolterstorff's criterion capable of including an infinite number of hypothetical irrational beliefs.

(ii) Could one demonstrate the falsehood of an enthusiastic

belief by pointing out internal contradiction? Even this is more difficult than it might appear.

The enthusiasts have beliefs which have their own internal consistency. They are not built up on the basis of a reasonable argument; rather they are founded on a claim to divine revelation. Once a statement is considered to be a revelation, there is an obligation to submit to it all other ways of knowing. If God has revealed something, then it ought to be believed. If these 'revelations' appear strange, then the enthusiast can retreat into mysticism and claim that God's words are bound to be beyond limited human understanding. Consequently, enthusiastic beliefs do have their own consistency, and so cannot often be ruled out on the grounds of internal contradiction. Even if one did find a discrepancy it is unlikely to be persuasive to the enthusiast because internal contradiction may be acceptable to a person who has rejected reason as the prime source of knowing. He can call it a paradox which is hidden in the mystery which is God's revelation, or else be even more extreme and rest content with logical contradiction.

(iii) Are there external means of 'demonstrating falsehood'? This is sometimes available, particularly when there is some didactic content, say if a person were to make a specific prediction about some future event such as the end of the world. This could be a way to provide adequate evidence of the falsehood of a person's belief. Perhaps this is the reason why movements that allow themselves to be directed by prophecy rarely survive for long before they collapse. The truth of their claims is too easy to check.

In most instances of religious and enthusiastic experiences, however, there are no external demonstrable grounds which could show that a belief based on a claimed encounter with God is false. The experience provides an internal conviction.

(iv) Is it possible to demonstrate that the enthusiast has an 'unreliable mechanism of belief formation'? This is an important qualification on the concept of a belief being innocent until proved guilty, and would seem to be the most promising of Woltersorff's suggestions on how to approach the enthusiast. In Wolterstorff's terms, once a person *knows* that his beliefs are being formed in an unreliable way, then he does have an adequate reason to give up that belief. One would presumably provide a lesson in church history and point out the many contradictory beliefs and problems which have arisen from the use of this method of belief formation.

Even this would be unpersuasive to the full-blown enthusiast, however. The enthusiast need not give up his claims to revelation. He can say that revelation does supply absolute authority, and where it has gone wrong in practice is at the times when people have made mistakes. They moved away from God, they did not listen properly to him, their sinful lives clouded the channels of communication, etc. Even admitting that there are false prophets, as Jesus led us to expect, does not rule out the possibility of the genuine; indeed it implies that there will be real prophets. The particular enthusiast, however, is certain that his own experience is a genuine encounter with revelation from God.

A more philosophically minded enthusiast could also point out that the 'mechanisms' of belief formation used by empiricism, rationalism and Wolterstorff also appear as unreliable in their own ways. Why should he submit his 'unreliable' ways of knowing to another system which may be no more reliable?

All of this raises the question, 'What standard could determine the reliability of such a belief-forming mechanism? The enthusiast assumes that God speaks, and that the Bible is infallible revelation. He therefore accepts the possibility of truth being revealed directly to him. He consequently concludes that he is within his rights to use a divinely-appointed method of forming beliefs. Why should he test his method against fallen, sinful, carnal, human claims to be able to sift rational from irrational belief?

At this point we find an attempt to talk across conflicting paradigms. The enthusiast and the sceptical (say, atheistic) observer are separated by differing presuppositions, methods, standards, and ways of testing claims to knowledge. The way in which they question each other's beliefs is determined by their own separate system, and so even Wolterstorff's suggestion of a demonstration that the enthusiastic method of belief formation is unreliable could not be achieved in the majority of circumstances.

If there is a mechanism which allows beliefs to be simply taken up, and there is no way to demonstrate that God was not the cause of an experience, and there is no way forward along the path of looking for internal contradiction, and no way of demonstrating that the mechanism of belief formation was false without begging the question; then one has been unable to sift enthusiastic belief by means of 'demonstrating its falsehood'.

This pushes one back to the route taken by Locke, and to the attempt to sift beliefs by arguing that a person *did not have good grounds for holding these beliefs in the first place.*

To summarize, it is difficult to see that an 'innocent until proved guilty' description of rational belief could be effective, because while this process may increase one's stock of true beliefs, it is not sufficient reliably to eliminate beliefs which are false. This is a particular weakness in the context of enthusiasm because (a) there is a mechanism which enables beliefs to be taken on in an irrational way, and (b) the subjective nature of these experiences of revelation (which are at the heart of enthusiasm) means that in most circumstances it is practically impossible to demonstrate that such experience did not come from God. Potentially, this could commit a person to a host of contradictory beliefs.

A revised definition of 'basicality'

A 'basic' belief is a belief which can be accepted properly without any external evidence or argument; 'I feel tired', or 'I feel pain' are examples. You are perfectly justified in believing those things, without providing strict rational proof, making reference to the external world, performing scientific experiments, mathematical demonstration, reference to probability, and so on. This much may appear straightforward, but what makes things awkward is that the conditions which are necessary and sufficient to define what ought to be allowed into this category are controversial.

Basicality is commonly determined on the grounds that a proposition is incorrigible, self-evident or 'evident to the senses'. Some writers, such as Descartes, have wanted to add certainty to these conditions.[11]

Some contemporary writers who are well aware of the arbitrariness of this have re-defined what constitutes a basic belief in a form that results in the inclusion of theistic belief within the category of that which can be described as basic. One such writer is Alvin Plantinga who argues that belief in God is properly basic, and that it is quite rational to start with belief in God as part of one's noetic foundation.[12]

Plantinga argues that the 'evidentialist' objection to theism is rooted in 'classical foundationalism', yet this is a system which turns out to be 'both false and self-referentially incoherent'.[13] According to reformed thinkers such as Calvin, being self-evident, incorrigible, or evident to the senses is not a necessary condition of basicality. Plantinga also takes this view.

Plantinga makes the general point that in normal perceptual conditions:

> being appropriately appeared to, in the perceptual case, is not sufficient for justification; some further condition – a condition hard to state in detail – is clearly necessary.[14]

However, this 'further condition' is not defined by Plantinga.

Instead of using a 'foundationalist' argument, Plantinga attacks the problem from the opposite end:

> the proper way to arrive at such a criterion is, broadly speaking, inductive. We must assemble examples of beliefs and conditions such that the former are obviously properly basic in the latter, and examples of beliefs and conditions such that the former are obviously not properly basic in the latter. We must then frame hypotheses as to the necessary and sufficient conditions of proper basicality and test these hypotheses by reference to those examples.[15]

Plantinga offers belief in other minds, or that a person had breakfast this morning as examples of basic beliefs, even though they are neither self-evident nor incorrigible:

> Of course it isn't properly basic on the criteria offered by classical foundationalists; but that fact counts not against you but against those criteria.[16]

Criteria should not be 'presented as *ex cathedra*, but argued to and tested by a relevant set of examples'. The obvious question to follow this is which set of examples? It is difficult to imagine that everyone would agree on which examples are acceptable. Plantinga suggests that a person should take examples that are 'basic for him'.

> The Christian will of course suppose that belief in God is entirely proper and rational; if he doesn't accept this belief on the basis of other propositions, he will conclude that it is *basic for him* and quite properly so. Followers of Bertrand Russell and Madelyn Murray O'Hare may disagree, but how is that relevant? Must my criteria, or those of the Christian community, conform to their examples? Surely not. The Christian community is responsible to its set of examples, not to theirs.[17]

A second example of an argument which is centred on the definition of basicality is provided by W.P. Alston in the context of discussing a practice of belief formation which is based on Christian experience of God. His later views are rather more cautious, but in the early eighties he argued that Christian beliefs could be formed justifiably on the basis of experience. This was to the extent that (given the right circumstances) 'experience can provide justification sufficient for rational acceptance' (acceptance that the experience was an experience of God). The justification of this order of experience would be that:

> By virtue of having the experience the subject is in a position such that she will be adequately justified in that belief unless there are strong enough reasons to the contrary, unless there are defeaters of sufficient strength.[18]

Christian experience of God is to be regarded as a 'direct perceptual practice', and therefore does not need any more justification than any other direct perception would. In other words, it can stand as basic knowledge without any external support.

Interestingly, as with the re-definition of 'reasonable belief', such a structure as this would also provide a significant support for seventeenth-century enthusiastic belief. The enthusiast would be in the position to claim that his experience of God was a direct awareness of God which was communicated directly to the consciousness, the light being 'infused into his being' without the mediation of other senses. It could therefore be accepted as a reasonable belief even in the absence of other support, because it could be classed as a direct perception.

Locke compares enthusiastic justification of belief with the conviction that one is seeing the light of the sun, because neither demand justification from reason. Locke's phraseology is different, but the process he describes is essentially what Alston would describe as a 'direct perceptual practice'.

> What they have a sensible Experience of admits no doubt, needs no probation. Would he not be ridiculous who should require to have it proved to him, that the Light shines and that he sees it? It is its own proof, and can have no other. When the Spirit brings Light into our Minds, it dispels darkness. *We see it, as we do that of the Sun at Noon, and need not the twilight of Reason to shew it us.* This Light from Heaven is strong, clear, and pure, carries its own Demonstration with it, and we may as rationally take a glow-worme to assist us to discover the Sun, as to examine the celestial Ray by our dim Candle, Reason.
>
> *This is the way of talking of these Men: they are sure: and their Perswasions are right only because they are strong in them.*[19]

As well as this 'direct perceptual practice', in most circumstances enthusiastic claims would be 'beyond disconfirmation', and if beliefs are 'innocent until proved guilty' then they ought to be believed. Knowing 'as sure as that I have being' is a good description of a belief which could be described as basic, and such a belief would have to be considered as rational to hold even though it is held without evidence or reason.

It is found by abundant experience that those who are led

away by impulses and imagined revelations are extremely confident; they suppose that the great Jehovah has declared these and those things to them; and having his immediate testimony, a strong confidence is the highest virtue. Hence they are bold to say, *I know this or that – I know certainly – I am as sure as that I have a being*, and the like; and they despise all argument and inquiry in the case.[20]

One can see the attraction in the approach of Alston and Plantinga. It allows a people to support their own Christian understanding of experience without reference to any possible falsifying experiences. One's religious claims are placed conveniently beyond the range of philosophical criticism.

There can also be no doubt that there is a need for an alternative to 'classical foundationalism' because, as Plantinga points out, this has proved to be inadequate as a definition of what should constitute knowledge. It would also be difficult to disagree with the assertion that there have not been adequate definitions of 'basic belief'. Neither has it been demonstrated that belief in God is *not* a properly basic practice.

Alston and Plantinga consequently offer an alternative to classical foundationalism which may be capable of avoiding the problems of excluding so much from one's epistemology that one is forced into scepticism. This would allow the inclusion of knowledge which seem to be evidently justifiable, in spite of it being unable to fulfil the rigours of classical foundationalist criteria. There is a contention here which has an internal consistency, and would seem as arguably acceptable, in this respect, as are the alternatives.

Despite these useful points, however, there are some significant difficulties with this 'particularist' epistemology.

To begin with, one of the characteristics of a basic belief according to Plantinga is that it is one which the person is unable to disbelieve. What is 'basic for him' is another definition which he uses.[21] Plantinga applies this to himself, and states that he is personally unable to disbelieve in God.[22]

However, what one is unable to disbelieve, and so class as basic, is intensely personal. The subjective inability to resist belief says little about whether such beliefs are in themselves objectively true or false. This could be no more than a demonstration of the human capacity to take on all kinds of beliefs; a capacity which can be frighteningly large and irrationally certain. Consequently the ideas recommended by Plantinga and Alston create a system with a capacity to include error in a person's beliefs which is as large as that person's capacity to believe.

There are two especially significant questions which need to be answered.

(i) The first crucial question is 'Should experience of God be classed as a "basic perception"?'

What is revealed in creation, for example, can be seen as the works of God, but this would not constitute a basic perception, because what is evident to the senses would be described as feeling wind, seeing sky, stars, rain, and so on. Even these terms are well beyond a direct perception because all of these statements have implicit interpretation. If we express these statements in the way that Chisholm has recommended, 'I am being appeared to bluely' would be a more accurate way to describe a perception of 'sky'.[23]

To take another example, to see the external world as the creation of God is to present a theory about its cause, and one which is open to discussion with other plausible explanations. Looking at the heavens and simply 'knowing' that they were created by God is not enough. To use an analogy, one may feel a sense of awe on looking at Glasgow University, and be appeared to 'stonily' but this would not constitute a basic experience of its builder or architect. Any understanding of its creation demands interpretation. Similarly, a particular belief as to the origin of creation being God is an interpretation of the evidence. One could offer well-thought-out alternative accounts of the origins of such religious belief which could be compelling; or else give objections to theism, for example, on the grounds of the existence of evil.

Furthermore, belief in God is a very complex set of beliefs; including justice, holiness, omnipotence, omnipresence, love, anger, and so on. It is a big jump from 'basic practice' to belief in such a God, and a jump which cannot be made without accepting some form of revelation. Granted, one could have an experience of God which could be classed as basic, but the moment one understood it as theistic experience, and *said* anything about it, then that statement could not be classed as basic, nor could it be logically derived from only the basic perception.

All verbal phrases are far more theory-laden than we are generally aware of. But the moment we use the term 'God' in relation to the experience we have added an immensely complex interpretation, one which is (perhaps deceptively) out of all proportion to the length of the noun.

Plantinga offers examples of what he describes as basic beliefs:

(6) God is speaking to me
(7) God has created all this
(8) God disapproves of what I have done
(9) God forgives me
and
(10) God is to be thanked and praised.[24]

If one defines a basic belief in the way that Plantinga does as being a belief which is (a) held without reason, and (b) one is unable to give up, then these could indeed be basic beliefs in the right circumstances.

However, it is a *huge* jump from a directly perceived 'religious experience' to the above statements. They entail a conviction that what was revealed in the experience was God, the creator of heaven and earth who will judge the living and the dead, who is holy, who speaks to people, who is interested in their morality, who forgives, who deserves to be praised, the God of Abraham Isaac and Jacob. It is certainly too big a jump from 'direct perception' for belief in such a God to be described as a 'direct perceptual practice'.

Since this definition of direct perception is capable of including such massively theory-laden statements as those above, then there must be a serious flaw in the way that basicality is being defined by Plantinga.

(ii) The second question is whether Plantinga and Alston supply an adequate description of basic perception.

What is needed to resolve all of this is a careful re-assessment of the general issue of the nature of basicality, as this is the heart of the issue, but this cannot be done satisfactorily only with reference to belief in God.

To seek to resolve the question of basicality only with reference to this particular belief is a dishonest approach, as it is the equivalent of changing the rules in the middle of a game in order to get the result that one wants to achieve. In other words, one particular conclusion is used to determine which methods will give that specific result. It would be fairer, if the issue of basicality were resolved with reference to a far wider application, instead of exclusively with reference to theistic belief.

Plantinga states that it is not 'within my power to cease believing in God',[25] which is revealing, because this is the starting point and the determining factor in his final conclusions. Basicality is used to describe a belief which one holds without external reason, but is unable to give up. There are conditions on justifying such a belief, but Plantinga is unable to define what these conditions are. But until these conditions can be defined, how could belief in God ever be justified on the grounds that it is a basic belief?

> . . . some further condition – a condition hard to state in detail – is clearly necessary.[26]

If this condition cannot be stated, then belief in God cannot be included in the category of direct perception, because this category has not been defined. Indeed, Plantinga's views vary over his different books and it is unclear what he considers to be essential features of a basic belief. His later writing seems more qualified and cautious.[27]

As we have seen, in discussing what kind of examples can be used to determine what can be classed as basic belief, Plantinga takes the following approach:

> The Christian will of course suppose that belief in God is entirely proper and rational; if he doesn't accept this belief on the basis of other propositions, he will conclude that it is *basic for him* and quite properly so. Followers of Bertrand Russell

and Madelyn Murray O'Hare may disagree, but how is that relevant? Must my criteria, or those of the Christian community, conform to their examples? Surely not. The Christian community is responsible to its set of examples, not to theirs.[28]

I would argue that the criteria of the Christian community certainly should also conform to other peoples' examples. If they do not, then one has an epistemological sieve which is excluding all examples which may be contrary to what one would prefer to believe.

This is similar to 'proving' a theory by using a method that ignores all experimental evidence which conflicts with the desired conclusion, and only includes evidence that supports what one would prefer the theory to say. It is a misleading and dishonest method because it is not only out of touch with the available evidence, but is consciously distorting it by omission. This is not acceptable as a way to define direct perception.

Even though empiricist and rationalist criteria have failed to provide a means of persuading the enthusiast or of resolving the 'problem of the criterion', its description and criticism of the epistemic structure of enthusiastic belief formation still remains acceptable. And though it may prove extremely difficult to examine the truth of persuasions 'by something extrinsical to the persuasions themselves', this is nevertheless what is needed, because there are many occasions where such beliefs will clash with each other, and will therefore need some other standard to be imposed on them in order to distinguish between their respective claims to knowledge. We need more than internal conviction, or claims to self-authentication, to justify a claim to know. Locke's description remains true, and applicable to Plantinga's, Wolterstorff's and Alston's thesis.

Every conceit that thoroughly warms our fancies must pass for an inspiration, if there be nothing but the strength of our persuasions, whereby to judge of our persuasions; if reason must not examine their truth by something extrinsical to the persuasions themselves, inspirations and delusions, truth and falsehood, will have the same measure, and will not be possible to be distinguished.[29]

What the 'something extrinsical to the persuasions themselves' could be is an issue that still needs to be resolved.

In the application to a reality where true and false beliefs are mixed up, unable to be disconfirmed, and held with such conviction that they could be described as being basic, these definitions of basicality and rationality are (a) inadequate in themselves because they are ill defined, and (b) incapable of distinguishing that which is true from that which is false. They consequently do not provide the means to assess charismatic experience.

Theological 'particularism'

Before we leave this chapter on 'particularism' it is important to consider the closely related arguments in theology which have also attempted to justify belief in God in the absence of rational foundations. They are related to the above philosophical views in the sense that they begin with what is putatively known (i.e. the existence of God), and so can be described as 'particularist'.[30]

Many reformed thinkers and theologians have rejected natural theology and its attempts to provide rational justification for the existence of God. What we must note is that it is argued, not only that the reasoning is flawed, but that the very idea of justifying belief in God in this way is intrinsically hopeless.

According to Calvin, God has created us in such a way that we have a strong inclination towards believing in him. This tendency has been distorted by sin, but still remains the natural and universally present human condition. 'The knowledge of God has been naturally implanted in the minds of men'.[31] Belief in God is revealed through Jesus and the scriptures; it is also declared by the heavens.[32] This belief is certain, but it is not reached on the basis of reasonable argument. The believer simply *knows* that God exists. This knowledge of God and of the authenticity of scripture is not established on the basis of reason, but by the witness of the Holy Spirit,[33] and by its own authentication.

> Such, then, is a conviction that requires no reasons; such, a knowledge with which the best reason agrees in which the mind truly reposes more securely and constantly than in any reasons; such finally, a feeling that can be born only of heavenly revelation. I speak of nothing other than what each believer experiences within himself.

This experience is related to the doctrine of election:

> Whenever, then, the fewness of believers disturbs us, let the converse come to mind, that only those to whom it is given can comprehend the mysteries of God.[34]

However, giving up on the arguments for the existence of God leaves a gap between the evidence for God's existence and the conviction that he does exist, which is filled by a variety of options which attempt to find refuge in 'faith'. So believing comes to be seen as an act of the 'whole personality', or to use Pascal's words it involves the 'reasons of the heart'. Kierkegaard repudiated objective assurance for Christian faith in preference for the 'proof of the emotions'. William James suggested a 'will to believe' which tipped the scales in a way which was consonant with our emotional nature. Such approaches to faith are an implicit rejection of natural theology.

Further into the twentieth century, this rejection of natural theology and replacement with fideistic structures has been argued by theologians such as Bultmann, Barth, and Niebuhr.

> If you really reject natural theology you do not stare at the serpent with the result that it stares back at you, hypnotizes you, and is ultimately certain to bite you, but you hit it and kill it as soon as you see it![35]

If we re-phrase the issues involved then what is argued is that belief in God need not (and should not) be based on argument or evidence from other propositions at all; that the believer is perfectly entitled to go on with theistic belief even in the absence of any rational arguments in support of the existence of God. If this is so, then the position is indeed similar to Plantinga, Alston et al., in the sense that it is deemed acceptable to believe in God without this belief being supported on the basis of any other beliefs or propositions. In other words, belief in God is being treated as properly basic.

This way of thinking has also been applied to the doctrine of revelation. According to Karl Barth, absolute authority could not be verified except with reference to itself. A person who believes in God's revelation does so because he has experienced the Word, and the Word has created faith in him.

> It is Jesus Christ Himself who speaks for Himself in it, [the word] *and needs no witness save His Holy Spirit* and is glad of the faith of His own in the promise received and grasped.[36]

> God's revelation has its reality and truth wholly and in every respect . . . within itself. Only by denying it can we wish to ascribe to it a higher or deeper ground. Obviously the adoption of revelation from the vantage of such a ground, different from it and presumably superior to it; – this can only be achieved by denying revelation.[37]

> The Word of God becomes knowable by making itself knowable. The application of what has just been said to the epistemological problem consists in the fact that we hold fast to this statement and not one step beyond do we take. The possibility of knowing the word of God is God's miracle on and in us.[38]

If this Barthian argument is correct it would be a dismissal of the present book because we are attempting to assess religious understandings of experience, such as claims to have received revelation, through a rational process. It is therefore important to meet this objection.

The issue can be put in the form of a dilemma:

> . . . either revelation is totally immune from rational criticism, or it is subject to such criticism. If the former, it is wholly discontinuous with our ordinary standards of what is reason-

able and right; if the latter, it can have no independent authority.[39]

Mitchell usefully points out that the kind of argument used by Barth, which has been very persuasive in current theology, rests on a false dilemma which relies on a distrust of reason. The assumption underlying this dilemma is that when reason has been applied to revelation, the revelation has been deprived of any independent authority.[40]

I would like to take this argument a stage further and take the opposite view to Barth and Niebuhr by arguing that the only way truly to submit to the authority of revelation which comes from God is to be as critical as possible of every claimed 'revelation'.

Imagine that an admiral in the navy sends orders to his ships. It is one thing to question the authority of the admiral, and decide to ignore the orders which one does not like. This would be mutiny and an attempt to undermine the admiral's authority, and so the sailors would be shot, keel-hauled or whatever is considered to be appropriate in the navy now. *It is quite a different thing to question whether these orders did in reality come from the admiral or not.* Indeed, if one was in a situation where counterfeit orders were being given, the only way to be certain of being under the authority of the admiral would be to examine critically any 'order'. If one were not to do this, then it is quite likely that one's commitment would be, not to the admiral, but to the giver of the counterfeit orders.

This is analogous to the situation in the religious context, where there are competing claims to be true revelation, between differing religions but also within Christianity, and particularly within enthusiasm. In such a setting, to submit to the authority of God would demand that one were critical of every putative revelation, and that one did *not* accept the words on the strength of 'faith'.

Part of the confusion here is concerned with the object of faith. If one is certain on the basis of some independent grounds (a) that God does exist, and (b) that the Bible is his revelation; then the requirement for unconditional faith in him would make perfect sense. What must be noted, however, is that this requirement for faith has its place *within* the system of Christian belief, and cannot properly be considered as an obligation to continue to embrace the system itself, because the reason for exercising such faith depends on this being a true system. How a person chooses to believe this system is one issue, and how a person exercises faith in God within its framework is quite another.

What we must be careful not to confuse then, are (a) one's belief in the existence of God and revelation; and (b) assuming that he exists and has revealed truth about himself, trusting in unconditional reliance upon him. They have different requirements when it comes to a response of faith.

If one exercises the kind of unconditional faith which is due to the person of God, and applies this to the issue of God's existence and revelation, then theology is cut off from all external support of criticism. It becomes fideist.

This step is taken by Bultmann.

> Our radical attempt to demythologize the New Testament is in fact a perfect parallel to St Paul's and Luther's doctrine of justification by faith alone apart from works of the law. Or rather it carries this doctrine to its logical conclusion in the field of epistemology. Like the doctrine of justification it destroys every false demand for it on the part of man, whether he seeks it in his good works or in his ascertainable knowledge. *The man who wishes to believe in God as his God must realize that he has nothing in his hand on which to base his faith. He is suspended in mid-air, and cannot demand a proof of the Word which addresses him.* For the ground and object of faith are identical. Security can be found only by abandoning all security, by being ready, as Luther put it, to plunge into the inner darkness.[41]

Bultmann's claim is that Christian theism must be accepted without rational support, and is an existential choice which is accepted without question or reason. This is a bizarre step to make, because there is no biblical or logical reason to proceed from the doctrine of justification by faith to the peculiar epistemological doctrine that faith needs no rational support. They are entirely distinct.

If we keep our analogy of the admiral, the unconditional obedience which is rightly given to him assumes that (a) there is an admiral, and (b) these are his orders. These two claims are, however, established independently of the sailors' 'faith', and should not be accepted on the basis of unconditional blind commitment. It is only after they are established and set within the framework of a naval command structure that unconditional obedience to the admiral has any meaning.

There is confusion here over the object of faith, one which arises from a false assumption. In reality, to submit to and endorse the authority of God and his revelation demands that all claims to revelation should *not* be accepted on faith, but should be subject to criticism. This is directly applicable to enthusiastic belief because it implies that it is necessary to be critical of all the claims it makes to knowledge. Accepting a putative prophecy on nothing but faith, for example, is both irrational and an abdication of the requirement to put one's faith in God.

Conclusions

(i) Many of the same criticisms we made of Plantinga, Alston and Wolterstorf apply to the fideistic views of writers such as Barth and Bultmann.

(ii) There are severe problems with the 'innocent until proved guilty' concept of faith. This implies that one needs some 'grounds' for theistic belief.

(iii) The inclusion of belief in God in the category of basic perception is not effectively argued; it does not avoid fideism, and so it is a system which can include too much error.

(iv) Therefore we need some other approach to the interpretation of charismatic experience.

6

Can Leaky Buckets Hold Water?

Probability, scepticism and a cumulative case

So far we have still been unable to discover a means of interpreting charismatic experience. Strict rational proof is not available. The 'methodist' approaches of the empiricist and rationalist philosophers seem to have been a dead end, and yet if we go to the other extreme, the 'particularist' means of resolving our question also seem to be unable to sift through claimed Christian experience. The significance of this ineffectiveness should not be underestimated. Epistemology is currently in turmoil, and our problems in understanding Christian experience illustrate the heart of the difficulties it faces at the present time. So where do we go from here?

Enthusiasm and probability

Perhaps we could make progress at this point and attempt to establish probability as a means of justifying a particular belief about the nature of a claimed religious experience.

However, Basil Mitchell points out a crucial problem which arises when one attempts to determine the probability that one's experience was genuinely 'religious'.

> For how could one estimate the degree of probability that an experience represents a genuine encounter with God when one is not in a position to compare the experience in question with others that are known to be experiences of God?[1]

One would have a way around this problem if one had biblical revelation as a presupposition, because one would have a large body of experience which could be relied on to represent experience of God, and therefore to act as a standard to which one can refer.

At this point, however, Mitchell is questioning whether the existence of God can be demonstrated to be probable, and what experience can contribute to this argumentation. It is therefore the theistic system in its entirety which is open to question. In the context of such a basic question, one could have no such reference points as 'revelation' which could be relied on for comparison, without begging the question.

Mitchell's conclusion is therefore that probability could not be used in justification of a religious interpretation of an experience.

It may be possible to explore this issue further, however, if we take medical diagnosis as an example of a means of establishing knowledge which is based on probability. Could this provide a model for the assessment of religious experience?

Diagnosis is a process which leads to a testable hypothesis, but which does not rely on strict rational proof. It is still, however, a reasonable process. A system which attempts to determine the cause of a physical or mental 'experience' in the form of illness could provide useful insights, because determining cause is our aim in the assessment of enthusiastic experience. For our purposes it is also useful to study a system which is forced to decide on a course of action on the basis of its diagnosis.

The procedure involved in diagnosis includes finding out the history of the patient, physical examination, and various technical diagnostic observations. The accumulated information becomes the data base from which conclusions emerge.

The history yields information concerning the patient's subjective sensations (direct perceptions), his emotional state, and alterations in his bodily appearance and function.

What is interesting is that as with the assessment of religious experience, one is faced with a variety of alternative ways to understand the symptoms. For a physician to resolve this, the process involves dismissing the unlikely, and trying to establish which of the alternatives is the cause.

The clinician tests each hypothetical diagnosis in turn, trying to dismiss the unlikely and to verify the correct. He does this by asking two questions: Does the diagnosis explain all the findings? Are expected findings present?[2]

What this describes is a process which looks forward and attempts to see if the illness fits a certain class of disease, and then reverses its approach to examine if the characteristics of such a disease are consistent with the illness which is under examination. In this way one is attempting to verify one's findings during, or arising from the examination of the patient.

One problem in the diagnostic process is that the information given to the physician is often inadequate, irrelevant, and of varying accuracy and precision. Consequently, the diagnosis is not a strictly logical and watertight procedure, but a matter of judgment which will grade from the less certain to the more certain. One could have a first order certainty in the case of gross anatomical defects, for example leg fracture, hairlip, and genetic abnormalities. At the other end of the scale would be groups or collections of signs and symptoms which make up a disease picture, but the etiology remains obscure, for example 'infectious mononucleosis, sarcoidosis, and systematic lupus erythematosus'.[3]

Observations consequently need to be assessed, because there is wide scope for error.

> The possible error in every diagnosis arises from the fact that all knowledge of human origin is uncertain. The distinguishing characteristic of scientific knowledge is not that is more certain than non-scientific knowledge, *but that the degree of uncertainty can be rather well determined.*[4]

This determination is made by deciding the probability that a particular illness is the cause of a set of symptoms in a particular person. A probability of 'o' would mean that an illness was quite impossible as the cause, and a probability of '1' would be a certain diagnosis. The physician often finds himself in the situation of having a number of plausible diagnoses of an illness, and it is by ordering their relative probability that the solution is determined. An example of a collapsed forty-two-year-old man is given:

Diagnostic list	Credibility of Diagnosis
Myocardial infarction	$C = 0.5$
Cerebrovascular accident	$C = 0.3$
Cardiac arrhythmia	$C = 0.1$
'Something Else'	$C = 0.1$[5]

The 'something else' ensures that the list is all inclusive, and that the sum of the credibilities is equal to one. In principal, he continues to make progress in the same way throughout the whole process by determining the *probability* that specific symptoms may indicate a particular disease.

> In essence this represents in a simplified manner the diagnostic function. Given a certain set of examination information that is consistent with a number of diagnoses, what is the most likely or most credible diagnosis? Logically, it is that diagnosis that has the greatest probability of association with the available information when compared to all the diagnostic possibilities.[6]

To explore the practicalities of such an approach in application, we will take an example of its use by a medic in the charismatic context. This comes from the report: *A Social Anthropologist's Analysis of Words of Knowledge, Manifestations of the Spirit and the Effectiveness of Divine Healing.*[7] Part of this report relies on probability for assessment. It gives an example of a 'word of knowledge' spoken at a Wimber conference in Sheffield in the early 1980s:

> 'There is a woman here whose name begins with L . . . She is thirty-two years old, has had a throat condition for eight years, and has taken medicine for it but it hasn't helped her.'[8]

The report excludes the possibility of prior information on those who attended the conference, and examines the possibility that this 'word' could have been a lucky guess. When interviewed it turned out that the girl who responded was called Linda, and that the information was slightly wrong in that she would not be thirty-two for a few more months.

In Linda's case we can estimate that if there were about 1,500 women present at the conference and if there are about twenty common initials of women's names (excluding initials like X,Z or Q) then about seventy-five women might have been expected to fit the first two specifications.

If most of those present were aged between twenty and sixty – but Wimber did have a discrepancy of one year (or a few months) in this detail – then we could allow thirteen age brackets of three years each, allowing for an error of one year on either side. This brings us down to about six possible women.

It is difficult to estimate the total 'universe' of possible organs, especially as left and right sides may be specified or details such as the 'fifth cervical disc' and so on may be included. Doctors or those with medical training might be able to list hundreds of different parts of the body, but for the present purposes let us take a very conservative figure and assume there are only thirty principal organs or parts. Even with a choice of only thirty bodily areas, we are down to 0.2 people who would fit these criteria by chance alone.

Then there is the detail of 'eight years', which is considerably longer than the average length of time for a throat illness to persist in a woman of this age. If we take an arbitrary figure of one in fifty throat conditions lasting as long as eight years then we find that on the basis of chance alone 0.004 people in the crowd might be expected to have such a combination of traits. In other words, even by using very conservative figures such as a choice of only thirty organs in the body, the crowd would have to have been 250 times larger than it actually was for just one person to have had such a combination of characteristics through chance alone.[9]

How should one view this report? It may be possible to question the details of it, for example, one would need to know whether 'L' is a less common initial than say 'M'. It is also important to discover how frequent illness of the throat is, rather than just the number of organs in the body. One would also need to know how many of such 'words of knowledge' were inaccurate. If one were allowed 250 guesses in this instance, then it would be probable that one of them would be correct.

This is beside the point at issue, however. Even if one has shown that it is very unlikely to be the result of a guess, then one has still not shown that this 'word of knowledge' was a genuine religious experience; one has simply determined that one of the alternative explanations is questionable, i.e. pure chance was an unlikely cause. This still leaves alternatives: telepathy? fraud? an unlikely possibility that turned out to be true? a person's subjective feelings about their illness distorting their perception? a religious experience? some unknown explanation?

Probability has contributed something useful in the negative sense of making one particular explanation unlikely. What it has not done, and could not do, is to determine the probability that a Christian theistic explanation was correct.

If one loosened up the kind of probability one allowed, and treated the assessment of religious experience in the way that, say, historical research is done, or a decision taken in a court, then one is allowing probability to be 'determined', even though this is not in a precisely quantifiable way. This could be a way forward, though it would be better described as a cumulative argument where on the balance of evidence, one decision is preferable to another. We will return to this possibility later, but in this section we are confining ourselves to mathematically definable probability.

How useful is probability in the assessment of charismatic experience?

Medical diagnosis is based on the mechanical predictability of physical functions, whereas religious experience is the claimed interaction of a person with God. On the one hand, God is personal and free to disclose himself at will rather than according to some formula or pattern. On the other hand, though, if he has made promises through biblical revelation, then these provide the possibility of predictable behaviour in the right circumstances.

Even making allowances for promises, however, an encounter with God could never be so predictable that it could be assessed adequately by a medical model. In such an encounter, one has the subject of the experience, a person who is himself very complex; relating to a God who is not only infinitely complex, but almighty, mysterious, and transcendent. Inevitably, the results of this experience would be unpredictable. Indeed, it would be far more surprising if an encounter with God was unsurprising and predictable.

The same difficulty would arise, for example, if a charismatic experience took the form of demonic oppression, as this would involve beings about which there is so little agreement or reliable information that it would seem impossible to determine probability in such a setting.

Charismatic experience is more analogous to the interaction between two unknown people, one of whom may not exist, than to the interaction of the body with disease.

Even more significantly at this point in the argument, there are difficulties in the use of the medical model because it is dependant on probability. This can be done effectively in medicine because there are clearly defined groups of illness and disease each with predictable associated symptoms which can be used to determine probability. Such a reference point would be essential if one were to determine probability in respect of any experience, because one would need a known point of comparison in order to determine what proportion of such experiences could be described in a particular way.

It may be possible to use 'diagnosis' to interpret charismatic experience in a loose form, but this is not strictly based on probability. It yields no more than an unquantifiable likelihood. The more radical is one's questioning, the less it is possible to use probability in the assessment of experience. This is because 'diagnosing' probability depends on accepting a body of data against which the probability can be tested. If one is attempting, as is this book, to assess a system in its entirety, then it is difficult to see that mathematical probability can be used in the interpretation of religious experience, apart from the negative function of narrowing down the field of possibilities by ruling out some other explanation, such as pure chance.

Enthusiasm and scepticism

I must confess that at this point in writing my own thesis I reached despair of being able to say anything meaningful about Christian experience. If it is not possible to argue the case that God has been revealed in an experience on the basis of strict rationality, nor possible to demonstrate the probability that one particular theory is the correct interpretation, nor to find a method which could establish knowledge, nor to have knowledge which can be believed with certainty – then can such experiences ever be interpreted in a reasonable way? Is one forced into scepticism?

A sceptic would conclude that we do not know what (if anything) we know, nor is there a way of deciding whether we know in a particular case.

This would rule out enthusiastic claims to knowledge as being irrational because they have such an element of certainty in them. Such claims to knowledge would be quite unjustified if one were a sceptic. Beyond this, the sceptic would have little to say to the enthusiast, because his scepticism would imply rejecting the available criteria which may be used to assess a claim to knowledge. Consequently, he has no criteria with which to assess the enthusiast's claims. This would leave conflicting interpretations of experience, and no way to decide which, if any of them, represents knowledge.

There are, of course, many problems with scepticism. It leads to conclusions such that a person who accepts them will be unable to live consistently with that acceptance. It also rests on a meticulous argument to justify that we know so little, with the result that its conclusions are a denial of its premises and methods.

However, there may be an escape from such a sceptical cul-de-sac. It would be a false argument that because alternative explanations are possible, no single explanation is at least to be preferred. It could be that we could at least see if charismatic experience fits better with one interpretation, rather than with one of the alternatives. Though this will be difficult in practice, at least it is an approach which would not rule out, in principle, the possibility of being able to make a reasonable assessment of a charismatic experience.

If we are correct up to this point, then enthusiastic experience must be assessed because it is unacceptable to make a fideistic existential choice, unsupported by reasons, for or against an understanding of experience. The option not to assess is effectively the option taken by the enthusiast. He is utterly convinced of the truth of his interpretation of his experience, but has little if any desire to support this with a reasonable argument. The experience is enough in itself.

A claim which is supported with this kind of justification could not be known to be a genuine experience of God, nor defended in a rational way. Virtually any experience could be given the same justification, as could a host of contradictory interpretations. If one took this route, then one would have to concede a division of knowledge between normal rational thought and acceptable religious argument, and admit that one's faith is, in the end, unreasonable, blind, subjective and existential. The potential of such thinking to include error means that this is not an acceptable epistemic position.

Religious experience must therefore be assessed. The difficulty is that such experience could not be rendered probable in any strict sense of the word; but neither could an interpretation of experience in itself be shown to be necessarily false or logically incoherent.

If we are to avoid a hopelessly sceptical conclusion, then we are pushed into exploring a route taken by Mitchell. This argues that it is, indeed, possible to make a rational case for and against a particular understanding of experience, but it is a case which is not justified by using the normal pattern of deductive or inductive reasoning.

Could the means of assessing such experience be rational, though in a form other than strict argument or proof on the basis of probability?[10]

Enthusiasm and the cumulative case argument

One of the common philosophical and theological objections to a claimed religious experience is that there can be no *rational* case in support of the belief that the particular experience was in fact an encounter with an objective God. This was the main objection of the church to the Montanists, of Locke and Leibniz to the enthusiasts, and has remained a common criticism through to the present day. The assumption is that for an interpretation of an experience to be rational, it must conform to the requirements of proof or of strict probability. If a theistic interpretation is unsupported by such a form of reasoned argument, then it would be unjustified to claim that a particular experience should be attributed to God.

It is argued by Mitchell, however, that this is a false assumption in relation to Christian theism. He makes the general point that in fields other than theology, we commonly, and justifiably, make use of arguments other than those of proof or strict probability; and that arguments in the realm of theology are also typically of this sort. If this is so, and such an approach to understanding experience is acceptable, then it could provide us with a useful way forward in the assessment of enthusiasm.

If we explore this route, then arguments that appear to be a series of failures (a) when assessed in terms of purely deductive or inductive content, and (b) in isolation from other support, could become more acceptable as contributions to what Mitchell calls a 'cumulative case'. When this approach is applied to an interpretation of enthusiastic experience, then one is arguing that one's own case is making better sense of all the available evidence than does any of the alternatives.

Mitchell illustrates this approach using an example of the debate between theists and atheists.

The debate between theists and atheists is unlikely to make progress, so long as it is confined to a single argument, such as the cosmological argument, or, indeed, to a whole series of arguments, if these are to be taken piecemeal without at any stage being brought into relation to one another. Here, at least, the Cartesian strategy of 'dividing the question' must be resisted. The debate, to be useful, must take the form of a dialogue in which, as John Wisdom observes (in relation to legal judgment), 'The process of argument is not a chain of demonstrative reasoning. It is a presenting and representing of those features of a case which severally co-operate in favour of the conclusion.'[11]

Mitchell points out that this process forms the basis of two other disciplines, critical exegesis and history; in both areas such a process of cumulative argument is perfectly acceptable. It is a rational procedure, and one which produces results which are capable of being true or false. In both of these settings, there are cases where an argument which does not purport to be a proof or to rely on strict probability is capable of providing reasonable grounds for a conclusion about a matter of fact.

There is an obvious danger inherent in the idea of using cumulative rather than inductive argument. This is the danger that one's argument has degenerated into a last ditch attempt to salvage beliefs which have ceased to be credible because they are unable to stand up to the rigours of rational proof. One is consequently providing a weak appearance of rationality for beliefs which are rationally indefensible. This pitfall is noted by Flew.

Nor, incidentally, will it do to recognize that of a whole series of arguments each is individually defective, but then to urge that nevertheless in sum they comprise an impressive case; perhaps adding a sop to the Cerberus of criticism that this case is addressed to the whole personality and not merely to the philosophical intellect. We have here to insist upon a some-times tricky distinction: between, on the one hand, the valid principle of the accumulation of evidence, where every item has at least some weight in its own right; and, on the other hand, the ten-leaky-buckets-tactic, applied to arguments none of which hold water at all. The scholarly and the business like procedure is to examine arguments one by one, without pretending – for no better reason than that they have been shown to be mistaken – that clearly and respectably stated contentions must be other than they are.[12]

This is no doubt true, but a cumulative argument is not undermined by this in principle. Such an epistemology does still remain a possibility; it is simply good to be aware of a possible danger inherent in the task. The buckets could be arranged inside each other in such a way that the holes do not overlap. This would be to create a 'synergism' in which the interaction of the components exceeds the sum of the individual parts.[13] This is analogous to a cumulative argument in which beliefs, experiences, methodology and other types of evidence *interact* with each other to support a web of highly ramified beliefs; beliefs which would not be justifiable in isolation from each other.

There is in fact increasing support for 'cumulative' reasoning, and this support is not confined only to a religious setting. Neither is it confined only to the writing of Mitchell, or indeed just to contemporary writers. Cardinal Newman's writing could also be classed in this way, at least in that he emphasizes the significance of judgment in making the choice between a variety of factors.

It is plain that formal logical sequence is not in fact the method by which we are enabled to become certain of what is concrete: and it is equally plain, from what has been already suggested, what the real and necessary method is. It is the culmination of probabilities, independent of each other, arising out of the nature and circumstances of the particular case which is under review; probabilities too fine to avail separately, too subtle and circuitous to be convertible into syllogisms, too numerous and various for such conversion, even were they convertible. As a man's portrait differs from a sketch of him, in having, not merely a continuous outline, but all the details filled in, and shades and colours laid on and harmonized together, such is the multiform and intricate process of ratiocination, necessary for our reaching him as a concrete fact, compared with the rude operation of syllogistic treatment.[14]

A cumulative argument is also used by Swinburne for the existence of God. He attempts to demonstrate a 'balance of probability', but the form of his argument is also what Mitchell would call 'cumulative'.

> I have argued that various occurrent phenomena are such that they are more to be expected, more probable if there is a God than if there is not. The existence of the universe, its conformity to order, the existence of animals and men, men having great opportunities for co-operation in acquiring knowledge and moulding the universe, the pattern of history and the existence of some evidence of miracles, and finally the occurrence of religious experiences, are all such as we have reason to expect if there is a God, and less reason to expect otherwise.[15]

Swinburne builds up an argument for the existence of God by examining the cosmological argument, teleological argument, arguments from consciousness and morality, providence, the existence of evil, and so on. What must be noted, however, is that he does not claim that any of these individually provide 'proofs' or a good inductive argument for theistic belief, but that they combine to form a persuasive cumulative effect.

> One unfortunate feature of recent philosophy of religion has been a tendency to treat arguments for the existence of God in isolation from each other. There can of course be no objection to considering each argument initially, for the sake of simplicity of exposition, in isolation from others. But clearly the arguments may back each other up or alternatively weaken each other, and we need to consider whether or not they do.[16]

Swinburne argues that the existence of God is the most probable explanation for the existence of a whole variety of factors. He attempts to determine the probability of this using Bayes's Theorem, but this does not seem to be possible.

> . . . as we have seen we just do not have the criteria for very precise estimation of probabilities in science or history or most other fields. However I now suggest that it is reasonable to come to the following qualitative judgment about the force of

the evidence so far considered (i.e. all the evidence apart from the evidence of religious experience). Theism does not have a probability close either to 1 or to 0, that is, on the evidence considered so far, theism is neither very probable nor very improbable.[17]

Swinburne's way around this problem is to suggest that one ought to broaden what is included in the argument, and then choose the most plausible hypothesis available.

The phenomena which we have been considering are puzzling and strange. Theism does not make their occurrence very probable; but nothing else makes their occurrence in the least probable, and they cry out for explanation. *A priori*, theism is perhaps very unlikely, but it is far more likely than any rival supposition. Hence our phenomena are substantial evidence for the truth of theism.[18]

Swinburne uses the claims based on religious experience as the clinching evidence.

The experience of so many men in their moments of religious vision corroborates what nature and history show to be quite likely – that there is a God who made and sustains man and the universe.[19]

The main difference between Mitchell's and Swinburne's cumulative arguments is that Swinburne takes a more traditional philosophical approach to his questions by attempting to justify one particular belief at a time, i.e. the existence of God. Mitchell on the other hand uses a cumulative argument to provide the required justification of religious belief, but he is also attempting to justify a whole set of traditional Christian beliefs on this basis. Mitchell thus provides a doubly cumulative argument because both the Christian beliefs in question and the justification of those beliefs are contended to function together in a provision of mutual support for each other. This results in a dialectical relationship between the premises and the conclusions. Swinburne does not push the possibilities of a cumulative argument so far as is done by Mitchell.

W.P. Alston has also adopted a cumulative form of argument in support of religious beliefs. He does not develop this in detail, but when he discusses issues such as the epistemology of religious experience, he does so in the context of what this experience could contribute to an argument which is based on many different footings.

> Perhaps it is a mistake to look for a foundation of one's faith that stands infallible, indubitable, and incorrigible, in no need of support from any other source. Perhaps no system of belief can be grounded in that way. Perhaps a more reasonable aspiration for the human condition is to have multiple sources of support such that although each can be questioned and none renders any of one's beliefs absolutely certain, they lend support to each other as well as to the beliefs they are invoked to support; so that in the way the whole assemblage fits together we have sufficient reason to take the beliefs to be true. Thus in order to answer the claim that one's putative experience of God is this-worldly only, one can appeal to the witness of others who are more advanced in the Christian life, to the revelation of God in His historical acts, and to general philosophical reasons for believing that God as constructed in Christianity does exist and rules His creation. Though each of these considerations can itself be doubted and though no single strand is sufficient to keep the faith secure, when combined into a rope they all together have enough strength to do the job.[20]

There is an impressive increase in support for the idea of a cumulative approach to the epistemology of religious beliefs. One could include all of the above writers, but also other figures as diverse as Charles Hartshorne, Elton Trueblood, J.R. Lucas, I.M. Crombie, and Austin Farrer. All of these have, in one form or other, deployed a cumulative argument to support the rationality of religious belief.

There are variations in the ways in which these arguments are individually constructed by their authors; however the same principle applies to all. This is the idea that the patient accumulation of various pieces of evidence can work in combination to provide rational justification for a belief, or in Mitchell's case, for a whole set of beliefs. Such arguments are not a theological peculiarity and they are also used in several other disciplines.

Theoretically, a defence of charismatic experience could be constructed in this 'cumulative' way. Often there will be a jumble of unusual physical phenomena to be assessed; healing, shaking, falling down, screaming, crying, jumping, etc. On their own these sensations are ambiguous, but they could be combined with a demonstration that the alternative explanations are less able to make sense of the facts than the hypothesis that they are caused by a direct intervention from God. There could be some biblical justification given for a particular experience. There is also an inner conviction as to the nature of the experience, and so one is then forced to reckon with the claim some people make that they have experienced God; that they have direct perception of him. Such a claim should not be dismissed outright without good reason. Following this experience there is the possibility of an altered life in terms of transformation of character, continuing peacefulness, generosity and changes in patterns and devotion in worship, and so on; characteristics which are unusual.

The charismatic Christian has an explanation for all of this even though it is one which could be questioned and reinterpreted in each of its component parts. If one is to dismiss a charismatic's understanding then it is not enough to claim simply that other explanations are possible. It is necessary to (a) demonstrate the faults in the charismatic understanding, (b) to produce an alternative and (c) to provide a justification as to the reason the alternative understanding is preferable.

Alternatives to a charismatic understanding are provided in the form of purely psychological explanations of enthusiastic phenomena, sociological examinations of the whole situation, differing theological ways of understanding these events, philosophical questions about the enthusiast's claims to knowledge, and so on.

The way to resolve this issue, therefore, would be to examine the content of each conflicting interpretation, and ask how each theory attempts to makes sense of the experience. Which of the options could more adequately explain the occurrence, character and effects of a charismatic experience?

The question raised by this is how can such a decision between varying hypotheses be made? What we must now examine is the way in which one can make a choice between these conflicting theories.

7

Can Ducks Turn into Rabbits?

Theories and paradigms

When we try to find out exactly what was the cause of a claimed religious experience, there will always be a number of competing theories which may be used to explain what was going on. The issue that needs to be addressed is how one can decide which of these hypotheses should be preferred. What criteria are on offer to assist in making a choice between conflicting theories?

This will become a more problematic issue than it may at first appear, and phrases we have been using such as 'making the best sense of evidence', or 'interpreting the facts' can begin to take on a more evident questionableness. In order to clarify the significance of these problems, we will take the example of a claimed 'prophecy' and see how such an event could be interpreted by people of differing views.

(i) At the simple end of the scale one is assessing the claim to prophecy in a context where there is broad agreement on the existence of God, on the attributes and purposes of God, on his capacity to speak, and on the means he uses to do so. If two people agree that the Bible represents God's revelation, and agree on its interpretation, and agree that God communicates to the church through prophecy; then one is asking a comparatively straightforward question, i.e. 'Is this prophecy from God?'

In such a situation one could find theoretically agreed methods which could be used to assess a particular claim to prophecy. The question could probably be resolved by appealing to the Bible which would be a mutually agreed source of knowledge. What is the character of the speaker? Does he have a reliable record in the past? What is the content of the prophecy?

Is it in conflict with other revelation? Is it supported by other revelation? If there is prediction involved, does it turn out to be accurate?

Many charismatic writers have written books with this internal level of questioning, for example, *Discerning the Spirits*, by Douglas Mcbain, *Come, Holy Spirit*, by Bishop David Pytches, or *Spiritual Gifts and the Church*, by Donald Bridge. These are books which aim to assess aspects of the charismatic movement. Indeed the subtitle of *Discerning the Spirits* is 'Checking for Truth in Signs and Wonders'. A claim to be able to determine what is 'true' in such a context would only be made from within the charismatic framework. This claim is only possible because the broader questions about authority, or interpreting religious experience, or what religious experience could contribute to the debate about the existence of God, are not at issue. These books are addressed to charismatic people by writers who share the same assumptions as their readers. Their scope and means of assessment are determined by the movement they aim to assess.

If we adopted the same assumptions and confined ourselves to such a level of difficulty, then we would have a resolvable and straightforward choice to make between possibly conflicting theories.

(ii) A higher level of difficulty in theory choice would follow from an increase in the complexity of the issue, while remaining within a Christian context. Say, for example, that both of the people who are attempting to assess this 'prophecy' still believe in God and agree on the authority of the Bible, but one claims that God no longer speaks directly to the church in this way since the completion of the New Testament. In order to resolve the issue of a disputed 'prophecy' in this context, one must ask, 'Does God speak through prophecy?' before one can ask, 'Is this prophecy from God?' This is an increase in complexity because there are more issues that would need resolution before the two sides could reach agreement on what the events mean.

On the other hand, one could argue that this would make assessment easier. If both sides stick to their assumptions, then they have no problem in analysing the prophecy. One side does the contingent assessment we have just outlined, and the other disbelieves the 'prophet' on the assumption that prophecy does not happen.

This will not suffice, however. Firstly because the two views share logically contradictory assumptions. One says that prophecy does occur, and the other says that it does not. One of them must therefore be wrong.

The second reason is more significant for this book. The assumptions of each side are not incorrigible or self-evident, and so each ought to allow their assumptions to be modified in the light of empirical evidence or of better theory. For example, experience can contribute something significant which could, in principle, modify a person's assumptions about how the world functions. Say that the prophecy turned out to be startlingly correct and to include knowledge which could only have come from God. In this situation it would be wise for the dispensationalist to re-think his assumptions about prophecy.

It is at this level of theory choice that the discussion begins to heat up, because some of the suppositions of each side are being questioned by the other. People tend to be rather ticklish about their presuppositions. Again much of the literature falls into this category of theory choice. There are authors, such as Peter Masters in *The Healing Epidemic*, or B.B. Warfield in *Counterfeit Miracles*, who accept cessationist presuppositions, and therefore rule out the possibility of current prophecy. Because the work of the Spirit is excluded as a possible explanation for a claim that an event is miraculous, or a prophecy genuine, then such authors tend to attribute dramatic events to Satan's work, or to deliberate deception on behalf of those involved. Where they are being more generous, they can ascribe the experience to psychological causes, or to mistaken beliefs.

Other writers defend charismatic experience from dispensational doctrine. For example, John Wimber argues that the church in the West needs to make a 'paradigm shift' in order to function properly in its use of the gifts of the Spirit. Views such as dispensationalism are a distortion of scripture, and the result of submitting true Christian thought, which allows room for God's supernatural intervention, to a Western rationalist strait-jacket. In order to recover the spiritual power of the New

Testament, then the church must break free from this unbiblical world view.

It is interesting that Wimber argues that this alteration in ideas constitutes a paradigm shift.

> Western Christians must undergo a paradigm (or perception) shift to become involved in a signs and wonders ministry. This is a shift towards a worldview that makes room for God's miraculous intervention. It is not that we allow God's intervention: he does not need our permission. The shift is that we begin to see his miraculous works and allow them to affect our lives.[1]

A paradigm shift may be an acceptable description of this level of theory choice because it involves looking at the world in a different way, interpreting the 'facts' in ways that were not done before and effectively making what is analogous to a 'gestalt switch'.[2] It also means accepting different methods of establishing what can be known, i.e. direct revelation in the place of reason.

It is still, however, a 'sub paradigm' shift because behind this alteration in views there remains a vast amount of agreement between the two sides over who is God, the person of Jesus, the church, the supremacy of biblical authority in resolving the dispute, and so on.

(iii) The previous two levels of complexity in theory choice are still internal choices within a web of Christian beliefs. Both sides have vast areas of agreement on many issues which are crucial to resolving the dispute. The problems in choosing between competing theories increase to the point where they become potentially insurmountable when the distance between the two sides becomes so great that the objection to a claim to prophecy comes from someone outside of the Christian web of belief. In this situation one is not just asking 'Is this prophecy from God?', and 'Does God speak through prophecy?', because the question, 'Is there a God?' needs to be resolved first. The distance between the two sides in this situation is so wide that they rarely address each other, because each has such differing presuppositions from the other. If these two sides are to reach agreement, then considerable modifications will be required in one or in both webs of belief.

Take the example of an explanation of a charismatic experience of 'prophecy' made by an atheistic psychologist. He may want to explore such issues as the psychological motivation behind a person's religious claims, or perhaps point out that this person had adopted the same beliefs as his parents. He will be aware that religious experiences have been understood in a variety of psychological or pathological ways which offer explanation of them without reference to God. They can be attributed, for example, to hyper-suggestibility or hypnotic techniques.[3] Our psychologist may point out that deprivation and maladjustment may account for some forms of 'religious' experience, as may mental illness or abnormal physiological states, such as those induced by drug taking.[4]

From the point of view of our atheist, whatever the proposed *mechanism* at work, the *content* of the 'prophet's' message is not an issue which needs addressing. To ask 'Is this prophecy from God?' would be meaningless if one were thinking within a paradigm that excluded the existence of God. The assumptions which determined the shape of this person's paradigm would also exclude the possibility or necessity of asking such a question. Consequently the prospect that this prophecy could have some true cognitive content which had been revealed by God would not even be an issue which would need to be addressed.

Because the truth of the 'prophet's' claim is not an issue, this tends to create a condescending attitude. One side assumes there is no God, and therefore these claims to be the receiver of revelation are of necessity false, and these religious people are deluded.

This conceptual gulf has significant implications for groups who intend to use 'signs and wonders' as a form of evangelism. Even if one does perform miracles, there is still a vast distance between world views which needs to be crossed in some way. In the context where Jesus performed his miracles, this gulf was not so large because these acts were done within a group of people who shared many significant beliefs with each other.

These three categories are arbitrary points along a gradation in the differences between theories. They do, however, help to illustrate the way that complexity in the choice between conflicting theories increases as the assumptions of the two differing views diverge. This reaches a point where the discussion is taking place across the gulf between two paradigms, and the contended issues are quite impossible to resolve until at least one of the two sides makes a major change in its web of belief.

Consequently the way in which a person answers the question, 'If a person claims to be encountering God in his experience, how can you tell whether he really is?', depends on his situation within a web of belief. As it was put by C.S. Lewis: 'What you see and hear depends a good deal on where you are standing: it also depends on what sort of a person you are.'[5] This is significantly more complex than a straightforward choice between conflicting theories, because it also involves a choice between different paradigms. There are difficult issues to face up to at this point, because it is disputed (a) whether it is possible to talk meaningfully across differing paradigms, and (b) whether is possible to make a rational choice between them at all.

Making the choice between conflicting theories

We will begin with the issue of simple theory choice before going on to the more complex question of the way in which the choice between paradigms can be made. There are many writers who have written on how the choice between rival theories can be made. For example, according to Thomas Kuhn, the 'only three normal foci for scientific investigation'[6] are (a) accuracy and scope, (b) predictive capacity and (c) fruitfulness.

A.J. Ayer take the opposite approach from Kuhn, in that he suggests focussing on ways in which a particular thesis could be *discredited*, rather than rationally supported. The main question to ask is, 'Is it free of internal contradiction?' 'Thus, *so long as it is free from internal contradiction*, it is hard to see how any philosophical thesis can be refuted, and equally hard to see how it can ever be proved.'[7] Internal contradiction would be the one clearly logical way to rationally disprove a particular theory.

Karl Popper gives primary importance to falsification. This follows in the path of Francis Bacon: 'Truth emerges more readily from error than from confusion.'[8]

A theory can be regarded as 'true' or rather 'corroborated' when it has withstood all attempts at falsification up to the present. This leaves science in a continual process of trial and error and therefore in a position of searching for the truth, but without the right to claim that it has the truth in its possession.

In *The Web of Belief* W.V.O. Quine suggests six 'virtues' which would be a feature (in varying degrees), as part of a successful hypothesis. These features are conservatism, modesty, simplicity, generality, refutability and precision.[9]

Although there is no uncontroversial and definitive list of criteria which automatically determine the selection of a particular hypothesis, when it is in competition with an alternative, there are broadly accepted 'values' which aid in making the best choice between conflicting theories. If there was a straightforward decision to make between theories, in assessing charismatic experience, then the process would be comparatively simple. One would apply the kind of values outlined above, and see which theory comes out with the most support on that basis. Limiting ourselves to assessing enthusiastic claims from within the system itself would therefore leave us with relatively few difficulties to resolve.

However, if we intend to face up to more complex levels of assessment, then the issue of paradigm and paradigm choice needs to be explored. The situation here is more problematic because the choice is not a simple two-theory choice within an agreed framework of values, facts and methodology. There are two or more separate *systems* of thought which underlie the differing theories, and which are in competition with each other to provide coherent understanding. Each has its own presuppositions and methods, and even its own definition of what counts as fact.

For example, one may be theistic understanding, and the other atheistic. These two paradigms provide radically different ways of looking at reality and compete with each other for supremacy in interpreting an individual experience. The same sort of conflict also occurs outside the religious context: for example, in the case of competing metaphysical systems, scientific paradigms, radical Marxist beliefs, or of Freudian and non-Freudian literary criticism.

This kind of situation creates particular problems when there is a dispute between such different paradigms. There can be profound conceptual differences between the two sides. Each tends to accommodate any evidence and arguments into its own system, and to re-assess them in the light of its own principles. They tend to talk across each other and be lost in mutual incomprehension.

Take, for example, the question of the reality of miracles in the New Testament. If one starts the examination of these events with a materialistic or Humean view of reality, then a report of a miracle should not be believed. That reported miracles ought not to be believed is assumed to be a fact, and therefore all evidence is interpreted in its light. Consequently, claimed 'miracles' must have some kind of mechanistic explanation, or are perhaps myths which have been added on to the story of Jesus by the early church. When such a paradigm-determined methodology is applied to, say for example, prophecy which seems to be accurate, it must have been written after the event. This is because it is assumed to be impossible for someone to know beforehand what is to occur. This will be given priority over the literary evidence as regards date or authenticity. From this point of view, for example, the predictions of the fall of Jerusalem in AD 70 could not have been made by Jesus, and must have been added at a later stage by some editor of the material.

The evangelical fundamentalist, however, complains at the unfairness of this approach to the evidence, and at the Humean assumption that determines the nature of the argument. He wants to ask, 'Why should one's attitude to the miraculous not be modified in response to the facts of history, rather than the facts being adjusted to suit an assumption about what is possible?'

What I want us to note in this argument, however, is that it is not just a simple difference of approach to literary criticism, but a clash between two different views of reality. Because of this, what is deemed to be possible, and what are regarded as the facts, are determined by the relevant paradigm. To one who is a Christian, his own interpretation seems the natural and obvious one, and the others will appear forced and unreasonable; while to one who is not a Christian, the reverse will appear to be the case. Each is astonished at the stupidity of the other view.

If we are going to be able to assess charismatic experience in a way that is more than mere conceptual relativism it is essential that we should see if it is possible to make a rational choice between different paradigms. If this is not possible, then in many circumstances one would be unable to make a rational choice between an enthusiastic interpretation of experience, and another competing explanation. This would imply that the possibility of assessment would be very limited indeed. One would not be able to say anything rational in support or in opposition to an interpretation of a claimed religious experience. You have your point of view and I have mine; not much more could be said. Consequently, we must give some thought to paradigms and to paradigm choice.

The nature of paradigms

'Paradigm' is defined in *A Dictionary of Philosophy* as:

> In the philosophy of science, a central overall way of regarding phenomena, within which a scientist normally works. The paradigm may dictate what type of explanation will be found acceptable, but in periods of crisis a science may exchange paradigms. *In its usual employment in the present context the term is both ambiguous and vague.*[10]

The truth of this last sentence is soon evident when one examines the various way in which the word is used.

Depending on the writer,[11] paradigm differences can be a combination of different presuppositions, different aims, different attitudes, 'absolute presuppositions',[12] 'basic commitments',[13] 'bliks',[14] different concepts of truth, the 'philosophic background' influencing the science of the time;[15] 'standards of rationality and intelligibility' which provide 'fundamental patterns of expectation' so that 'we see the world through them to such an extent that we forget what it would look like without them',[16] different stand-points, a gestalt switch, different views of reality, a different set of beliefs, a different model, or different methods. According to Hans Küng, a paradigm is an 'interpretive model', an 'explanatory model' or a 'model for understanding'.[17] The word has also found its way into computer science, psychology, sociology, theology and other disciplines who each adapt its meaning to their own purposes.

'Paradigm' is being used in rather slippery ways, and so one needs care in interpreting a particular writer's use of the word, because it seems to be defined by its context.

If we go back to the beginning, we find that the Greek root of the word is a 'pattern' or 'example', and this was how the word was used in England until the latter half of the twentieth century. A 'paradigm case' would be representative or typical of something; a standard form, or a classic example. One example would be 'paradigms' of regular nouns and verbs.

The meaning of the word took a new twist in 1963 with the publication of *The Structure of Scientific Revolutions* by Thomas Kuhn. In this book paradigm was used to describe a basic conceptual model of reality. The two meanings are connected in that they could both be described as a 'model'. However, in the way that Kuhn used it, this 'model' is that of a large-scale pattern to which the physical world or its appearances are argued to conform. It is this later 'large scale' sense of the word with which we are concerned here.

In *The Structure of Scientific Revolutions* Kuhn argued that the scientific community was dominated by paradigms, by which he meant: 'standard examples of scientific work which embody a set of conceptual, methodological and metaphysical assumptions'. A paradigm is an entire constellation of beliefs, values, techniques, and so on shared by the members of a given community.[18] The concept of paradigm is used by Kuhn to describe a complex (and controversial) mix of ideas, and there is a well-known history of conflict over these ideas, particularly with Karl Popper. Kuhn's description of paradigm could be summarized briefly as follows.

Kuhn uses the word paradigm to refer to a scientific theory which has a dramatic degree of predictive power in a situation where older accepted theory has become unable to keep up. It is important that it should be so striking that other scientists will attempt to develop further successes by modelling their own explanations and predictions on the same paradigm. Sometimes a paradigm can be so significant that it will create a whole field, such as celestial mechanics which was a product of the Newtonian paradigm.

The paradigm is an achievement, in the sense that it provides an accepted way of resolving problems more effectively than its predecessor.[19] He also maintains that a paradigm has considerable immunity from falsification, and can only be overthrown by a new paradigm. A paradigm will not be given up simply because of a few awkward observational results, but only when a better all-encompassing theory is available.

The most controversial and interesting aspect of Kuhn's idea of paradigm is his description of the process by which a paradigm is replaced. The choice between paradigms here is determined by such considerations as 'faith', 'elegance' and 'conversion', rather than by purely rational argument.

> there is another sort of consideration that can lead scientists to reject an old paradigm in favour of a new. These are the arguments, rarely made entirely explicit, that appeal to the individual's sense of the appropriate or the aesthetic – the new theory is said to be 'neater', 'more suitable', or 'simpler' than the old.[20]

> The importance of aesthetic considerations can sometimes be decisive.[21]

His description of the process by which a paradigm is replaced is analogous to conversion; 'Scientists then often speak of the "scales falling from their eyes"'.[22] This 'conversion' cannot be objectively assessed, because there are no neutral historical or methodological canons to which one can appeal. Kuhn describes this 'conversion' in terms of seeing the world in a different way:

Nevertheless, paradigm changes do cause scientists to see the world of their research-engagement differently. In so far as their only recourse to that world is through what they see and do, we may want to say that after a revolution scientists are responding to a different world . . .

What were ducks in the scientist's world before the revolution are rabbits afterwards . . . Therefore, at times of revolution, when the normal-scientific tradition changes, the scientist's perception of his environment must be re-educated – in some familiar situations he must learn to see a new gestalt. After he has done so the world of his research will seem, here and there, incommensurable with the one he had inhabited before. That is another reason why schools guided by different paradigms are always slightly at cross purposes.[23]

Kuhn uses the analogy of a 'switch in visual gestalt' (such as the patterns which can be seen in a necca cube, or a 'magic eye' picture), but suggests that a change of a scientific paradigm has even more variables. In the case of a gestalt switch, it is appropriate to say that the subject interprets the data differently when he sees, say, a duck or a rabbit. He can learn to direct his attention to the lines on the paper and can come to see these lines without seeing either of the figures. But this is not the case with a scientific paradigm. Here even the data are not unequivocally stable, and it is therefore more than a change in interpretation. A change in paradigm can also be a revision of the 'basic facts'. At this point he has been accused of being radically subjective, and even irrational.[24]

Not only does Kuhn use the language of Christian conversion to describe a paradigm change, but the establishment of the new paradigm even requires *faith* if it is to succeed.

The man who embraces a new paradigm at an early stage must often do so in defiance of the evidence provided by problem-solving. He must, that is, have faith that the new paradigm will succeed with the many large problems that confront it, knowing only that the older paradigm has failed with a few. A decision of that kind can only be made on faith.[25]

When a paradigm is established, one is in a period of 'normal science'. This normality continues until it is superseded by a new theory which can more successfully deal with problems which have arisen under the old system.

Kuhn's writing refers specifically to scientific paradigms, but the same issues arise in other disciplines, for example where there is a conflict between competing metaphysical systems, or between different theological systems. It is quite possible to describe the major changes which have occurred in theology over the centuries as changes in paradigms. For example, the systems of thought initiated by Origen, Augustine, or Martin Luther were radically distinct from previous systems of thought. The same could also be said of post-modernist theology in the current theological context.[26]

John Watkins draws some other interesting parallels between theological and scientific paradigms:

> Consider a theological scholar working on an apparent inconsistency between two biblical passages. Theological doctrine assures him that the Bible, properly understood, contains no inconsistencies. His task is to provide a gloss that offers a convincing reconciliation of the two passages. Such work seems essentially analogous to 'normal' scientific research as depicted by Kuhn; and there are grounds for supposing that he would not repudiate the analogy. For *The Structure of Scientific Revolutions* contains many suggestions, some explicit, others implicit in the choice of language, or a significant parallelism between science, especially Normal Science and theology. Kuhn writes of a scientific education as a 'process of initiation' which 'prepares the student for membership in the particular scientific community'. He says that 'it is a narrow and rigid education, probably more so than any other except perhaps in orthodox theology'.[27]

There are distinct similarities between theological and scientific paradigms. This implies that the choice between religious and non-religious interpretations of experience will have similar problems to those which are inherent in the choice of different paradigms in other contexts, but it also implies that the resolutions of these difficulties could also be of use in theology.

Within the paradigm of Christian thought there is a sub-paradigm called 'enthusiasm'. It has its own communities, methodologies, means of assessment, and internal consistency. It manifests the cross purpose conversations which are typical of communication between paradigms, and it has its own constellation of beliefs. Enthusiasm has its own means of defining that which should be considered to be a fact and has its own ways of reaching knowledge. Consequently it is so different from traditional Christianity, that it is entitled to be described as a distinct paradigm.

Difficulties in making a rational choice between competing paradigms

It is obvious that paradigm choice in any context is complex. The difficulties can in theory be overcome, but in a short book such as this there are too many issues involved for us to be able to provide a comprehensive discussion on all of them. For example, there is a problem of language difference, problems of paradigm related facts, methodology and evaluative procedures. There is a lack of criteria which could be specified *in advance* which would determine the paradigm change. The choice is therefore sometimes considered to be a sociological issue, which would leave any paradigm choice as a relativistic and irrational conversion.

One key problem which needs to be resolved if a rational choice is to be made between paradigms is the issue of paradigm relative 'facts'. This issue is raised by Kuhn's description of a paradigm, which impugns the neutrality of facts. If he is correct, then it would imply that paradigm choice could *not* be made in the way that a normal theory choice can be made. This is because subjecting the hypotheses to the facts, and then abandoning those theories that fail the test, is not possible because what are considered to be facts are paradigm relative.

For the scientist this problem is particularly acute because he will have to choose between unusually high level theories. When this situation occurs, then a decision has to be made, but this decision cannot be determined simply by the 'facts'. Some of the 'facts' could also be seen as interpretive theories in relation to other 'facts', and it is therefore always possible in principle to call them into question.

For example the cornerstone of modern cosmology is the theory that the space and time have been expanding since the 'big bang' a few billion years ago.

So when did the big bang occur? This could be determined by measuring the rate at which the other stars are receding from us, and therefore the rate of expansion of the universe. The methods used to establish this seem increasingly point to a lower age for the universe than was thought, even down to 8 billion years according to some physicists.

This creates a problem because there are stars in our own solar system which are 'known' to be over 14 billion years old. The ages of stars are determined by mature and self-consistent physics, using well-established methods, but they give results which are quite at odds with a universe which is only 8 billion years old.

The difficulty is that these 'observations' of the stars and the expanding universe are not strictly speaking 'observational'. They are arrived at on the basis of a variety of complex experimental techniques which are based on differing theories.

So what do you do now? The means of dating a star can be used uncritically as background knowledge, but why shouldn't contradictory data indicating a young universe throw this open to question? In this situation, the measurement of the rate of expansion of the universe is treated as providing the facts, and the methods used to date the age of a star are falsified.

Yet again one could treat the age of the stars as being factual, and let this undermine the evidence which would date the universe at only 8 billion years.

Another way of resolving the problem would be to throw everything into the air and attempt a theory which is different from the big bang theory, but more able to cope with anomalies between the apparent age of the universe and the age of the stars. In this case the basic theory is overthrown while the 'observations' of the age of stars and the rate of expansion of the universe are both treated as being facts. However, one would be very reluctant to do this because the theory is supported by accurate mathematical prediction of how the universe has turned out to be. Consequently most physicists would rather treat this theory as background knowledge and question contradictory 'observations'.

This interesting concept of factual relativity creates a knotty problem, and yet it can be overcome in a number of ways

First, while this paradigm-relativity is true of some facts it is not true of all of them because there are also neutral facts which are comparatively reliable as reference points. The idea of 'paradigm relative facts' is only true up to a point. Decisions are made within a framework of agreed facts, such as specified scientific language, and 'common-sense' facts of the sort that are presupposed in all scientific inquiry. It is important to emphasize this, because this idea of paradigm relative facts has been overstated at times. A particular paradigm has very many facts which are *not* wholly relative to that paradigm, and so its facts are not all paradigm relative.

Secondly, it is also important to note the historical point that a particular paradigm does not stand in total isolation from other systems of thought. In reality it will come to be preferred because it is able to make the best sense, not only of its 'own' facts, but also of the 'facts' which were part of the alternative paradigm. Its ability to do this is indicative of a rational link between two separate systems.

A particular paradigm will have very many close connections with that which superseded it, and a large part of its theory and 'factual' content will be in continuity with other world views. This is described by Quine as the virtue of 'conservatism' in the decision to adopt a particular hypothesis.

> Conservatism is rather effortless on the whole, having inertia in its favour. But it is a sound strategy too, since at each step it sacrifices as little as possible of the evidential support, whatever that may have been, that our overall system of beliefs has hitherto been enjoying.[28]

There is always a significant element of continuity when a new scientific paradigm is appropriated. The new paradigm continues to use the same methods of observation, reason and hypothesis, and is adopted, not just because of its ability to comprehend its own 'facts', but because it offers a more coherent interpretation of facts which belonged to the previous paradigm.

The way in which the theory of relativity superseded Newtonian physics provides a good example of this process:

> The aftermath of the famous Michelson-Morley experiment of 1887 is a case in point. The purpose of this delicate and ingenious experiment was to measure the speed with which the earth travels through the ether. For two centuries, from Newton onward, it had been a well entrenched tenet that something called the ether pervaded all of what we think of as empty space. The great physicist Lorentz 1853–1928 had hypothesized that the ether itself was stationary. What the experiment revealed was that the method that was expected to enable measurement of the earth's speed through the ether was totally inadequate to that task. Supplementary hypotheses multiplied in an attempt to explain the failure without seriously disrupting the accepted physics. Lorentz, in an effort to save the hypothesis of stationary ether, shifted to a new more complicated set of formulas in his mathematical physics. Einstein soon cut through all this, propounding what is called the special theory of relativity.[29]

The theory of relativity is therefore adopted because it is better able to make sense of the facts which were observed *under Newtonian science* and of the anomalies which had arisen. It replaced a system which had become overburdened with supplementary hypotheses and unnecessary complication to the point where it was *itself* aware of a crisis.

While one can understand what he means, Kuhn is consequently being rather misleading when he says that 'What were ducks in the scientist's world before the revolution are rabbits afterwards',[30] and that the new paradigm will

> gather up large portions of that experience and transform them

to a rather different bundle of experience that will thereafter be linked piecemeal to the new paradigm, *but not to the old.*[31]

There has been no scientific revolution, at least not yet, which was radical enough to loose its links with what has gone before. Indeed, two of the features of a new hypothesis which would make it more likely to be of value, are (according to Quine) not just the virtue of 'conservatism', but also 'modesty'.[32]

> What is thus illustrated by Einstein's relativity is more modestly exemplified elsewhere, and generally aspired to: the retention, in some sense, of old theories in new ones. If the new theory can be so fashioned as to diverge from the old only in ways that are undetectable in most ordinary circumstances, then it inherits the evidence of the old theory rather than trying to overcome it. Such is the force of conservatism even in the context of revolution.[33]

If we apply all of this to a paradigm change, then we are viewing such a shift as being a change in hypothesis; one which functions in principle the same way as all theory change would. Granted, the leap is greater, as is the extent of the implications and the risks, but the process is fundamentally the same. The confusion in the debate about the subjectivity of this change is partly a result of language, as paradigm shift is being used in an unrealistically absolute sense; one which does not seem to occur in reality. Paradigm is not an ontologically unique category, it is a particularly complex group of theories. Ironically, the more absolute one's concept of the change is, the more subjective is the decision to adopt it.

All of this implies that the facts of a particular paradigm have a substantial overlap with other systems of thought, and are only paradigm-relative to a limited extent. The possibility of a rational choice between conflicting paradigms is therefore not undermined by the existence of some paradigm relative facts.

How this tricky choice between paradigms can be made is by using our old friend, the mechanism of a cumulative argument. Consequently this is not a choice which is made on the basis of strict logic, but this does not render the process inevitably irrational or 'irreducibly sociological'. Kuhn describes the way in which the conceptual revolution operates in these terms.

> . . . if the paradigm is one destined to win its fight, the number and strength of the persuasive arguments in its favour will increase. More scientists will then be converted, and the exploration of the new paradigm will go on. Gradually the number of experiments, instruments, articles, and books based upon the paradigm will multiply. Still more men, convinced of the new view's fruitfulness, will adopt the new mode of practising normal science, until at last only a few elderly hold-outs remain.[34]

This is clearly not an exercise in strict logic, but it could still consist of more than a description of the psychology of philosophers and scientists. There is a progressive accumulation of evidence from many different directions which give support to the new theory.

The choice between paradigms is not therefore an irreducibly sociological or irrational decision. Neither is the choice rendered irrational by the issue of paradigm relative facts. The other suggested difficulties in overcoming paradigm choice are also in principle capable of being overcome, and so it ought to be possible to make a rational choice between conflicting paradigms.

Some implications and analogies

We have argued that a theological system of thought can be considered as a paradigm, and in particular that enthusiasm is distinct enough in its characteristics that it is entitled to be called a paradigm. There are considerable problems in choosing between paradigms, but the main objections to paradigm choice being a choice which can only be accounted for sociologically rather than evaluated epistemologically, can be overcome, at least in principle.

This is important, because this implies that it is also possible to make a rational choice between conflicting interpretations of charismatic experience, even when they are at the more complex level of theory choice where one needs to be able to make a decision between competing conceptual systems.

If this is so then it is not good enough to rely on one's own assumptions without facing up to the challenge that an alternative paradigm presents to them, because the issue of paradigm choice is, in principle, capable of rational resolution.

Kuhn usefully used the analogy of a switch in visual gestalt to describe paradigm change. We will explore some other analogies to see if they can further clarify our thoughts on paradigms.

Paradigms as a group of circles   Perhaps it would be possible to describe a paradigm by using the analogy of circles drawn on paper. Some of the circles overlap others by various amounts, and others are concentric, thus taking the form of onion layers.

This helps to illustrate the way that paradigms relate to each other, as it allows for an overlap between aspects of distinct paradigms such as acceptance of rational methods, use of empirical evidence, inductive reasoning, and so on.

For example, it would be possible for a cosmologist to work within the framework of relativity, and also hold a set of Christian beliefs. This could be thought of as three overlapping circles. Newtonian physics is part of the picture because of the large area of overlap which exists between these two systems. Our physicist may be doing this work motivated by a desire to understand the work of the Creator in his creation. This would provide him with a constellation of Christian beliefs with their own distinct character, as well as having additional areas of overlap with cosmology. If he is also a member of a particular denomination, then he may have a concentric circle within the overall system of Christian beliefs.

This is helpful, but not sufficient to cover all the aspects of paradigm we have discussed.

Paradigm in the web of belief   The conception of a web of belief is an analogy which is attributed to Quine. I would like to develop the notion of this structure and use it to explore ways of describing the concept of paradigm. To adopt the idea of a web of belief is to imply that there is no need for an incorrigible foundation which functions in support of the beliefs contained within it. Rather, beliefs are acceptable because of the way in which they relate to the other parts of the conceptual scheme; beliefs, 'facts', theories, methodology and (most significantly for this thesis), experience. Placing the concept of paradigm into such a 'web of belief' is useful because it provides a continuity with the 'cumulative approach' we intend to take.

To consider the anatomy of this web we will begin, so to speak, at its periphery. In these outer edges of the web we have beliefs which are more willingly surrendered than the increasingly influential and firmly embedded beliefs which are encountered as we move towards the central areas. The outer edge consists of the most tentative beliefs.

For example, a person hears an engine roaring down a road behind him and thinks it is a motorbike. When it comes into sight, however, it turns out to be a car. The original guess was wrong, but insignificant in the sense that other areas of the web of belief are hardly influenced by the renunciation of the first idea. A belief in this outer edge of the web could really be little more than a guess. It may be correct, but the believer holds his opinions in this part of the web in a very tentative fashion. Even if the original guess is wrong, it really doesn't matter (unless, of course, the car runs the believer over!).

Moving into the depths of the web we begin to encounter a more significant realm of theories. These are held with more conviction than would be a mere guess. A guess may well be the first stage of developing a theory, but in this area of the web, the guess is potentially consequential, and so needs to be put to a more rigorous empirical test.

Imagine a person who suspects that he has been adopted into the family that raised him, even though he was never told this by his acting parents. This suspicion leads him to do some research, and through this, he discovers that he was in fact left on the doorstep of the adoptive family. The confirmation of the original suspicion alters other parts of his web of belief in terms of the way those who were thought of as being blood sisters, brothers, and parents are related to him.

Further into the web we reach the province of 'laws'. These are still theories in essence, but they are more significant and firmly embedded. They are also applied inductively to the whole of the universe. An example of this would be the speed of light being 186,000 miles per second, which is a universally applied law. If it were to be found unveridical, it would have widespread effects on many branches of science.

Deeper still we come to the domain of what is described as paradigm. It still has the same basic nature as the outer theories, in that it could be described as a 'story' which is made to fill up the gaps in the empirical evidence, or as a particular understanding of reality. A paradigm is, however, more significant than other theories because it is held with such conviction that it is presupposed; and so widespread in its implications, that to alter it would create upheaval throughout the rest of the system. The classic examples which are often given of two separate paradigms are Newtonian physics or Einstein's relativity.

This means that as one moves deeper into the web there is a gradation in the extent of the theory's influence, and in the strength of conviction in the believer who accepts these increasingly consequential theories. When viewed in this way, rather than a paradigm being an ontologically distinct category, it is in continuity with all other theories. The words we are using; guess, theory, law, and paradigm are imposed on the web of belief in an artificial way in the sense that there is a gradation of consequentiality through the model. They do not, in reality, describe sharply defined areas within the web of belief.

As has been discussed, some writers, particularly Kuhn, appeared to put quite extreme emphasis on the concept of paradigm by treating it as being absolute, or as an 'absolute presupposition'. Where there is a paradigm change there are no links with that which came before; ducks even become rabbits in the new world.[35]

If paradigm differences were as absolute as these images imply, then there *would* indeed be no logical road between paradigms. There would be no agreement on what are the facts, or on methods by which disagreement could be resolved. The choice would be a leap in the dark dependent on the scientific culture in which one's thinking has been shaped.

If we imagine a paradigm that was so different from its predecessor that it lost all the basic assumptions of the previous world view, it would be such an extreme change that it would be incomprehensible. It would use a different language in different ways, and have a different concept of what is rational. Indeed, it would be an implicit rejection of all that counted as knowledge before its arrival. It would accept none of any previous experimental 'fact' or theory, and would mean demolishing and rebuilding every method, fact and hypothesis used by science in the past. It could be internally coherent, but such a paradigm would be so unrelated to every other form of knowledge or pattern of thought, that it would appear as much like insanity as like progress in understanding. There would be no extrinsic means of testing which of these two appearances was correct.

The way to avoid such an unrealistic description of a paradigm change is to start with a less extreme definition of paradigm. This also has the benefit of being a more accurate description of the way it functions in reality. As we have seen, there are still many assumptions behind paradigms; ones which remain in continuity when the new world view is adopted. In principle changes in absolute presuppositions would be paradigm changes, but an 'absolute' change does not accurately describe the way that scientific changes have occurred in reality. Newtonian physics was never an 'absolute' presupposition.[36]

This leaves us with a gap between the degree of upheaval involved when paradigms alter in the real history of science or theology, and some of the extreme descriptions of what is involved in those changes. To clarify this situation we need a modification to the web of belief we suggested earlier. Paradigm is not at the centre of the web, because there are absolute presuppositions at a stage further in towards the centre. During a paradigm change these remain in continuity between the two world views and ensure significant lines of communication between them.

As we have already discussed, there is a vast amount of common ground between paradigms. For example, Newtonian physics shares with relativity a common scientific method, relativity is adopted because it makes better sense of the facts observed under the previous world view, it uses the same means of observation, and so on. This is very important, because it implies that there is a theoretical possibility that the adherents of differing paradigms can communicate coherently with each other because they share significant suppositions. In principle the two paradigms can work back through the web of belief until they find enough shared assumptions on which to base a discussion about which world view is the better description of reality.

A change in absolute presuppositions would be far more significant than such an alteration in a scientific paradigm.

Say, for example, one moved from a paradigm which accepted that events needed causes, into a situation where a large community of people believed, as a presupposition, that events were wholly disconnected from causes. This would be much more basic an alteration that has occurred in any historic paradigm change. Even more fundamental than a rejection of causation would be a rejection of the use of reason. If reason were to be replaced by a system which rejected all rational thought, then one would be in such a different world view that all discussion that made a claim on anyone would be ruled out, because reasoning is a condition of any cognitively useful dialogue.

Such changes may be possible in principle, though the degree of upheaval within the web of belief that would be required to adopt them makes it very unlikely that we will ever see such a fundamental paradigm shift in reality.

If the concept of paradigm is understood as being an area which is embedded deeply in a web of belief, then the word is to some extent vague in its use, because it describes a reality where hypothesis grades into theory which grades into law, on into paradigm, which in turn grades into absolute presupposition.

If one also assigns the more extreme 'absolute' descriptions of paradigm to an abstract realm at the furthest end of the spectrum from the guess, then they do make sense. One does need more moderation, however, in describing the real history of scientific discovery, and real changes in theological paradigms. The element of continuity between real paradigms is stronger, the changes are not absolute in nature, and there is growth in knowledge as a result.

Paradigm as an arch of belief Using the analogy of an arch holds good in a number of useful ways.

In the structure of an arch each of the stones in the arch is unable to hold up the entire structure alone. An arch does not preserve its shape because it has some 'incorrigible' stone which creates a single span. It is an entire 'constellation' of stones which are arranged into a system which is capable of providing the necessary support. It has a cumulative strength created by stones which individually would be unable to support the structure as a whole. The arch exists because of the relationship the stones have with each other.

This description of the way in which an arch maintains its existence bears a resemblance to the way in which a paradigm functions. A paradigm has its own internally consistent relationship between the beliefs, assumptions, methodology and experiences that make it up. The paradigm has a set of assumptions which can support a whole constellation of beliefs, and it is when these elements are functioning together in a proper relationship that the paradigm is strong.

In an arch the material supported by the arch contributes to the strength of the whole structure because the more weight that is put on it, the more tightly the stones are forced together. There is a complex set of internal stresses which contribute to the strength of the structure as a whole.

This is an interesting concept when compared with the structure of a paradigm, because this is also the situation there. What occurs is a constant dialectic between the assumptions of the paradigm, its 'facts', its theories, its means of assessment, its ability to predict, its experiences and so on. The paradigm exists in a constant process of trial and error, where each part of the system is adding support to each other part.

What is crucial to note here is that this mutual support can also occur between paradigms. One has, in reality, numerous sub paradigms which operate on the basis of larger ones. For example, Newtonian physics and relativity operate within a larger paradigm which would include the rationality of scientific method itself in terms of experimental methods, induction and deduction, trial and error in the refinement of theories, and so on.

The choice between two sub paradigms is made within the context of a more basic collection of beliefs. This is what makes mutual dialogue a possibility.

If we retain the analogy of an arch, then this may be compared with a situation in which there are smaller arches supported by a larger one. The ground could be compared with absolute presuppositions.

The significance of the widespread mutual dependency that exists within, and provides support for, belief systems does not seem to be generally appreciated. For example, in *Battle for the Mind* by William Sargant there is an analysis of conversion and Pentecostal experience which explains these phenomena in terms of brain washing, hypnosis, and other psychological mechanisms. The book begins as follows:

> It must be emphasized as strongly as possible that this book is not concerned with the truth or falsity of any particular religious or political belief. Its purpose is to examine some of the mechanisms involved in the fixing or destroying of such beliefs in the human brain.[37]

If Sargant's point is simply that causal questions and evaluative questions are logically distinct from each other, then this would be quite acceptable. However, a total separation between these two factors is unrealistic in the context of a large-scale conceptual system, such as Christian belief, because it envisages a set of almost incorrigible reasons for beliefs which exist in isolation from experience. The reality is of mutual interconnection between all the factors which support the particular set of beliefs. Consequently, an inexplicable and dramatic conversion experience is something which contributes to a person's system of beliefs as a whole. He believes the Bible's account of conversion partly because it accords with his own experience, and he interprets his own experience in the light of what the Bible leads him to expect. Stated like this it is far too simple, and clearly circular. However, added to this simplistic account may be other supports in the form of historical evidence, a coherent philosophy, other people's experience, existential evidence in the shape of an unusual change in life and personality, a claimed direct perception of God, and so on. It is the entire accumulation of factors working together which supports the system of beliefs. This means that an alternative way of understanding a mechanism of experience can potentially have a significant effect on the system of beliefs as a whole.

Darwin faced the same issue when he published *The Origin of Species*. His aim was not to undermine theistic belief, but rather to understand the works of the Creator:

> There is grandeur in this view of life with its several powers, having been originally breathed by the Creator into a few forms or into one; and that, whilst this planet has gone cycling on according to the fixed law of gravity, from so simple a beginning endless forms most beautiful and most wonderful have been, and are being evolved.[38]

Although he did not intend to undermine Christian faith, the effect was that he weakened a part of the arch which was central to many people's theistic belief, i.e. the argument from design. The loss of this was enough to call into question the entire system, because it created an intellectually credible explanation for the extreme complexity which is found in nature, whereas previously, the only available explanation for this was to attribute this apparent design to an intelligent creator. This is not a moral judgment; it is simply pointing out that a constellation of beliefs functions in mutual relationship, and that in practice individual parts of this do not separate out into neatly distinguished and logically distinct parts.

When a paradigm begins to collapse, each part of the system is calling the rest into question. Eventually, there is so much internal strain that the supporting assumptions begin to collapse. Just as a weakened arch will need scaffolding to hold it up, so the paradigm uses supplementary support for its assumptions until it reaches the point of collapse. This can happen quite suddenly even when a few stones are removed. It falls as an entire structure because the individual stones could not support the whole without one another.

Describing a belief system in this way has the advantage of being an accurate description of the way in which Christian beliefs fall apart in reality. When a person ceases to believe in Christianity, there are almost innumerable individual beliefs which are given up; for example, belief in God, in Jesus, in judgment, in the Holy Spirit, revelation through the Bible, conversion, Creation, etc. However, this renunciation is not performed in an individual way where each of these beliefs marches before a person in a detached manner for assessment. More commonly a person will say, 'it just fell apart', or perhaps someone close to them suffers, and they say, 'I just can't believe in a good God any more.' The system then collapses in its entirety.

If paradigms do function in ways which are analogous to an arch, a collection of circles, or a web, then this implies that the way to assess a paradigm is with a constant dialectic between theories, facts, methodologies, experiences, and other paradigms. This is how such a complex system of beliefs is structured, and this is how its 'claims to know' are supported. To assess such a structure we need a cumulative argument, and one which uses a whole group of criteria to examine a whole group of beliefs. Given the structure of a paradigm, any other approach will be inadequate. This is the way in which religious experiences need to be assessed. It is also the way in which the whole jumble of enthusiastic experiences needs to be appraised. These phenomena recur as a whole in history, and in the context of their own theories which attempt explanation. They need to be assessed as an accumulation and on the basis of a cumulative argument.

Conclusions

(i) A religious world view can be described accurately as a paradigm.

(ii) Enthusiasm is a sub paradigm within Christian belief.

(iii) Each paradigm can give an account of the experimental evidence.

(iv) Which of the competing systems gives the best account of the evidence is determined by 'judgment'.

(v) The criteria on which this judgment is based are not themselves all paradigm – relative.

(vi) The issue of 'paradigm relative facts' and 'paradigm relative evaluative procedures' is sometimes overstated, as there are very significant elements of continuity between real, differing paradigms.

(vii) Paradigm is not an ontologically unique category. It is a complex and especially consequential group of theories. The decision between two paradigms is therefore, in principle, resolvable in the same way as is all theory choice.

(viii) In reality, a conceptual system can be placed within another larger paradigm, or have significant areas of overlap.

(ix) A choice between paradigms can be made in a rational way. No road in a strictly logical sense does not necessarily imply that there can be no rational discussion between two parties.

(x) There is more than an 'irreducibly sociological' choice to be made between differing paradigms, because it is possible to make a reasonable judgment which takes the form of a cumulative case argument. A variety of criteria can be balanced in an assessment of a new paradigm's beliefs, theories and methodologies. Therefore the choice between paradigms can, in principle, be made rationally.

(xi) Charismatic beliefs and experiences must be assessed as a whole constellation, and by using a cumulative case argument.

8

Attempting to Build an Arch with a Brick

How not to interpret charismatic experience

What we are aiming to do is to discover a way of answering the question: Suppose people claim that they have encountered God in their experience, how can we tell whether they really have? In order to answer this we have sifted through the possible epistemological options, and concluded that the best available way in which this could be resolved is by using an argument which takes the form of a cumulative case.

Interpreting such claims to have had a religious experience significantly increases in complexity because its resolution depends on making a rational choice between conflicting paradigms. It is questionable whether this is possible at all, but we have argued that it can be done by using a modified cumulative case. The modification is necessary because the decision involves more than just accumulating reasons to take up a particular belief in the first place, in the way that it is done, for example, by Swinburne. We are also considering 'fact', methodology, evaluative procedures, other paradigms, theory, and experience to be part of the process of justification. These all function together in a constant dialectic as they jostle to provide coherent understanding. An argument which takes this form is neither simple nor capable of rapid construction. This would lead us to expect that an attempt to interpret charismatic experience is unlikely to be successful if it is based on too few criteria, and even less so if it is based on a single criterion of assessment.

In spite of this, however, there is a vast amount of contemporary literature which is written both in support of and in opposition to charismatic experience with the assumption that assessment can be done in a simple way. Some literature takes into account more complex issues such as dispensational theology, but there is nothing in contemporary writing on the charismatic movement which would handle these issues with the kind of complex argument that would be needed if it is to provide an adequately comprehensive assessment.

To explore this necessity for complexity, we will take a sample of the criteria which are in common use as means of assessing charismatic experience, and then demonstrate their ambiguity. For the moment we are seeing how each of these criteria functions on its own, which is how they are presented, rather than how they might contribute to a cumulative argument.

Because the aim of the book is not primarily to assess charismatic experience, but to show how this assessment could be done in principle, the list will not be exhaustive. Although it would be fun to develop a comprehensive application of criteria which are used in assessment with reference to more examples, there is not space to do this. This is acceptable, however, because the purpose of the book is rather to set out in general terms how a programme to evaluate charismatic experience should look, and this can be achieved without covering every particular example.

A substantial portion of this section explores biblical objections to the various criteria which are commonly used to assess the charismatic movement. It is important to do this, because even if one does not share the same presuppositions about biblical authority, those whom we are describing *do* treat the Bible as their premise. Consequently, if they do not conform to their own standards, then the result is internal contradiction. According to Ayer, this is the one logically certain way to undermine a particular thesis.

Does unusual physical healing signify that a person has encountered God in his experience?

There is an emphasis on healing which permeates the charismatic movement. It is also an emphasis which has increased significantly over the past twenty years, and has expanded from a straightforward Pentecostal 'laying on of hands' or 'anointing with oil' into more varied theologies and practices. There are claims for 'healing of memories', healing of bodies, 'deliverance', 'lifting curses' as a form of healing, psychological healing, leg lengthening, etc. Some behaviour which has traditionally been thought of as sin, such as homosexuality, is also treated as sickness which needs to be healed. There are many books of 'testimonies', or systems of 'ministry' which address the issues raised by healing, along with conferences and magazines specifically aimed at this area.

The following is taken from the information sent out nationally to advertise what is described as 'An Advanced Course in Healing'.

> Workshops will explore the whole spectrum of healing: healing of sexual brokenness, healing of the homosexual, healing of memories, healing those with multiple personality disorders, healing of physical bodies, and deliverance.[1]

Given our analysis of the nature of charismatic experience, this emphasis on healing is quite predictable. Healing exemplifies many of the enthusiastic traits outlined in chapter 1, such as belief in the immanence of grace, expectation of the supernatural, anticipating the transformation of the personality, as well as a sense of status. God intends his people to be healthy, happy and wealthy.

The effect of these enthusiastic emphases in practice is that the success of healing (whether physical or emotional) has come to be one of the central criteria which is used to assess the spiritual status of the individual believer, as well as the success of particular churches and the charismatic movement as a whole. The significance which is given to the question of healing has lead to a number of books, many written by medical doctors, which address the question, 'Is healing actually taking place?'

Of course, if one is claiming that healing is taking place, then it is important to explore this question. And if one is simply asking 'Does miraculous healing occur today?', then this is a perfectly suitable approach. However, there is more to it than this, because such healing is being presented as a 'Sign of the Kingdom'. When this happens the success of healing becomes a criterion which can determine whether or not it is justifiable to believe that God is working in a person, church or movement. Just as in the life of Jesus, the authenticity of his message is evidenced through accompanying miracles, so current claims to experience miraculous healing are used to demonstrate that a person has encountered God in his own experience. If healing comes from God, and illness comes from Satan, then the success of healing becomes a criterion which is used both to justify a particular theology, and to justify the theological claims of a church or a person to have had an encounter with God. The converse is also applied, in that lack of healing becomes a sign of sin or unbelief.

Even writers who are opposed to the charismatic movement do not seem to question this assumption that healing is a criterion which could determine whether the Spirit is at work or not. Consequently Peter Master's book *The Healing Epidemic*, a book which is virulently opposed to the charismatic movement, includes an assessment of the effectiveness of claimed healing. He argues that if healing is not taking place, then this is a sign that the charismatic movement is not caused by the Holy Spirit. This carries with it the implication that if healing is taking place, then the Spirit is working within it.

The aim here is not to take this frequently trodden path and assess whether there really is healing taking place or not; but to question the significance of healing as a criterion for assessment. *Even if there is healing, what does it prove?*

There are some interesting historical differences of opinion on this issue. If we take the example of the New England Revival there was no particular expectation of healing, because the accepted sign that the Spirit was at work was not that a person was healed, but that he remained faithful through suffering until death.

Formerly there was a longing to die with something of impatience; but lately, since that resignation forementioned, about three years ago, an uninterrupted entire resignation to God with respect to life or death, sickness or health, ease or pain, which has remained unchanged and unshaken, when actually under extreme and violent pains, and in times of threatenings or immediate death.[2]

In other words, if one asked the question 'Is the Spirit working in this ill person?' within the current charismatic movement, the inclination would be to look and see if he or she had been healed, whereas in Edwards' day, one would look and see if he or she was being faithful. 'Though he slay me yet will I trust him' was viewed as being as less ambiguous indicator of a work of the Spirit than healing. The same attitude to suffering and healing is also found in the work of Wesley and Whitfield.

Edwards could find a strong biblical justification for his views. Such biblical evidence should be considered here too, because if a movement is basing itself on the Bible, then it is important for it to be consistent with this in order to avoid internal contradiction.

In the Bible illness can come from God. Such an idea is unthinkable for a significant proportion of people within the current charismatic movement, because illness is considered to be caused, either directly or indirectly, by evil forces. Sickness is part of the evil, sinful realm which belongs to the devil, and an area of life which is healed by Jesus. An entitlement to physical healing is sometimes included in the doctrine of the atonement: 'with his stripes we are healed'. Healing has consequently come to be seen as a 'right' which should be 'claimed' by faithful Christians who want to take up all that they have inherited from the Father.

If all of this were true, then effectiveness in healing would indeed be an accurate criterion to measure the work of the Spirit. The biblical view, however, is rather more complex than this, and there are many examples of illnesses which are part of God's plan. 'Who is it who makes men deaf, dumb and blind, is it not I the Lord' (Ex. 4.11); 'An evil spirit from the Lord tormented Saul' (I Sam. 19.9); 'the angel of death' which was sent by God, along with all the other 'plagues', such as boils (Ex. 12.29). There are also examples of the Israelite people being led by God to kill vast numbers of people in battle, which obviously involves physical injury.

It would also be difficult to dismiss these ideas as being merely an inferior stage in the development of man's religious awareness, because these same ideas also find parallels in the New Testament. Zechariah is struck dumb by an angel (Luke 1), Jesus allows Lazarus to die by deliberately waiting for three days after hearing the news of his illness (John 11). Saul is blinded on the road to Damascus (Acts 9.9), Ananias and Sapphira are struck dead for 'lying to the Holy Spirit' (Acts 5.1–11), Herod was 'eaten with worms and died' as a judgment from God (Acts 12.20–23). The church at Corinth also faced this issue, in that some of its members were to be 'handed over to Satan for the destruction of the flesh' (I Cor. 5.5). The Corinthians also faced death and sickness as a result of their abuse of the Lord's supper: 'this is why some of you are ill, and some have died' (I Cor. 11.30).

Therefore one cannot assume on biblical grounds that it is always God's will to heal. Sometimes (according to the Bible) he will have a very different plan. Consequently the authenticity of a work of the Spirit cannot be assessed solely on the grounds of a simple question such as 'was the person healed or not?' God could be at work in illness as well as in healing, and so the success or failure of healing is an ambiguous sign which does not point in a clearly defined theological direction.

Another ambiguity is encountered in the practical difficulties inherent in the attempt to assess claims to miraculous healing. If one takes the track trodden by current writers such as John Wimber, Dr David Lewis, and many others, and depend on healing as a support for one's theology, then, apart from the biblical issue, one has to face considerable problems both theoretically and practically. It is quite feasible to attribute 'healing' to Satan, or to God, or to purely physical processes, mistaken diagnosis, spontaneous remission, mental effects on the body due to stress etc. To demonstrate which of these or other factors was the cause in a particular situation can be extremely difficult. The effect of this is that it is often difficult to demonstrate that unusual healing has taken place at all, and even harder to 'prove' that its cause was direct intervention from God.

The problem can be illustrated by using some of the books which analyse this theme in the context of charismatic healing. Two books, John White's *When the Spirit Comes with Power*, and David Lewis's *Healing: Fiction, Fantasy or Fact* were written by a psychiatrist and a medical doctor respectively. Both examine the evidence of healing in meetings led by John Wimber, and both conclude that there is strong evidence that miraculous healing was taking place. A third book, Peter Masters' *The Healing Epidemic*, has sections written by Professor Verna Wright, who is also a medical doctor. Though his training and methods of assessment are similar, and all three share Christian beliefs, Professor Wright's conclusion is that there is no evidence of healing in this context, and that psychological manipulation is a preferable explanation for the observed phenomena. Perhaps significantly, Professor Wright has a cessationist view of the Bible, and so his research confirms his view that miracles do not take place now. Dr Lewis and Dr White work from within the charismatic movement, and their research is consistent with their own particular ideas about what is possible.

It appears to be the inevitable situation that an individual's beliefs interpret the empirical evidence in the light of his or her respective paradigms, rather than the paradigm being upturned by the 'facts' of the situation. The issue is put clearly by B.B. Warfield.

> A Catholic believing first in the divinity of the church as the organ of the Holy Ghost, in which He is made a deposit for the whole world, and from which alone He can be obtained and believing, next, in the truth of all the distinctive teachings of this church, as to monasticism and asceticism, relics and saints, transubstantiation, and the like, in honour of which the alleged miracles are performed – will naturally be predisposed to believe these miracles real. A Protestant, believing none of these things, but looking upon them as corruptions of the Gospel, will as naturally be predisposed to believe them spurious.[3]

The same issue is illustrated later by Warfield in the context of 'Lourdes Superstition':

Even though we should stand dumb before the wonders of Lourdes, and should be utterly incapable of suggesting a natural causation for them, *we know right well that they are not of God*. The whole complex of circumstances of which they are a part; their origin in occurrences, the best that can be said of which is that they are silly; their intimate connection with a cult derogatory to the rights of God who alone is to be called upon in our distress, – stamp them, prior to all examination of the mode of their occurrence, as not from God. We are far more sure that they are not from God than we can ever be sure, after whatever scrutiny, of precisely how they are wrought.[4]

What to note is that the possibility that there could be a miracle in this context is ruled out by Warfield's presuppositions. He goes on to discuss the way that the 'miracle' relates to doctrine.

Of course as R.H. Benson puts it, 'those who believe in God and His Son and the Mother of God on quite other grounds, may declare that Lourdes is not enough'. But this is not to make the miracles carry the doctrine, but the doctrine the miracles in accordance with J.H. Newman's proposition that it is all a matter of point of view, of presuppositions.[5]

This illustrates that healing cannot be used as an unambiguous criterion to assess a movement, or a person's individual claims to have encountered God, because it is the healing claim *itself* that is in need of assessment. 'Did it happen'? is the first awkward question, and 'How did it happen'? being even more awkward. The elusiveness of hard evidence in such a context means that the judgment given in answer to these questions depends in which paradigm one is situated. It is consequently a criterion which cannot be applied in real situations with confidence.

Perhaps there could be instances of healing which were so dramatic that they did provide good evidence of the miraculous – if one were to have an arm grow back, for example. A clear case of mongolism which was healed would demand a change in the genetic structure of every cell in the body. Healing such as this would at least be the kind of sign which would indicate an omnipotent creator at work. In this situation the evidence could theoretically be so dramatic that it could force an upturn in a person's paradigm. According to Locke a true miracle which attested a claim to revelation would have a character, such that it 'can be performed by none but a divine power, and require the immediate hand of the almighty'.[6]

In practice, however, this less ambiguous kind of healing is not commonly in evidence. For example:

> John Wimber claimed to have prayed over more than 200 children with Down's Syndrome. To his genuine disappointment only one of the 200 have shown any sign of healing. This one child still has many of the symptoms of his problem (i.e. visual features), but has been able to reach 'the lower end of the normal range' in educational attainments. John was careful to emphasize that it was the lower end, but within the normal range.
>
> The healing rate for Down's Syndrome is 0.5 %, and the healing that did take place was only partial (unlike Jesus' healings). Why this disease is so resistant John has no idea. On further consultation with doctors working in this area, we have been assured that for a Down's Syndrome child to be in the lower end of the normal range of academic achievement is not unusual or remarkable, let alone miraculous. From a medical viewpoint, John Wimber's 0.5% success rate with Down's Syndrome is less than is achieved through the efforts of health professionals.[7]

The implication of this for claims to heal is rather devastating. If it could be demonstrated that all the apparent healing is taking place in an area which can be caused by psychosomatic processes, or else fall within the range of normal remission, then the most plausible hypothesis is that the healing taking place here is determined by the normal forces of nature. If this is so then there is no unambiguous 'sign' which is indicating the work of omnipotence.

It is even questionable whether one could ever justify a theological position on the basis of miraculous claims. Certainly Hume rejected the possibility that one should ever believe a person's claim to have witnessed a miracle, and his views have been extensively influential since then. Even without accepting this sceptical view, though, the whole issue of claims to miraculous physical healing takes its place within the framework of the charismatic movement, and is part of that which needs to be assessed. It can contribute something in support of the system in its entirety, in the sense that if there were no healing when one's theology led one to expect it, then this would be a difficult anomaly which would put a strain on the credibility of one's thinking. It is also possible, in principle, for an example of healing to be so inexplicable that it could have a significant effect on a person's whole web of belief. However, healing has a dubious over-emphasis in current thinking, and too much is being claimed for particular examples which turn out to be so ambiguous that they are of no use as a means of assessment.

As we would expect, on biblical, theological, practical, and epistemological grounds, one could not normally assess whether the Spirit was at work on the basis of claims for the success of physical healing, when these claims are separated from reference to a broader context. Both healing and illness could theoretically be caused by the Holy Spirit, or by numerous other possible causes.

Is an encounter with God in experience indicated by a psychological level of well-being?

The issue of psychological well-being is closely connected with the previous issue, because it is another form of healing, and consequently the same arguments apply to this area too. It is, however, given such a prominent position within the charismatic movement that it demands separate treatment from physical healing.

There have been claims that an encounter with the Holy Spirit results in transformation of the personality. Such claims can be found right back through the Pentecostal doctrine of baptism in the Spirit, and into the variety of enthusiastic movements discussed earlier. The names for the experiences vary, but one of the claims for its effects which remain constant through these enthusiastic experiences is that an encounter with the Spirit leads to a permanent alteration in personality and is indicated by the fruit of the Spirit; love, joy, peace, and so on.

This emphasis has diversified within the current charismatic movement and come to be evidenced in a variety of counselling styles, such as healing of memories and deliverance. All of them have a common assumption that God intends people to feel mentally calm and peaceful. Feelings such as these are therefore an indication of a genuine encounter with God.

For example, according to Kenneth Copeland, it is even sinful to feel grief over anything such as bereavement:

> As a believer, you've been redeemed from the curse of grief and sorrow by the blood of Jesus Christ. You don't have to put up with them any more than you have to put up with sin or sickness or disease.

> So don't do it any more. When the devil tries to burden you with grief and sorrow, resist him. [8]

In the case of Copeland (and Urquhart), faith is being treated as a mental effort, really as a form of positive thinking, and one which is under the control of the believer. In practice this means that a mood which upsets this positive state of mind is damaging to faith, and so ought to be resisted.

Such extreme views are not held throughout the whole charismatic movement. However, what is more common is the similar assumption that God wants all Christians to have a standard type of personality and an uninterrupted psychological smoothness.

The effect of this emphasis is that the work of the Spirit in the believer has come to be assessed in terms of the level of psychological well-being which he enjoys. Peacefulness, happiness, contentment and so on are a sign of the Spirit, and anxiety, pain, grief, tension, etc., need to be 'dealt with', through prayer, or faith. To put it crudely, God always wants everyone to feel good.

As with physical healing, one can find strong strands within the Bible which can be drawn on to attempt a justification of this attitude to peace of mind. After all, Jesus did say that his followers were to 'be anxious for nothing' (Matt. 6.34); 'Let not your hearts be troubled', he said (John 14.1). Jesus promised peace: 'peace I leave with you, my peace I give unto you' (John 14.27). The Holy Spirit is sent as a 'comforter' who will dwell with the disciples (John 14.15). St Paul says 'let the peace of Christ rule in your hearts' (Col. 3.15), and describes Christian maturity in terms of 'the fruit of the Spirit' (Gal. 5.16–25). Indeed, there is such a large body of biblical material which can be used in support of the idea that God intends people to have a sense of peace that it is easy to see the reason why it is treated as an indication of the work of the Spirit.

However, there is more to be said about the biblical view point on peacefulness than this. The Bible does state that one day there will be no more tears, sorrow or pain (Rev. 21.1–4), but this is not be so until after death. One can see a typically 'impatient' enthusiastic concept of grace at work here. The problem with using psychological health as a means of assessment is that this represents only part of the biblical picture, and there are many examples of grief, sorrow and psychological pain which fit in with God's plan.

One example of this would be the experience of Jeremiah. He was afflicted with a morbid depression, wishing that he had been aborted (Jer. 20.17), suffering physical illness (Lam. 3.4) and bitterness (Jer. 3.15). He says that God 'seduced' him, 'raped' him, lied to him (Jer. 15.15–21), and that God is merely using him as target practice in a game (Lam. 3.12). One could quote Jeremiah's misery extensively.

The interesting thing to note here is that his personality would be unacceptable in many current charismatic churches. An attempt would probably be made to cast out his demons, as they could be seen as the obvious cause of his nearly blasphemous attitude to God; to lift his curses, as they could be viewed as the reason for his consistent lack of success in ministry; to heal his memories, as he has such a low self-image that there must have been a problem in his relationship to his parents; to criticize his lack of faith, as he has not healed himself, and is not living in material or emotional prosperity.

None of these approaches would have worked, however, because his personality was especially shaped by God for the specific job to which he was called (Jer. 1.5). In fact, his whole genetic history has been shaped and supervised to fit this God-given role. This is the reason why his temperament remained constant throughout his life. Jeremiah's last recorded words are, 'Or hast thou utterly rejected us? Art thou exceedingly angry with us? (Lam. 5.22)'

According to the Bible, the reality of Jeremiah's encounter with God is not demonstrated by mental certainty, calmness or good feelings towards God, nor in success in prayer or service; but in *perseverance*. In spite of all the difficulty, both internal and external, he remained faithful to a calling for around forty years. This is markedly different from the popular view of faith mentioned above, as Jeremiah certainly does not get all he wants; he is simply tested by fire, and yet survives. Mental well-being is irrelevant to his primary role.

A second example of the ambiguity of psychological well-being in the Bible is the parable of the tax gatherer and sinner in Luke 18.9–14. The Pharisee stands confidently before God, with no sense of guilt, and a very positive attitude towards himself. Psychologically he was A1, and yet he goes home 'condemned'. The opposite is true of the tax collector. He 'stands at a distance', feeling unworthy, beating his breast in an expression of bitterness, guilt and regret, and yet he goes home 'justified'.

The paradox is that the man who *felt* innocent was in fact guilty; and the man who *felt* guilty was pronounced innocent. There is a distinction made here between guilt as a feeling, and the fact of objective guilt before God. The parable provides an example of self-delusion. What I want us to note here is the implication that there are times when it is positively dangerous to feel 'good' or 'innocent', and one of those times would be if one were actually guilty before God. In this situation an encounter with God is indicated not by peacefulness, but by guilt.

This distinction between true and deluded feelings towards oneself and towards God was one which was made clearly in the time of Edwards and of the Puritans. Indeed, this concern is one of the motivating forces behind Edwards' writing of *The Religious Affections*, because it was seen as crucial to be able to distinguish between reliable and misleading personal convictions, particularly those which concern a person's status before God.

> And it is the concurring voice of all orthodox divines, that there may be religious affections, which are raised to a very high degree, and yet there be nothing of true religion.[9]

> And so it is ever likely to be in the church, (that Satan destroys the work with confusion) whenever religion revives remarkably, till we have learned well to distinguish between true and false religion, between saving affections and experiences, and those manifold fair shows and glistening appearances by which they are counterfeited; the consequences of which, when they are not distinguished, are often inexpressibly dreadful.[10]

Feelings are an ambiguous indication of a religious experience, because one could easily be deluded, for example, about one's safety (in many contexts), and happily sail into danger or overtake a car on a twisted road on the strength of that conviction. Feelings of anxiety or depression can be quite disconnected from 'spirituality', and have organic causes. Hypnotic experience can create a sense of peacefulness. Vallium or anti-depressants could create a feeling of calmness.

There is a need to distinguish genuine religious affections from non genuine, but this is not a characteristic concern which marks out the current charismatic movement. The simple experience of 'feeling' peaceful can be treated as being enough of a criterion to indicate a real work of the Spirit. Consequently, if a person thrashes around in anguish in a charismatic service, this would be attributed to the demonic, whereas in the time of Wesley, or Edwards, it would be as likely to be seen as a sign of deep conviction of sin. This is because allowance was made for unpleasant emotion being caused by God. Today, the aims of modern psychology seem to have been broadly accepted, even though these may not always be consistent with biblical aims for personality. By contrast, the scriptures often indicate that God may not want a person to 'feel good' all the time. While 'peacefulness' may occur in many instances, it is not the primary aim of a work of the Spirit.

One can conclude that the simplistic criterion which equates the work of the Spirit with psychological well-being is inadequate as a means of assessment. It fails because feelings of well-being or otherwise are not necessarily caused by a religious experience. On top of this, according to the Bible there are times when it is not God's plan for a person to feel good. Again we are confronted with an inconclusiveness which undermines this criterion for assessment. Both mental health and mental anguish could theoretically be the result of an experience of the Spirit, or else come from some other source, spiritual or psychological.

Does material prosperity indicate an encounter with God?

It seems strange that this question needs to be asked, because this concept has little in the way of historical parallels. Perhaps the monasteries of Cluny in France came close to it with their elaborate rituals and expensive furnishings for worship, but to claim that God wants everyone to be materially wealthy is unusual. The major proponent of this view is the American Kenneth Copeland, but similar views are found in some parts of the English Charismatic movement as a result of other figures, such as Reinhard Bonnke.

> Leave foolishness behind and stir within you the faith to reach out and receive what you, as a redeemed child of the living God have a divine right to – not the curse of poverty, but the blessing of prosperity.[11]

The degree of one-sided biblical interpretation and strained exegesis necessary to support such a view of wealth is blatant. 'My God shall supply all your needs' (Phil. 4.19) is taken to include such 'needs' as a new car. 'And if you be in Christ then you are Abraham's seed, and heirs according to the promise'

(Gal. 3.29) is interpreted as meaning that every Christian should be as materially prosperous as Abraham.[12] 'He became poor that we might become rich' (II Cor. 8.9), is interpreted to mean that Jesus intends all poor people to be materially wealthy.[13] The whole idea is so badly supported that one is inclined to dismiss it outright, and yet the widespread influence of these views indicate that they must be taken seriously. Copeland's 'ministry' seems confined to wealthy Western countries. It would be difficult for him to get beyond these areas because the poverty and starvation of much of the world would have to be attributed to a sinful lack of faith and expectation. One suspects that these concepts are a result of biblical exegesis being filtered through an American cultural grid which imposes the aims of success and materialism on to the church. Copeland's views are certainly not the result of anything resembling balanced biblical interpretation.

Again, the heart of the issue is that wealth is inconclusive as an indication of the work of the Spirit. Jesus' teaching on wealth and poverty is sometimes difficult to apply, and part of it does include promises of having all one's 'needs' supplied and of 'overflowing blessing' (Matt. 6.25–34). There are also rich people in the Bible who are Godly, such as Abraham and Solomon. The fault comes in exaggerating this side of the argument, and in ignoring the other sides of this issue, or of reinterpreting the issues to suit a particular culture. There are strong biblical strands which warn against riches as a 'snare' which will rob a person of the kingdom of God; riches are 'unrighteous mammon' (Matt. 6.24); there is a warning not to 'store up treasures on earth' (Matt 6.19), 'the love of money is the root of all evil' (I Tim. 6.10), and so on. There are many rich people in the world who have become rich through immoral means such as the exploitation of slaves, drug trafficking, organized crime, etc. Wealth in itself is no unambiguous indication of goodness nor of the work of the Spirit.

Taking the example and teaching of Jesus has more generally led to a stress on poverty as an expression of spirituality, rather than accumulation of wealth. The rest of the Bible describes many impoverished people who were faithful, as does the whole history of the church. If one looks to the future, then the New Testament expectation seems to be for increasing hardship and persecution for Christians, rather than a comfortable material prosperity. According to Peter suffering is a calling which is part of Christ-likeness; 'do not be surprised when suffering comes' (I Peter 2.21).

The effect of all this is that both wealth and poverty may or may not be signs of an encounter with God. We can conclude that since both wealth and poverty may, or may not, be part of God's plan, neither can be a useful single criterion to detect the work of the Spirit.

The three preceeding sections of this chapter rather nicely illustrate the characteristic impatience of 'enthusiastic grace', since they cover forms of prosperity (physical, psychological and material) which are more traditionally seen as being reserved for eternity. The way of suffering, more commonly understood within Christianity, is that while God ultimately intends perfect health and wholeness, there is only a foreshadowing of this before death: 'it is too much for us to determine that God shall never bring an outward calamity in bestowing a vastly greater spiritual and eternal good'.[14] Evidently this is a biblical attitude, and yet there is still more to be said; it can be taken one stage further. There is an assumption in this argument that God ultimately intends 'a vastly greater spiritual and eternal good' for individual people. This must be questionable on biblical grounds because the existence of heaven is also balanced out with hell. Perhaps one of the reasons there is such resistance to this doctrine of damnation in contemporary theology is because it unpalatably envisages God doing something which is not ultimately to the benefit of those who find themselves in that situation. Hell provides no therapeutic element, nor a possibility that a person passing through would emerge as a better, reformed and more complete character at the end. It is pure judgment and retribution.

Arguably such a concept upholds God's justice, holiness, and righteousness, and in that way is to his benefit. However, there is no benefit to those who undergo this fate. This is no doubt unpleasant for the inhabitants, and yet is consistent with the purpose of creation given in the Bible and taken up by the creeds.

The chief end of humankind is to glorify God and serve him forever; it is not the chief end of God to serve humankind and to keep it happy forever.

If this understanding is correct it would provide an insight into the theological issues which are raised by issues of mental and physical healing, and prosperity. Enthusiastic grace is not only impatient, it is also short sighted, in the sense that it focusses on the 'nice' things that God will do for people, especially now. If one were to refocus one's theology into infinity, it would become evident that the purpose of all healing, and prosperity, indeed, the purpose of all creation, is to glorify God.

This glorification may be achieved through individual faithfulness, through miraculous healing, or else through suffering patiently until death. It may be achieved through Shadrach, Meshach and Abdednigo's deliverance, or through Stephen's martyrdom. The glorification of God is the reason for healing, and for non-healing, for illness which comes from God, for the intense psychological pain of Jeremiah, and so on. It is also the common unifying reason for the existence of both heaven and hell. The glory of God is the purpose of existence itself.

We therefore have an ascending order of hypotheses within theology on the issue of healing. The enthusiastic understanding of events is (a) that God wants us to be well, and (b) that he wants it now. It is both short sighted, and impatient. One stage up from this is that God wants us to be well, though this may have to wait till eternity as there can be other priorities for the present. It is only short sighted. Stage (c) is that God may not plan for us to be well at all, at least, where this is not glorifying to him. The 'greater eternal good' of any individual will not be allowed to take priority, if this will be at the cost of God's eternal righteousness or his justice. Of these choices it is only the latter hypothesis that is able to provide a coherent explanation for suffering, both in this life and the next. If one takes this view then non-healing, which is an uncomfortable anomaly for many charismatic writers, ceases to be a theoretical problem.

One can conclude on biblical, moral, epistemological and theological grounds that a claim to have encountered God in experience should not be assessed in terms of material, physical or emotional well-being. Individually, each of these criteria is ambiguous.

'Peculiarity' does not provide a means of assessing claims to have had a religious experience

That an experience is 'peculiar' is not argued *per se* as an objection to charismatic experience, but one suspects that it does have a significant influence on the attitudes of those who object to the phenomena associated with charismatic experience. Enthusiastic experiences can appear to be so strange and dramatic that they demand an explanation; one which is not always available. Because these experiences are out of the ordinary, they have created a strong reaction in people, both for and against attributing these phenomena to direct intervention from God. Consequently, the idea of their 'peculiarity' does need consideration.

There is certainly a variety of peculiar experiences which accompany enthusiasm, and these have always been highlighted by the opponents of a particular movement. They have been mentioned above, but they include falling over, shaking, shouting, crying, laughing, jumping up and down, crawling on the floor, roaring, barking, and screaming. Through the 1980s Wimber has encouraged such phenomena by exhorting people to be free to experience whatever comes along, and to have the nerve to speak out the 'words' or 'pictures' that occur to them, however strange they may seem to the person at the time. The 'Toronto Blessing' has been associated with the same phenomena, but in a more extreme form. All of this can be picked up by those outside and dismissed as emotionalism, hypnotism, mass hysteria, or even insanity, and indeed these explanations may well be correct at times.

What I want to point out here, however, is that sheer peculiarity in itself is not, of necessity, a sign of a non-genuine religious experience. It could equally well be the sign of omniscience, only appearing strange to us because of our lack of understanding. Indeed, unpredictability is what one ought to expect. In biblical terms God is transcendent, well beyond our complete understanding, and 'his ways are not our ways' (Isa. 55.9). As well as this mystery we have the awesome complexity of the human mind, which is also hardly understandable to us. If we suppose that there is indeed an interaction between God and man taking place in some event, then both sides of the interaction are complex and only partially understood. The results of such an experience must be frequently varied and unpredictable. The sheer oddness and peculiarity may be a sign of insanity, but this could also be the sign of a God who is almighty and mysterious, at work. Perhaps the only thing one could predict with any confidence in such a setting is that the results of the encounter will be unpredictable.

There is a distinct precedent for peculiarity throughout the Bible on which to draw; for example, Eziekiel's prophesies and actions, swimming axe heads (II Kings 6.5), Jesus putting mud on to a blind man's eyes (John 9.15), the burning bush (Ex. 3.2), and Moses's staff turning into a snake (Ex. 7.8–13).

According to the Bible, God has made promises which do provide commitments that he will behave in predictable ways. His behaviour could therefore be relied on in many circumstances, as could the motivation and consistency which would underlie his actions. However, these promises do not cover every particular eventuality, and there is still scope for a large amount of unpredictability.

One could also argue that unpredictable experience is more in line with the character of God than, say, traditional Pentecostal doctrine, which has the whole relationship between God and man pinned down to a set formula of conversion, baptism in the Spirit, and speaking in tongues. It would be surprising if God were so predictable in his action, and also that people were so uniform in their needs.

The effect of all this is that peculiarity can point to the almighty and mysterious, as well as to emotional manipulation, insanity, or to a variety of psychological states. Oddness is consequently too ambiguous to be of use as a criterion to assess the work of the Spirit. It is the peculiarity which needs assessing.

That it works or does not work does not provide unambiguous justification

To put the issue in the form of a question: 'Does success justify a person's theology?' The assumption that it does is prevalent throughout the church, and revealed in phrases such as, 'I don't understand the theology of it but it works', or 'Its success speaks for itself'. Take the example of Yonggi Cho's church in South Korea. This church began as a normal Pentecostal fellowship, but has developed its own brand of charismatic theology and grown into what is considered to be the largest church in the world. What I want to point out is that the reason its theology is taken seriously is, to put it crudely, to be found by counting the hundreds of thousands of people who attend: the equivalent of the advertising slogan 'a quarter of a million people can't be wrong'. Whenever the pastor's books are introduced they include a reference to the size of his church. There is a tendency to give more credence to all of the theological views of a person who is successful in terms of gathering numbers. If we state it blatantly, the assumption is that if all those people are affected in this way when an individual speaks, then he must know what he is talking about.

This would appear at first sight to be a useful criterion of assessment. After all, one of the marks of a good theory is that it is 'fruitful' and that it has predictive capacity. When events are in line with what one's theology would lead one to expect, then this is a positive indication of its veracity.

However, in isolation from the other marks of a good theory, a criterion such as predictive capacity can be misleading. The difficulty arises because one has omitted to develop the explanatory element of the theory.

Take, for example, a theory which stated that 'the movement of the moon is caused by the tides'. This would have mathematically precise predictive capacity, in spite of being entirely false. Or to take another example: if one supposed the existence of a little man in the fridge who turned the light on and off when the door was opened and shut, one could justify it by saying, 'My theory works. When I open the door the light goes on, just as I predicted.'

Mesmer justified his theory of the effect of the 'magnetic fluid' in the 'ether' by pointing to the way people fell down when apparently exposed to it.

The problems come to light when one moves beyond the level of a guess, and attempts to provide a detailed explanation; at this point these original theories become strained to breaking point. Predictive ability must be combined with explanation where this is available, because in isolation from this, an ability to predict can be deceptively misleading as an indication that a theory is correct.

Take, for instance, the enthusiastic example of 'falling in the Spirit'. One side could justify its understanding of experience by saying. 'This is a work of the Spirit, and I know this because when I pray in a certain way, this happens. I don't understand the theology of it but it works.' The other side, however, could develop a theory which attributes the effects to hypnotic technique, and could also justify its explanation by arguing that 'it works', in the sense that one is able to predict the experiences by using the particular theory.

The two alternatives will continue to be unresolved until a more detailed explanation of cause and effect is developed. In other words, a justification, testing, and more thoroughly worked out explanation is needed. As stated above, we have two opposing guesses, and if one is content to rest with 'I don't understand the theology but it works,' then that theory will always retain its inherently uncertain status. 'That it works' will be quite obvious, 'why it works' will be more elusive, but essential, and this is what must be answered if an experience is to be understood and interpreted in an accurate way.

If we continue to consider the same example of 'slaying in the Spirit', we will find that there are logical gaps in the discussions which have not been carefully bridged. Take Wesley and Whitfield as examples of this issue. Both had experience of people falling over in a dramatic way while they were preaching, but Wesley used this as justification of his Arminian theology, whilst Whitfield interpreted the events as a sign that he was correct in his Calvinism. Such an attempt at justification contains a sizeable leap between the experience and the conclusion. The occurrence of falling down is taken firstly to be a mark of God's grace, and then secondly, to be a justification of a person's entire theology. Since the theology taken by each person to be justified by these events was in part contrary, one must suspect that there is a problem in these large jumps between experience and interpretation. Both Wesley and Whitfield distanced themselves from such thinking in later years. One is beginning with the experience of people falling down during a religious meeting, and moving from there to the conclusion that all one's theology must therefore be correct. This jump is not justified on logical or epistemic grounds. This is particularly so when a God of grace is presupposed, one who does not demand perfection as a precondition of blessing.

This is simply a particular issue which I am using to illustrate the point that because something 'works', this does not necessarily justify one's theory regarding the reason why it works.

There are also significant moral difficulties with such an approach to justifying experience. Lots of things 'work'. Hypnotism works, acupuncture works, voodoo works, witchcraft may be quite effective, 're-birthing' New Age techniques may work, as does mass hysteria, positive thinking, and all kinds of psychological manipulation. The 'Children of God' cult managed to grow in number using 'hookers for Jesus', and the Moonies are accused of exploiting brain-washing techniques. They are effective; they work. The Mafia is a successful organization, as is the Mormon sect, and the Islamic religion. Arms dealing could make one successful in terms of monetary reward. Hitler was successful in persuading large crowds of people by using oratory.

Consequently, 'that something works' is morally neutral, and one needs not only to ask the questions 'does it work?', and then 'how does it work?' (explanation), but also 'is it morally justified or not?' This last question would be disastrous for a Christian to omit. If 'that it works' is a sign of divine approval, then some of the most apparently demonic ideas and movements in history have been approved by God. Success does not justify theology nor imply moral impeccability.

The Bible is also suspicious of the criterion 'that it works' as a justification for theological interpretation of experience.

For example, this same issue arose when Moses went to meet

Pharaoh. In the context of seeking to justify their beliefs, both Moses and the court magicians were able to turn staffs into snakes, the implication being that success in this task was a justification of their differing views. In spite of their success, neither was successful in terms of persuading other people to adopt different views.

Jeremiah provides an example of a person who was called to be unsuccessful for an entire life. He was constantly in opposition, and ignored for his entire ministry. He preached repentance, and the people did not repent, but preferred to ignore him or treat him as a joke. If one applied the criterion 'did it work' to Jeremiah, then he was wasting his time.

One would have the same problem with the life of Jesus. In comparison with other world religious figures, he comes off badly. Only three years teaching, always an outsider, deserted by his friends at the end, who even denied that they knew him. His death was in the form of a public execution, and at that stage he felt deserted even by God himself.

Many biblical characters look like failures. Abraham giving up security in Ur, Nehemiah building a wall in the desert, Paul giving up a successful university life in favour of facing insecurity, imprisonment and death. Hosea's marriage could hardly be described as successful. The book of Job addresses the reasons why the innocent suffer while the ungodly are prosperous. The same issue recurs throughout the Psalms.

In the biblical view of reality, success and failure can only be judged from the stand-point of eternity, and as a result one could easily be misled by drawing conclusions on an issue prematurely. Apparent success could be ultimate failure, and apparent failure could be ultimate success.

In the light of this, one is forced to differ with Gamaliel's defence of the apostles.

> So in the present case I tell you, keep away from these men and let them alone; for if this plan or this undertaking is of men, it will fail; but if it is of God, you will not be able to overthrow them (Acts 5.38–39).

One feels sympathy for him as a tactful, diplomatic and impartial person who has cleverly secured the release of the apostles. However, even though his words sound generously liberal, they are based on the false principle we have been discussing, which is that theology can be justified by assessing whether it is evidently successful or not. This leads Gamaliel on to the position of neutrality in response to the apostles' message and to sit in the centre with a detached and 'academic' view of Jesus. 'Let them alone,' says Gamaliel. He is urging appeasement and compromise. This is clearly not a response to which Jesus or the apostles would be sympathetic: 'he who is not for me is against me'. Jesus uses absolute categories of choice; sheep and goats, wide and narrow paths, hell and heaven, light and dark. Obviously, one would not expect a Pharisee to have his thinking determined by Jesus, but irrespective of this, Gamiliel's defence is based on a premise which is inconsistent for a person who believes in an inspired Old Testament. It is also a defence which Christianity could well do without; Jesus would not approve.

It is reasonable to conclude that 'success' alone cannot be used as a criterion to assess one's understanding of experience. On biblical, moral, logical and epistemological grounds, both success and failure could point to a genuine religious experience, or to innumerable other causes. It is too ambiguous to use as a means of assessment.

Does a mixture of good and bad indicate that an experience is not genuinely religious?

This criterion of a 'mixture of good and bad' can operate on a number of levels and it is potentially applicable to individual experience, to a church, or to the charismatic movement.

For example, this criterion can operate on a personal and irrational level. Someone says, 'I went to a charismatic church once, and it was terrible.' On such a basis, the entire movement throughout the whole world is dismissed. Clearly it is unfair, but then people are not particularly fair and this is used as a means of assessment.

Another example of this process can be found in *The Healing Epidemic*, as people are lumped together under phrases such as 'charismatics believe that'. This is such a general statement that it is meaningless, but because Masters presupposes a homogenous unity which is either all correct or all incorrect, the effect on his assessment of the movement is to attribute extreme views to the whole spectrum of thought. The whole is then written off on the basis of abuses in parts.

This same presupposition also underlies other books. One example is *John Wimber Friend or Foe*. Even the title has an implicit categorical assumption, i.e. Wimber is all right or all wrong, for or against, wholly right or wholly wrong:

> John Wimber's teaching on 'The Third Wave of the Holy Spirit' proposes that the Pentecostal movement at the turn of the century and the Charismatic movement of the 1960s were truly movements of the Holy Spirit. However, John Wimber thinks that some of the central teachings of these two movements (concerning baptism in the spirit and the place of tongues) were wrong. *So the movements which taught error were inspired by the Spirit of truth!*
>
> This kind of confusion of truth and error is reflected in his books.[15]

The assumption underlying this criticism is that there are 'movements of the Spirit', and that such movements can contain nothing but truth, because they are inspired by the Spirit of truth. Error or sin signifies absence of the Holy Spirit.

Is this a fair assumption?

If we begin by assessing this assumption in biblical terms, then one could argue that such criticism may have a cumulative force in that there could be a point where there is so much that is wrong with the claimed religious experience that the good is outweighed by the bad. However, this point may be further down the road to antinomianism for many people to feel comfortable.

Consider as an example the church at Corinth during the time of Paul. This was a 'charismatic' church, but also one which needed to be warned against prostitution (I Cor. 6.15), incest (I Cor. 5.1), and drunkenness at the Lord's supper (I Cor. 11.17ff.). Some groups were undermining marriage (I Cor. 7), there were extremists on the issue of charismatic gifts, and on celibacy (I Cor. 7). Parts of the church had become 'partakers with demons' (I Cor. 10.20), and there were also doctrinal heresies to the point of 'baptism on behalf of the dead' (I Cor. 15.29), and even more significantly, denial of the resurrection of Jesus (I Cor. 15.1–19). This undermined Paul's gospel, as without the resurrection there is nothing from which to be saved, nor anything for which to be saved. The message thus becomes futile. It was a church which was accommodated to the spirit of its age, with a love for 'the wisdom of the world' (I Cor. 1.18ff.), and an idolization of clever public speaking. There were also numerous internal divisions, notably focussed around the personalities of Paul and Apollos (I Cor. 1.10–17), but also between rich and poor (1 Cor. 11.22).

A church with an accumulation of such excessive moral, doctrinal, and spiritual problems would be dismissed outright as a hopeless case by many traditional and charismatic Christians. In some ways it seems hardly Christian. Paul, however, never urges anyone to leave, and introduces his letter to them by thanking God for all the gifts that they have, and describing them as 'the church of God, loved, called, sanctified in Christ Jesus' (I Cor. 1.1–2).

One has to conclude that if the Spirit could be at work in the Corinthian church, then the work of the Spirit can co-exist with some very strange people, doctrines, practices, and morality. According to Paul, none of these failings debarred these people from being a genuine church, nor from experiencing the work of the Spirit.

One is therefore on thin biblical ice to argue that a church or movement must be perfect in order to experience the work of the Spirit, and one would have to conclude that some ideal of perfection is consequently a dubious criterion for assessing such a work, because the Spirit could be active in spite of failure. Agreeing criteria could prove to be a complex task if theology, morality, and spirituality turn out to be equivocal.

Such a mixture can also be seen vividly in a number of biblical individuals. David was capable of sublime psalms, but also of committing adultery and murder (II Sam. 11). Peter could say 'you are the Christ the son of the living God', and yet shortly after, Jesus is forced to say to him 'get behind me Satan' (Matt. 16.16–23). Paul the apostle is capable of strong theology and powerful evangelism, but also quite capable of having a 'sharp disagreement' with Mark (Acts 15.39). Indeed, it is the claim that one has reached perfection that would indicate a denial of the work of the Spirit: 'He who says he has no sin deceives himself and the truth is not in him' (I John 1.8).

In biblical terms one ought to expect that individuals and churches will always be a mix of good and bad.

According to the New Testament one would be disappointed if one expects to find a perfect 'movement of the Spirit', a perfect church, or a perfect believer, and this is demonstrated throughout church history. The historical reality is of movements which are made up of people, and therefore of a complex mix of sin, holiness, mixed motives, lust, pride, spirituality, etc. The movements with which they are involved may start comparatively well, but then commonly deteriorate. It is rare for a movement to retain the fervour of its founders as it moves into the next generation. This has been particularly true of enthusiastic movements which usually splinter into different groups, or else retreat into mysticism.

It is an ambivalent situation such as this which is assumed by Edwards in *The Religious Affections*. The circumstance he envisages is of a movement which contains a mix of good and bad, and to ensure its survival it must learn how to sift out that which is unhelpful. This is more biblical, more realistic, and also a better start to an assessment than an assumption that one could have a perfect theology or movement of the Spirit involving people. If the existence of imperfection in a believer or church or movement is enough of a criterion to determine that the Spirit does not operate there, then one is forced to conclude that there have been *no* individuals, churches or movements which have been inspired by the Spirit. Edwards observes:

I have had opportunity to observe many instances here and elsewhere; and though there are some instances of great affections in which there has been a great mixture of nature with grace, and in some, a sad degenerating of religious affections; yet there is that uniformity observable, which makes it easy to be seen, that in general it is the same spirit from whence the work in all parts of the land has originated.[16]

He ponders on this issue in later years in *The Religious Affections*:

> There is indeed something very mysterious in it, that so much good, and so much bad, should be mixed together in the church of God; just as it is a mysterious thing which has puzzled and amazed many a good Christian, that there should be that which is so divine and precious, viz: the saving grace of God, and the new and divine nature, dwelling with so much corruption, hypocrisy, and iniquity, in the heart of the same saint.[17]

Edwards provides an example of balanced criticism on this issue because he does not allow an indication of abuse in a single part to undermine the credibility of the whole. He is consequently freed from having to defend every experience and doctrine in order to justify the claim that the Spirit is at work. Consequently he is able to incorporate the best of Chauncey's harsh criticism in his own work on 'the religious affections'. It is a good assumption with which to start, and one that enables a balanced conclusion. The alternative black and white view which is often attempted leads to outright and (misguided) acceptance or rejection of the whole mix.

There is no logical reason to suppose that because a person is correct on one issue he is always correct on all other issues. Nor that if a person is wrong in one instance he is invariably wrong on all others. Up to a point, each part of a set of beliefs and practices must consequently be assessed on its own merits. Eventually there will come a point at which the set of beliefs are so confused that one must judge the entire system is called into question. However, in normal circumstances there are no grounds to assume that a mix of good and bad theology or experience would indicate that a movement was all wrong, or that this would exclude genuine religious experience.

Do parallel experiences in other contexts imply that an experience is not genuinely Christian

There are some apparent similarities between enthusiastic experiences and those in other contexts. It is important to consider this issue, because comparison is often used in assessment of such experiences, usually by its opponents, to undermine the nature of charismatic experience. One can find, for example, experiences which seem to parallel charismatic experiences in other religions and occult based sects; or discover parallels between a variety of alternative therapies, and forms of 'miraculous' healing within the church.

The aim of this section is to illustrate briefly some of these connections in order to demonstrate that the question is relevant. The primary issue here is not to explore them all in detail, but to determine their significance. The questions are, even if there are parallels, what do these parallels mean? How important are they? Do they provide a useful means of assessment?

D. Hunt and T.A. Mcmahon are two people who take such a line of argument based on parallels in other contexts in their book *The Seduction of Christianity*. They assert that the charismatic movement is a form of apostasy, synchronism and idolatry. They place the mix of charismatic experience and theology into an American eschatological context where the movement is considered to be part of the work of antichrist in his attempt to seduce Christians away from the truth in the last days.

The main thrust of the book is in pointing out a variety of parallels between charismatic experience and teaching, and a number of questionable areas of belief. For example, the use of hypnosis is dismissed on the grounds that it is used by the occult.[18] The following quotations are other examples which are cited and criticized in *The Seduction of Christianity*.

Taking 'authority' over situations such as financial difficulties is discussed, and the book cites an example of this technique.

I began to see that I already had authority over that house and authority over the money I needed to purchase it. I said, 'In the name of Jesus, I take authority over the money I need. (I called out the specific amount.) I command you to come to me . . . in Jesus Name. Ministering spirits, you go and cause it to come. [19]

The criterion used in opposition to this technique is that it 'promotes concepts that cannot be found in the Bible, but are found in occult literature and practice'. [20]

Another practice called 'visualization' is used in some sections of the charismatic movement. 'Healing of memories' is one example of this.

> In your imagination allow your spiritual body, shining with light, to rise out of your physical body. Look back so that you can see yourself . . . and reassure your body that you will return momentarily . . . [21]

> Go deeper and deeper into outer space until there is nothing except the warm presence of the eternal Creator. Rest in his presence.
> Listen quietly . . . [to] any instruction given. [22]

Such practice is used as a therapeutic technique. One imagines Jesus going back into one's past, perhaps even as far back as birth, and one then allows him to alter the experience which is seen as the cause of present-day mental or physical illness.

> Jesus, as Lord of time, is able to do what we cannot . . . [we] ask Jesus to walk back with us into the past . . . it is the inner child of the past who is being healed. [23]

Richard Foster promises in *Celebration of Discipline* that through visualization we encounter the real Jesus Christ:

> . . . You can actually encounter the living Christ in the event. It can be more than an exercise of the imagination, it can be a genuine confrontation.
> Jesus Christ will actually come to you. [24]

This practice is dismissed in *The Seduction of Christianity* on the grounds that Hindus use similar techniques, [25] and that visualization is also used in the occult, particularly in Shamanism. [26]

Yonggi Cho recommends the following method of prayer:

> We have taught our people how to . . . visualize success . . .
> Through visualizing and dreaming, you can incubate your
> future and hatch the results.[27]

Hunt and Mcmahon see this as an aspect of the original
shamanistic religion of Korea, and having nothing to do with
authentic Christianity.[28] It is dismissed on the grounds of this
parallel.

The view of Hunt and Mcmahon is that because of the parallels
between these techniques used by parts of the charismatic
movement, and other sects and religions: 'It should be clear now
that what is being taught is a Christianized form of the mental
alchemy that lies at the heart of shamanism. This is basic
sorcery.'[29] It would be hard to find another book which combines
so much information with so little reasonable assessment (apart
from the telephone directory). It is predominantly a list of who
does what and where, and generalizations about 'charismatics'
and 'psychologists'. In the place of argument there are exclama-
tions that a person 'should have known better', or quotations
from 'authorities' in the form of orthodox ministers. It has one
main criterion for its argument, which is that a parallel practice in
some dubious context undermines its use by Christians. It is
heavily criticized in a response to the book edited by Robert Wise
and others called *The Church Divided*, particularly for its
distortions of the writers it claims to be assessing.

My aim here is not to defend the experiences and methods
discussed or to analyse whether the writers quoted are being
distorted. The crucial point as far as we are concerned is that
finding 'parallels in other contexts' is inadequate as a criterion of
assessment. Apart from any exegetical inadequacies of *The
Seduction of Christianity*, its main argument is flawed *in
principle*. Just because a practice finds its place in the occult or in
other religions, this does not imply that it is wrong for a Christian
to use.

For example, Islam demands commitment and belief, Hindu's
worship and pray, Buddhists meditate and write books,
Jehovah's Witnesses knock on doors, Mormons drive cars and
extol family values, the 'Children of God' do evangelism, etc.

Once one has said all this, however, one is still left with the question, 'But is this practice right or wrong?'

The mistake is in attempting to determine acceptable practice by looking in this negative way at what other religions do, and allowing them to become the standard of what is right and wrong for a Christian. Christian morality is traditionally determined by *God's* law rather than by the practices of a variety of sects and religions. It is a peculiarly perverted system of thought which allows the 'evil' side not only to be viewed as being capable of the miraculous, but also to become the law giver, and therefore the determining factor in Christian morality.

That a practice such as visualization is used in the occult, or in other religions, is consequently quite irrelevant to the morality of practising a particular technique. One may have good objections to it on other grounds, but parallel use is one which ought not to be used.

What is lacking is an assessment and explanation of the nature of the links between these different parallels. Are they examples of neutral psychological techniques? Are they manifestations of the occult in some form? Are they counterfeits of a Christian experience? These are large gaps in the argument which would need to be bridged if the issue were to be resolved one way or another.

Simply to point out that there is an alternative explanation for an experience is not enough. If the alternative is to be preferred, then one needs to demonstrate, not just that another explanation is *available*, but that the other explanation is *preferable* to the charismatic one; that it is making better sense of the evidence, and the evidence is being faced up to more honestly. The approach in *The Seduction of Christianity* is to point out that witchcraft explains ESP as being a devilish technique, and then to treat this as an explanation. This is thoroughly self-contradictory, because it is using the explanations provided by people whose views are rejected, as the explanation for experience within the Christian community.

As a result of these problems, the parallels pointed out by Hunt and Mcmahon are of limited use as a criterion to assess charismatic experience. It is the parallels themselves that need assessing, and this needs to be done on some other grounds.

Such argumentation is not confined to Hunt and Mcmahon and an excess of emotion in worship often creates suspicion of charismatic worship because of its apparent similarity to 'pagan worship' or to hypnotic techniques. People are getting 'carried away with their emotions', 'they may as well be at a football match'. The new songs are 'just like pop songs', you 'could as well be at a disco as it would have the same effect', people say, as though this settles the issue. These similarities are used to dismiss *emotional* worship within the Christian context.

However, people may become very emotional watching football, and different religions do indeed have emotional forms of worship, but it would be irrational to argue on this basis that, for example, shaking, trembling and shouting are therefore intrinsically wrong within Christian worship. One's initial response to such an accusation can be that there is extensive emotional expression in the Bible, and so it would be inconsistent with his premises for a person attempting a biblical assessment of such phenomena to reject such manifestations outright.

The mistake is to look for an intrinsic moral content in an emotional or physical response. For example, what is immoral about tears or trembling? Should a widow repent of crying for her husband, or an explorer in the arctic cease to commit the sin of trembling? Obviously not. This would suggest that these reactions are separate from their differing causes, and so in order to determine what is right or wrong about them, one must look to the cause, and to the effects. They may have good or evil causes, and they may have good or evil effects. This is also the line taken by Edwards in arguing that such emotional phenomena are neutral psychological responses.[30]

For example, tears may result from a death, a burglary, a homecoming, worship, fear, or onion peeling. Laughter may be caused by disaster, insanity, a joke, nervousness, or the fall of an enemy. Trembling may be from fear, tension, or cold. Laughing may lead to offence, or to relief; tears may ease painful emotions. One may cry through affliction from Satan, or cry with relief at deliverance from God. Either way, one cries; one may be 'good' and the other 'bad', but only in terms of cause and effect. If one is to assess what is 'good', or 'bad' then the causes are where one ought to look. The experiences themselves are morally distinct from the causes and the effects, and are human reactions to a variety of stimuli.

This does imply that they are not directly 'spiritual' phenomena, and that they cannot in themselves be dismissed as being either satanic or Godly, pagan or Christian, moral or immoral. One can say, however, that they are 'psychological'.

It is much more coherent to argue that this is the reason why such similar experiences crop up in such a variety of contexts; in psychology, in the occult, as well as in church. Rather than experiences being examples of demonic influence, as the authors of *The Healing Epidemic* and *The Seduction of Christianity* assume, it may well be because people in both pagan and Christian contexts have a similar psychological make up, reactions, and means of expression, and when deeply moved in some way, these are the responses that emerge.

I have said enough to indicate the inconclusive significance of these parallels, and this is adequate to demonstrate that they are unreliable as a means of assessment. Lack of emotional response could be an indication of unresponsiveness to the Spirit, and very emotional reactions could indicate the work of the Spirit, or a host of other causes. It is consequently the emotional reactions which need assessing on some other grounds, and what needs to be asked is, 'To what is this emotion a response?' Edwards considered this issue in discussing the extreme emotional and physical effects observed during the revival in his church.

All affections whatsoever have in some respect or degree an effect on the body. As was observed before, such is our nature, and such are the laws of union of soul and body, that the mind can have no lively or vigorous exercise without some effect on the body.

Great effects on the body certainly are no sure evidences that affections are spiritual; for we see that such effects oftentimes arise from great affections about temporal things, and when religion is no way concerned with them. And if great affections about secular things, that are purely natural, may have these effects, I know not by what rule we should determine that high affections about religious things, which arise in like manner from nature cannot have the like effect.

Nor, on the other hand, do I know of any rule any have to determine that gracious and holy affections, when raised as high as any natural affections, and having equally strong and vigorous exercises, cannot have a great effect on the body. No such rule can be drawn from reason: I know of no reason why a being affected with a view of God's glory should not cause the body to faint, as well as being affected with a view of Solomon's glory.[31]

An argument which includes a contribution from 'parallels in other contexts' is not ruled out by this ambivalence. What to notice is that a comparable experience in another context does not *resolve* the issue on its own. One still needs do much more work in order to decide which is the best of the available explanations.

This is done more effectively than the above two writers by Sargant in *Battle for the Mind*. This book was first published in 1957, and was seen by the evangelical community as a damaging attack on the nature of conversion. It is an examination of the processes which lead the individual to a rapid change of belief, and an observation of the way in which similar techniques are at work in animal behaviour, and also in a variety of human, religious and secular contexts. Sargant points out the comparison between religious conversion experiences and political systems of indoctrination, brain-washing techniques, and religious conversion experiences.

Sargant sites the example of the well known 'Pavlov's dogs', who were almost drowned in their kennels. Although they survived, all the behavioural patterns that they had learned seemed to have been erased from their minds. He goes on to examine the relationship between animal and human psychology in terms of their physical and emotional reactions to extreme stress, using particular examples, such as the reactions created by battle fatigue in soldiers, or the physical and emotional states reached as a result of prolonged fasting.

Though 'men are not dogs,' it would be foolish indeed to

continue to disregard entirely experimentation on the higher nervous activity of dogs as irrelevant to human psychology, or to the question of how a man's thoughts and beliefs can be effectively changed.[32]

The difference between Sargant's work, and that of Hunt and Mcmahon is that the latter point to a parallel in some context which is considered to be unwholesome, and their assume that this settles the issue. Sargant, however, points out these parallels, but then he argues in detail that there is a psychological alternative which is a *preferable* explanation to considering the events he discusses as being miraculous. The alternative explanation is not only available, but it is also preferable.

This is not a discussion on whether Sargant is correct or not, or on whether his argument is overstated. It is simply making the point that in principle, the issue was approached in the right way.

Conclusions

There are many other topics that could be chosen to illustrate the inconclusiveness of using a single criterion of assessment. For example:

The character of the preacher does not validate or invalidate a particular claim.

Subjective states of mind, such as enthusiasm, sincerity, emotion or internal conviction do not validate or invalidate specific claims.

False or correct theology does not validate or invalidate experience.

Physical manifestations do not validate or invalidate connected theology.

That it seems reasonable or unreasonable does not validate or invalidate an experience.

That it can lead to a variety of dangers does not validate or invalidate an experience.

That it leads to division, or unites in love does not validate or invalidate a claimed experience of the Spirit.

Manifestations of spiritual gifts do not validate or invalidate a theology.

Renewal in worship does not validate or invalidate all that is connected with the 'renewal'.

Outward expressions of godliness do not validate or invalidate the person's inner life or theology.

All of these would be fun to pursue in detail, and I would have to if my aim was to assess the charismatic movement. However, I have made the necessary point already, which is that it is right to expect that a single criterion of assessment will turn out to be an ambiguous means of assessing charismatic experience. This follows from the need to use a cumulative argument and reinforces the case for using such an argument. It predicts accurately that the above arguments would be inadequate in the ways in which they actually are. I have illustrated that there are biblical, theological, logical, and epistemological grounds why a single criterion of assessment is an inconclusive means of assessing charismatic experience.

This is a significant point to make because so much of the contemporary literature which assesses charismatic experience does not take this into account. There are many arguments which oppose or support charismatic experience on the basis of a single criterion of assessment, and these arguments are based on a false assumption.

This leads us to the next issue, which is to explore more useful criteria and see how they could function together in a cumulative case.

9

How to Shave Hairy Theology

Criteria for interpreting charismatic experience

So far I have demonstrated that the way in which charismatic experience can be interpreted in principle is by the use of a cumulative case argument. This demands judgment from the person who is attempting to make the best sense of the available evidence by using a variety of criteria to assist in the decision. Such an argument is not simple to construct, and does not easily justify claims to certainty.

Along the way to reaching this conclusion we have come across differing criteria which can aid in making an informed judgment on an interpretation of a particular experience. In this chapter I would like to pull these criteria together, and apply them specifically to examples of charismatic experience. None of these criteria individually could 'prove' much, but they do create useful building blocks which can work together to construct a rational assessment of charismatic experience.

We will begin, so to speak, at the bottom with a discussion on some dangers which need to be avoided if one is to construct a useful cumulative case in this context. Following this we will examine some criteria which can contribute positively to interpreting charismatic experience.

Justifying beliefs on the basis of a solitary criterion

If Smith claims to have encountered a wallaby on his way home at night from a country pub, the claim may be defeated by the successful challenges that it was dark, he had had a lot to drink, and the alleged percept is *a priori* very improbable. If, however, it is learned that a wallaby has escaped from a nearby wildlife park, then Smith's claim becomes very probable, despite the challenges. Indeed, Smith's experiential report now becomes important evidence for there having been a wallaby on that road, evidence which may help people to track the animal down. We now have a 'cumulative argument'.[1]

This is a useful illustration of the interaction of the components of a cumulative argument, especially in that the experience eventually becomes supporting evidence for what was initially a rather improbable belief. What it also illustrates, however, is how easily one can be misled by putting too much stress on an isolated piece of evidence. Darkness, drink, and improbability would *each* be strong evidence against the truth of Smith's claim.

A mistaken reliance on a single criterion of assessment has just been illustrated extensively in the previous chapter because it is one of the most important implications of the necessity of using a cumulative case argument. Relying on too few criteria, or on a single criterion, is a mistake which is often made in the assessment of charismatic experience. If a particular interpretation of any religious experience is picked out and isolated from its associated conceptual framework, then this interpretation will always be potentially misleading and capable of reinterpretation in a different way. It is as much use as an individual stone is if you would like to build an arch, or as helpful as an individual strand of thread is for the construction of a web.

Take, for example, the claim that one's beliefs can be justified by a 'miraculous' event. As an individual piece of evidence the event will be ambiguous because there is a whole conceptual framework within which the putative miracle occurs, and this framework will need justifying by more than the original experience. Consequently seeing a 'miracle' will not necessarily force a person to accept a Christian theistic interpretation of this event, and (according to Hume) a report of a miracle will be even less convincing.

Even before Hume, however, Jesus was aware of this reasoning, and knew that the Pharisees would not respond to miraculous events because they had already made up their minds about what was occurring; 'Neither will they be convinced if someone should rise from the dead' (Luke 16.31). The fact that seeing a 'miracle' is not necessarily believing is also evident in the contemporary instances of people who have observed the same events in the context of charismatic gatherings, but reached contradictory conclusions on whether there has been a miracle or not. On its own a 'miracle' is limited in its power to convince.

If, on the other hand, the 'miracle' were to be presented as part of a wider group of criteria and used as an element in a cumulative argument, then it may demonstrate a claim more persuasively. Say that the event is so well reported and so unusual in its character that there is no other available explanation but direct intervention by God, and it never does become adequately explained in natural terms. Its forcefulness is such that it even calls into question the credibility of world views with which it conflicts. The effect of the event on the individual is that he or she becomes unusually holy, loving, committed to fellowship, and over a lifetime demonstrates faithfulness even through suffering until death. He or she also claims to have had direct perception of God.

If one is in a situation where a strongly attested 'miracle' cannot adequately be incorporated into a body of secular beliefs, however much the antecedently held belief system is altered, then one may be justified in arguing that intervention from God was the best explanation of the available evidence.

In this example the putative individual proof that one's theology was correct was a claimed 'miracle'. It illustrates the difficulty of providing an individual 'proof' which will, *on its own*, justify a particular interpretation of experience. The 'miracle' needs to be incorporated into a cumulative case because beliefs cannot be justified adequately on the basis of a solitary criterion.

Reliance on direct perception

Direct perception should not be used as the sole justification of a claim to have had a religious experience. Whether direct perception is capable of providing warranted belief in other contexts is debatable, but when one's aim is to be able to choose rationally between competing theories, even when they form part of different world views, such an approach is not helpful. It is too subjective, and is too inclined to include error. To say that I know because I know is not a good enough reason to accept a particular theory.

Using direct perception as the basis of a claim to knowledge is the heart of the criticisms made against the enthusiasts in the days of Locke. The words used to describe this form of epistemic justification were different, but seventeenth-century enthusiastic belief formation, and current claims that religious belief can be justified on the basis of direct perception, both share a similar structure. The enthusiasts were quite sure of their beliefs on the grounds that they had a certain internal conviction which came from a claimed direct experience of God.

This justification of belief based on a claim to direct perception is also the central and determining feature of contemporary charismatic experience. For example, the acceptability of a particular experience, say for example a prophecy, is assessed on the basis of 'discernment'. In other words, an internal conviction is used to declare that the prophecy is real or false. The cognitive claims of the 'prophecy' are justified on the basis of direct perception.

For all the reasons mentioned in chapter 5, this way of claiming to know is not good enough when isolated from other values. It is unable to provide a warranted belief about a charismatic experience. Consequently, one ought to be suspicious of an argument which justifies religious belief only on the basis of direct perception.

Fideistic interpretations of experience

It is not uncommon for church people to treat quality of faith as being inversely proportional to the evidence. In other words, the less grounds there are for faith, the better that faith is. If one is capable of believing for no reason whatsoever, then one has the strongest faith possible. This is quite insane! Any belief is justifiable in those terms. However, a more refined version of this way of thinking is not new in theology and is called fideism.

Fideism has a long history. According to Kierkegaard, for example, faith is a passion and commitment which is so intense that any objective assurance would be inadequate to support it. One should therefore not look for objective reasons to sustain faith.

Such views have been extensively influential in twentieth-century theology. Bultmann also repudiated the quest for rational support for faith, denying that faith should have factual grounds. Barth rejected the possibility of support for revelation on grounds other than those which are given in Jesus, and thereby cut his beliefs off from objective basis: 'Jesus loves me this I know, for the Bible tells me so'. Fideistic belief continues to be supported by the 'post modern' theology of writers such as Lindbeck and Hans Frei.[2]

Plantinga and Wolterstorff et al have argued that direct perception alone can justify Christian belief. If this is so then belief in God could be held without evidence or reason. Whether this should be described as fideism is debatable because the 'grounds' of direct perception could be considered as 'reasons' even though they are of a non-propositional sort. Consequently Plantinga can be put at the least fideistic end of the spectrum.

The above writers are in many ways diverse in character, and the only point of similarity which is claimed here is that in each case faith is detached in some way from reason or objective evidence. A theology which is cut off from objective support would have been described by Locke as enthusiasm. Its manifestations through history are different; for example in the case of Kierkegaard, faith is a passion which is turned inwards, and doesn't have the common enthusiastic trappings. What it considers to be acceptable belief is, however, similar to enthusiasm, in that faith is to be held without 'reason' or evidence.

This separation of faith from reason also links these apparently different theologies with contemporary charismatic experience. A connection with existential theology such as that of Bultmann's would be a horrific thought for many people within the charismatic movement, as they would consider themselves to be fundamentalist in their attitude to knowledge. However, in that the concept of faith in both areas is one which is disconnected from empirical evidence, then there is also a significant similarity. 'Beware of analysing what is going on with your rational mind', warned Wimber. Again from within the charismatic movement Bishop David Pytches describes the gift of faith as an 'irresistible knowledge' which comes from inside a person, and as:

> . . . a supernatural surge of confidence from the Spirit of God which arises within a person faced with a specific situation or need whereby that person receives a *transrational* certainty and assurance that God is about to act through a word of action.[3]

If we put this concept of faith alongside that of Bultmann, we can see a similar detachment of internal conviction from external evidence:

> For man is not asked whether he will accept a theory about God that may possibly be false, but whether he is willing to obey God's will.[4]

> For faith cannot permit (as theology since Schleiermacher more or less definitely demands) the nature of its content to be dictated to it by a 'scientific doctrine' or a 'system of reason'.[5]

Faith is defined by Bultmann as 'the continual overcoming of unbelief',[6] and even more; true 'existence' 'believes only in the constant overcoming of unbelief'.[7] It is not a faith which is determined by objective facts or reasons.

Kierkegaard's conception of faith is that faith is a costly infinite passion. According to Kierkegaard one of the (many) reasons why it is inappropriate to look for objective assurance for faith is that the strength of passion in the man of faith is shown by its capacity to take risks which are beyond the available evidence.

> The intensity of a passion will also be measured by the sacrifice made in persuance of the passion, by the passion's costliness; and a passion which lacks objective appropriateness will be

more costly, in respect of anxiety and/or rational autonomy, than a passion which has some objective basis.[8]

Again, this is a conception of faith in which quality of faith is inversely proportional to objective evidence. The less grounds for faith implies that more risk is involved. This makes unsupported faith better than reasonably supported faith because it is more costly to hold.

Such an attitude to faith is similar to that which is held by some charismatic writers. According to Wimber, for example, faith is spelt R.I.S.K., and involves stepping out and playing one's hunches without being restrained by 'Western Rationalist' thinking. Another charismatic, Urquhart, writes about faith as follows:

> If I had faith for my healing, my prayer would be different: 'Lord, please heal me, according to the promise of your Word and I thank you for your faithful answer.' After that it would be a question of continuing in thanksgiving: 'Thank you, Lord, for my healing.' And I would need to persist in that faithful attitude until the healing was manifested in my life. That would mean continuing in thanksgiving through all the times *when assailed by doubts, when the circumstances seemed unchanged or when it appeared that the prayer had made no difference.*[9]

This manner of prayer involves thanking God for healing even though the symptoms of the illness are still there. If one were to exercise the right kind of faith for long enough then one has already been healed. The interesting thing to note at this point is that it is a conception of faith which is quite divorced from adjustment in response to empirical evidence. *To allow a belief that a person had been healed, to be undermined by the fact that they are still ill, would be to show weak faith.*

It is only fair to point out that there are also significant differences between theologians such as Bultmann, and charismatic enthusiasts. Bultmann, for example, would certainly have nothing to do with claims that demonic activity was a reality: 'It is impossible to avail ourselves of modern medical and surgical discoveries, and at the same time to believe in the New Testament world of daemons and spirits.'[10] There is another difference, in that this kind of 'detached' faith is applied by Kierkegaard and Bultmann to the foundations of Christian belief, whereas this is not usually done by charismatic or evangelical writers. Charismatic writers could have rational justification for Christian beliefs as a whole, but retain a readiness to 'step out in faith' because of having other reasons to believe that God will be faithful to his promises. This is less radical than Bultmann or Kierkegaard.

In spite of the differences, however, there is a significant similarity between the existential theology of Kierkegaard and Bultmann and charismatic thinking, at least in their conceptions of faith. What is argued here is only a single connection between these diverse writers. This is that they retain the possibility of exercising faith which is detached from objective/reasonable support.

We have already argued that although a fideistic attitude to belief has a capacity to include that which is true, it has too large a capacity to include that which is false for it to be useful for the purpose of choosing between competing systems of belief. Fideism is incapable of distinguishing between contrary beliefs, because it is justified by an internal conviction which must simply be accepted. It provides a certainty which is disproportionate to the available evidence. It produces beliefs which have conveniently detached themselves from external criticism. It is an unacceptable epistemic position.

One also needs to question the reason why there is a need to establish the rationality of religious belief in such a subjective way. If one has been forced into justifying a belief without empirical evidence, then it begins to appear like a last ditch attempt to preserve a belief which has ceased to be credible. If one is describing the activity of an omnipotent, omnipresent creator working in the universe, one who expects belief in, and obedience to that which he has revealed what possible reason could there be for there being so little external evidence in support of his activity? The process has removed one so far from the empirical evidence that even the need for evidence is questioned.

It also forces one into a strange image of a God who seems primarily prepared only to reveal himself directly to the consciousness. He is a God who leaves no adequate experimental evidence for belief, and then demands belief as a condition of salvation from Hell. Why should he make these conditions, and then do such a thorough job of hiding himself from empirical enquiry?

The alternative explanations are simpler and more coherent. Let us assume for the moment that there was no God involved in a claimed 'religious' experience. The internal conviction of the person can be explained in terms of family background, conversion experiences, stress, varied psychological forces etc. Such an explanation would have the advantage over a theistic interpretation in that it can also explain the lack of external evidence which could verify the experience, because it does not demand the existence of an external being who is involved in the experience.

The non-theistic interpretation predicts well, as it can expect that such processes will produce equally strong convictions for varied and contradictory beliefs; people have a capacity to believe for inadequate reasons. It also remains in contact with the available evidence. A non-theistic interpretation would explain more of the facts than the theistic approach.

If the only support for a theistic belief were to be fideistic, then one would be forced to conclude that atheism would make better sense of the available evidence.

Consequently a fideistic justification of a belief should be treated as being suspect. Even if the faith is exercised within a framework of theistic belief which has been justified on some other grounds, one still requires some reasonable grounds for exercising strong faith in regard to a particular contingent claim within that system; the faith should be accountable to other factors.

Talking nonsense about faith

An example of this nonsense would be to extend the doctrine of justification by faith and use it to justify belief in God and Jesus, as done by Bultmann. One finds a similar extension of this doctrine within evangelical or charismatic churches. For example, a person is asked why he or she believes, and the reply is that one does not need reasons because one is saved by faith: 'Where would be the need for faith if we had reasons to believe?' Effectively it is version of fideism: 'I know because I know.'

When people sing, 'You ask me how I know he lives, he lives within my heart', it can be hard to resist the urge to stand up and shout, 'No it isn't how I know!' It is far more rational to believe in Jesus because of the resurrection, because of historical evidence, because of a coherent philosophy, because of some apparent direct perception in experience, because it is livable, because it is less improbable than are the alternatives; in short because it is *reasonable*.

Thankfully, the disciples were not woolly headed enough to 'just believe' that Jesus had risen from the dead. They had given up on him after his crucifixion and were returning to their own jobs. It was meeting Jesus after the resurrection that changed them into people who believed. They had faith because they knew that it was true, and they were persuaded of this in response to evidence.

The current confusion about faith is that if God is who the Bible says that he is, then unconditional faith, even in the face of difficulties, is justified. What is not justified, though, is applying this kind of faith to the foundations of Christian belief, and assuming that the entire framework can be justifiably accepted on this basis. It could be seen as a confusion between necessary and contingent truth.

Even more confusion about faith

This confusion about faith is the opposite error to the previous one. It is offering the unconditional trust in God which may be justified if one has strong rational grounds for adopting Christian belief as a whole, but then gives the same strength of belief to a less certain contingent part of this system.

Take, for example a person who would like to be healed by God of an illness. A prophet in the church gives him a 'word of knowledge' which is that if he will only trust that he has been healed, then God will heal him of this illness. The person tries as hard as he can to believe that God is healing him, dismissing the continuation of symptoms as temptations which could undermine his faith. Not to believe that he is healed is seen as being equivalent to doubting God himself.

We will assume that God is as he is described in the Bible, and that he is capable of, and willing to, perform miracles today. Within the story above are hidden two different beliefs around which hinges a confusion. The first belief is that God is faithful and so his words should be trusted. The second belief is that God has spoken directly and declared that he intends to heal this person now. It is these two beliefs that have become confused in the mind of our person who would like to be healed.

If God is as he is revealed to be in the Bible, then there is a requirement for unconditional trust in a God who is just, righteous and omnipotent. This is a necessary requirement. What is also being asked, however, is that the person should believe that God has spoken and intends to heal in this particular instance. The second belief does not have the right to the unconditional acceptance that the first belief does, because doubting the second belief is not to question God's words, but to question whether these particular words do in reality come from God.

If a person is in a situation where there are conflicting claims to revelation, and there is the possibility of making a mistake in deciding to accept a particular claim, then to doubt the claim is a necessity. In order to put your faith in God's word, you must not accept the word of a 'prophet' on nothing but faith.

Giving a *contingent* claim unconditional commitment is not only an unjustified epistemic position, it is also an unbiblical response to a prophetic claim, 'test everything, hold fast to the good' (I Thess. 5.21).

This provides another useful criterion of assessment. One ought to be suspicious when unconditional commitment is given to a contingent claim to knowledge.

The ad hoc *use of a supplementary hypothesis*

An *ad hoc* hypothesis is one which is plucked out of the air as an attempt to explain the failure of one's original theory and provide for it some supplementary support. Such a hypothesis has the epistemic status of a guess, and while it may be a correct guess, one could never know whether it is correct until it has been tested in some way. It is the first stage in the formulation of a theory, but if the theory is to have any justifiable claim to be knowledge, it is crucial to carry on beyond this stage with the process of testing. Think back to the analogy of an arch; but here we have one which is beginning to crumble and so we have desperately to grab whatever scaffolding is to hand in order to try and hold it up. *Ad hoc* theories are the conceptual version of emergency scaffolding.

An excellent recent example of *ad hoc* justification of belief is supplied by the 'mystic astronomer' Sofia Richmond who placed quarter page adverts in the national press. These predicted global destruction during the run up to Comet Shumaker hitting Jupiter in July 1994. According to her predictions a huge fragment would head towards earth, planes would stop flying, many people would die, governments would fall, there would be starvation and world-wide destruction. Her basis for these claims are that 'God has placed a Prophetic Telescope inside her mind'.[11]

This provides a curious contemporary example of full-blown enthusiasm which is almost mediaeval in character. None of these events occurred on the appointed day. However, her enthusiastic belief system is far too certain to modify itself in response to evidence, and it is revealing to see how these beliefs continued to be justified. The way that she coped with the situation was by using *ad hoc* theories.

> Sister Marie is very glad that all the prayers of people who asked God to stop any dangerous effects from the Comet/Jupiter Collision, were answered in July 94.[12]

She then predicted another collision with earth, because the 'cosmic day of judgment' now has two parts.

> However the 2nd PART of THE COSMIC DAY OF JUDGMENT refers to Comet now heading towards earth . . . The second

Part of God's COSMIC WARNING will occur when HALLEY'S COMET APPEARS IN THE SKY IN A FEW MONTHS.[13]

'Sister Marie' can continue to believe that her original predictions were correct by invoking two *ad hoc* supplementary hypotheses. The first is that God modified his original plans for judgment in response to the prayers of people, and the second is that the Jupiter collision was only the first part of the expected judgment day. The evidence remains constant; nothing has happened. However, the theories develop in an uncontrolled, *ad hoc* fashion.

Having said this, the prophet Jonah faced this issue in Nineveh. He was annoyed with God for responding to the people's repentance, and for not destroying the city. Jonah was aware that this made him look foolish, because in fulfilment of his prophecy, nothing evidently happened.

The church is certainly not beyond using *ad hoc* theories, particularly in a charismatic context. Say, for example, a sick person asks for prayer at the front of a church after a talk on how God heals people today if they will only have enough faith. After praying, there is no evident improvement in his illness, and so the 'healer' says that God has told him that this failure to become well is the result of hidden sin which needs to be dealt with first.

In order to preserve the original, but struggling, hypothesis that God always wants to heal sick people who ask to be made well, the supplementary hypothesis that hidden sin prevents healing is invoked. In fact this is a way of milking the failure of one's original hypothesis when the interpretation of the experience has lost touch with the empirical evidence; which is that nothing has happened. Virtually any belief could be justifiably held if such a method is acceptable.

When one becomes aware of this process, one begins to notice unusual theoretical gymnastics occurring, where, for example, absence of healing is ascribed to a lack of faith, to the influence of demons, to memories which needed healing before the physical body can be effected, to curses put on the family, to oppression over a town, to not enough prayer, and so on. Indeed, a significant portion of preaching consists of attempts to explain why what was expected has not yet occurred. These theories are often, however, *ad hoc* because of their loose connection with empirical evidence. They twist and develop into different forms while the actual situation remains unchanged.

Such *ad hoc* theories may be true, but:

(i) This process needs to be kept on a tight rein, because it has such a capacity for abuse in practice. All manner of fanciful beliefs are possible if they are not put under the constraint of relating them to experience.

(ii) When a theory has become overburdened with supplementary hypotheses, then this calls into question its assumptions.

(iii) A theory needs support from evidence if it is to be anything more than a guess. If one permits such a justification of belief, then one is allowing beliefs to exist in free-floating detachment from the world of experience. These beliefs must be forced to be answerable to other parts of a belief structure if they are to have any claims to constitute warranted knowledge.

Again this provides a useful criterion of assessment. If a theory is *ad hoc* then it ought to be awarded the epistemic status to which it is entitled; it is a guess.

Beware of the ghost in the machine

The 'Ghost in the machine' is a concept which is attributable to Gibert Ryle.[14] Its original use is as a description of a what he considered to be a category mistake which is sometimes used when talking about the mind, i.e. that people have both a mind and a brain. Here, what what I am doing is taking the phrase to describe an 'unnecessary entity' which is invoked when there is no need to look for an explanation beyond mechanical processes.

Let's play with the idea and hypothesize a 'ghost' in the form of a small man who puts the light off when the fridge door is closed. I could grant that the theory has good predictive capacity; however, being a moderately sceptical person I may be, as yet, not entirely persuaded by this theory, and so I ask why it is that I am unable to see this small person in the fridge. The reply is that he is a spiritual being who is invisible. I then ask for any other kind of evidence which may persuade me to believe that there is such a character. The reply is that because this is a spiritual being, he could not be subject to the normal processes of scientific evaluation. Another more philosophically inclined believer in the little man argues that his beliefs are innocent until proved guilty and so leaves me with the onus to prove that the invisible man who is beyond scientific evaluation is not there. At this stage in the discussion I decide to point out that there is in fact a small switch which is triggered by the fridge door; but this turns out to be unpersuasive because I am told that it has been put there to test my faith, and that I should not deconstruct or explain away ideas which are so important to people. Still unpersuaded to believe in the little man, I am told that I will never have the kind of proof that I am looking for, but that I should still believe by making a leap of faith. I remain unromantically attached to my notion that the switch is the reason for the light going on and off.

Such a combination of dubious justification is not confined to such a silly example. Say, for example, that a group of enthusiastic people are sent out by their church to do evangelism in a town centre, and are prayed for by the church. Travelling in their minibus, however, they have a flat tyre. They conclude that this is the devil trying to stop them from doing the Lord's work, especially since they are now stuck beside the road as a result of having no spare in the van. They pray about this, and find that a nearby garage has exactly the tyre they need. This is interpreted as being God's protection, and so they rejoice at being protected from attack.

In order to explain the 'failure' of the original prayers made by the church for their safe arrival, the supplementary hypothesis that the Devil is attacking them is invoked, even though there is no empirical evidence to support this particular explanation over some other. In other words a complex realm of supernatural beings is being used as an explanation for a course of events.

The most simple way to understand the events is that they ran over a sharp object on the road, and the bus was badly maintained, as evidenced by the lack of a spare tyre. The 'protection' needs be no more than the fact that garages sell tyres. While their interpretation of events may be true, there is no reason to suppose that it is. There may be a ghost in the machine.

The same is true of the predictions made by Sister Marie mentioned above. The obvious explanation for there not being a 'cosmic day of judgment' is that her predictions are nonsense. They are supported by imputing supernatural activity into this apparently natural event. There is a 'multiplication of entities', combined with an '*ad hoc* theory', which add up to an unnecessary ghost in the machine.

The criterion provided by this issue is that one ought to be wary of the ghost in the machine.

Methods which are dependent on probability

If one uses 'probability' in a loose way in the sense of passing a judgment on which of two views is correct, then this can be a useful criterion in the right circumstances.

One could argue, for example, that a person is 'probably' guilty on the basis of the available evidence. Or one could argue that there is a probability that if Great Britain had made peace with Hitler in 1940–41, Europe would have become Russian-ized. This is not, however, a mathematically determined probability. In this form it is a description of a cumulative argument. The balance of evidence falls in a particular direction.

If one uses probability in a strictly mathematical sense, however, then there would be difficulties in its use in relation to religious experience. How could one estimate the degree of probability that an experience represents a genuine encounter with God when one is not in a position to compare the experience with others that are known to be experiences of God, without begging the question?

This could limit the use of medical diagnosis as a model in this context, as it is based on determinable probability. It is, however, sometimes used as a means of assessing charismatic experience. One should be cautious of specific claims to have determined the 'probability' that an experience was a genuine encounter with God, and ask how this probability was determined.

Unjustified certainty

Certainty has always been a feature of enthusiasm, and continues to be a significant trait of the charismatic movement. For example, there are claims to have a certain knowledge that God will heal in particular instances, and prophets who are willing to use the phrase 'thus saith the Lord'. This is an implicit claim to certain knowledge.

In epistemological terms, however, there are no grounds yet discovered which would justify a claim to know absolute truth. Indeed, all the systems which seemed to provide this, and the criteria which have been used to aid in the quest for truth, have proved to be defective in some fundamental way. This does not necessarily preclude commitment to a course of action, even though one is not certain of the foundations, but it does mean that a claim to *know* truth with absolute certainty goes beyond that which is justified by evidence.

This certainty is not only disproportionate to the evidence, but unbiblical in the context of religious experience. For example, the point is effectively argued in the context of prophecy by Dr Wayne Grudem in his thesis *The Gift of Prophecy in I Corinthians*. He defines this Corinthian form of prophecy as being an intuitive insight given by the Holy Spirit for public declaration, but possessing neither the nature nor the authority of scripture. The prophet was a person who tentatively offered his words to the church who then tested them to see whether they were significant or not. Sometimes an accepted prophet was legitimately ignored, and sometimes what they said was wrong or only partially true.[15]

Prophecy in I Corinthians is therefore quite different from prophecy in the Old Testament, where prophets did not submit their messages to the people to see if they were acceptable or not, but declared them with the claim that they spoke with the authority of God.

In content, prophecy of the type found in I Corinthians will not include any claims to divine authority (such as 'thus saith the Lord'), but will include material which would be thought to have come through a revelation and which will edify the congregation.[16]

If this distinction between the nature of prophecy in the Old and New Testaments is not made, then this results in claims to certainty on the basis of prophecy. Such certainty is unjustified in epistemological or biblical grounds.

This is just one application of a generally useful criterion, which is that claims to be *certain* about the interpretation of religious experience are usually unjustifiable.

The lack of an available alternative does not necessarily justify a supernatural understanding of events

Not having an alternative theory could indicate a failure of understanding and an inability to find a coherent explanation for some event, rather than imply a miracle. The onus is consequently *not* on the critic of charismatic claims to find more plausible alternatives, although if he could it would be helpful. It is up to the person making assertions about an experience to justify his own theory by pointing out its strengths.

The point is made by B.B. Warfield:

Nature was made by God, not man, and there may be forces working in nature not only which have not yet been dreamed of in our philosophy, but which are beyond human comprehension altogether. Simple inexplicability, therefore, is not an adequate ground on which to infer miracle. There must be something else about an occurrence besides its inexplicableness to justify us in looking upon it as a direct act of God's.[17]

Lack of an explanation could be a useful starting point, as it indicates an event which raises suspicion. One could also have the best available explanation at a particular time, and so this belief would be justifiable at that stage.

Historically, however, claiming to have encountered a miracle because there was no available alternative explanation has led to a significant degree of disillusionment, as it is the essence of a 'God of the gaps' mentality. There are innumerable 'inexplicable' events which have gradually become explained as scientific knowledge has increased. Consequently one is unjustified in assuming that the lack of an explanation automatically implies the presence of a miracle. A claim made on such a basis should be treated with caution.

Psychological motivations presented as reasons for belief

There is a need for more careful definition here. For example, a person may prefer to hold a set of beliefs because they are ingrained by his upbringing, or perhaps because they continue to provide a feeling of peace or security. These would be psychological motivations or 'reasons' for this belief.

However, such motivations to believe are misleading if the question one is asking is 'why should I be confident that these beliefs are true?' Indeed such a psychological motivation could be considered as a temptation which seduces a person into believing a proposition, even when this belief is not fully justified by the available evidence.

Once one has pointed out that some psychological motivation was the 'reason' to believe, one is still left with the question, 'but is this adopted belief true or not?' Such a process of belief formation describes a neutral mechanism which could facilitate either taking up or disregarding a particular belief and so this motivation applies to both belief and to 'unbelief'.[18]

Consequently the presentation of psychological motivation needs watching because in the context of religious experience there is often confusion surrounding the meaning and significance of such 'reasons'. For example, in *Battle for the Mind*, William Sargant describes a mechanism of belief formation which explains conversion and Pentecostal experiences in terms of brain-washing techniques. He does *not* claim, however, that these explanations indicate the veracity or falsehood of the particular beliefs which are adopted. They are explanations of mechanisms, and not assessments of the cognitive claims of the new belief system.

Unfalsifiable statements

An example of an unfalsifiable statement would be the Freudian claim that religious experiences are the product of sublimations of blocked sexual or aggressive impulses which cannot be expressed directly and which reactivate the repressed impulses of the Oedipal period. A theist could counter this by offering alternative explanations, and examples of subjects of religious experience who lead perfectly normal sex lives which show no indication of blocked sexual impulses. However:

> Such counter-evidence is unlikely to impress those Freudians who see attempts to disprove their theories as merely further proof of the theist's repressed impulses. Freudian theories thus often appear impossible to test empirically, for they can be stretched to explain any state of affairs (a charge more often levelled against religious beliefs).[19]

Charismatic examples of unfalsifiable statements would be a claim to know what God is doing in a person's life, imputing motives to people, or claiming that the reason why someone has not been healed was due to 'lack of faith', 'hidden sin', or some other 'failing'.

The difficulty with such statements is that a theory ought to be refutable in some way. If it is to be considered meaningful, then there should be some conceivable way in which the theory could be disqualified. This is particularly applicable to charismatic healing, because if this criterion of refutablity is abused, the success or failure of virtually any 'experiment' could be used in support of one's thesis.

For example, if a person is healed, then it could be considered to be a miracle; if he was not healed then this can be attributed to hidden sin, or unbelief; and if he dies then this is the perfect healing. One needs to question whether anything meaningful is being said in the first place, or whether anything has happened which related to the initial theory, when all possible outcomes support one's theory.

Another example of the need for refutability arises in the practice of 'healing memories' where it becomes questionable whether the 'memories' which are reclaimed in this process are real, or implanted by the imagination or created by pressure from the counsellor. The nature of the situation means that it is usually impossible to perform an objective check on the past events, and so the theory is unfalsifiable. Consequently it is virtually impossible to sift out veracity from falsehood in the process.

This provides a useful means of assessing charismatic claims as it illustrates the dangers of (a) re-defining terms such as 'healing' in mid-argument, and (b) the tenuous epistemic status of unfalsifiable statements.

Anti-rationality

For some writers, such as Popper or Ayer, anti-rationality would be synonymous with unfalsifiability. Even if this is not so, however, there is always a suspicion of reason at the core of an enthusiastic movement. The reason why enthusiasts were opposed by Locke was because they rejected reason in favour of claims to have received direct revelation.

However, it is impossible in practice to dismiss reason completely; if one were to reject reasonable thought, then it would not be possible to say anything cognitively meaningful. Consequently those who *claim* to reject reason as a basis for knowledge in a Christian context do not escape the use of reason. What happens is that reason is rejected or retained wherever this suits the argument which is to be supported.

For example, a person argues that the biblical view of creation can only be that the world was created in six days in 4004 BC. His opponent suggests reasons why this could not be so on the basis of the archeological record, geology, carbon dating, and so on. If our creationist finds himself stumped, then he can fall back on the argument that his opponent is relying on the arm of the flesh, trusting in 'Saul's armour', and that he should submit his fallen reason to God's revelation.

The point I am making is not to justify the theory of evolution in preference to special creation, but to point out that as stated above, the argument illustrates a selective reliance on reason. There is an attempt at reasonable exegesis, but a rejection of a rational conclusion which is based on other evidence. The same creationist would be happy to accept a scientific finding which supported his view of the origin of the world, even though he prefers to dismiss the same kind of evidence where it conflicts with his already established conclusions about the origin of creation. It is the equivalent of only retaining experimental results which support the hypothesis that the experimenter would like to believe.

For a Bible-using enthusiast, a denigration of reason would also be inconsistent with his premises, because the use of a 'sound mind' is considered important, and reason is used in discussion throughout the Bible. The appropriation of biblical concepts also demands rational reflection.

The existence of a parallel in another context does not mean that a practice is necessarily wrong for a Christian

There are a number of examples of this process cited in chapter 8. Another example is provided by a discussion on the use of hypnosis, written by Dr M. Bobgan. He argues against hypnosis on a number of grounds, but a central part of the argument is that 'Hypnosis has been an integral part of the occult. Therefore a Christian should not allow himself to be hypnotized for any reason.'[20] One may have other reasons for being wary of hypnotism, but it is dubious to argue that because it is used in the occult it is *therefore* wrong for a Christian. People in the occult wear clothes, worship, cry, drive cars, sing, sleep, dance, pray etc. Once this has been pointed out one is still left with the question of the morality of each action. It is quite feasible that hypnosis could be a neutral psychological technique which can be used or abused in many different contexts.

The charismatic movement is often criticized on these logically flawed grounds of 'parallel use'. We have already cited examples of opposition to 'healing of memories', specific forms of prayer, and styles of worship which are based on this ground. It is a commonly used criterion in this context, but an unfair means of criticism.

A confusion between the spiritual and the phenomenal

The charismatic movement along with other enthusiastic movements is replete with phenomena such as falling down, trance-like states, feelings of ecstasy, sensations of electricity, screaming, and so on. These are commonly considered to be indications in themselves of the Spirit's power.

However, this is not the only way in which such phenomena can be interpreted. It is suggested by Nigel Wright, for example, that these 'supernatural' events may be natural psychic phenomena.[21] Dr Andrew Walker offers another possibility; that they could be the result of psycho-social effects created by the group dynamics of a crowd.[22] Dr D. Lewis assesses the possibility that these phenomena are the result of mass hysteria, or of learned behaviour, or the result of the power of suggestion.[23] John White suggests four possible ways of explaining enthusiastic manifestations:

1. People do it to themselves. That is to say, the manifestations have a psychological explanation, or are consciously or unconsciously self-induced.
2. Preachers do it to suggestible listeners – producing a so-called mass hysteria or mass hypnosis.
3. The devil does it – the phenomena representing some form of demonic control.
4. Or else God does it.[24]

There is also a strong possibility that hypnosis is a mechanism which could produce these effects.

Perhaps none of the above suggestions individually can explain all the phenomena that occur, but in combination they provide a significant erosion into claims that such phenomena should usually be considered as miraculous interventions from God.

The issue is illustrated by Edwards' experience of revival. In his earlier writing he was more ready to attribute these phenomena to the work of the Spirit.[25] However, his interpretation is more cautious in his later work, *The Religious Affections*.

> Great effects on the body are no sure evidences that affections are spiritual; for we see them oftentimes arise from great affections about temporal things, and when religion is in no way concerned with them. And if great affections about things purely natural may have these effects, I know not by what rule we should determine, that high affections about religious things, which arise in like manner from nature, cannot have the like effect.
>
> Nor, on the other hand, do I know of any rule to determine, that gracious affections, when raised as high as any natural affections, with equally strong and vigorous exercises, cannot have a great effect on the body. No such rule can be drawn from reason.[26]

It would seem that Jonathan Edwards was on the right track in refusing to consider these events as being a sure sign of the direct intervention of the Spirit. Rather he considered them to be neutral psychological phenomena. Given some strong emotional impetus, this is how people respond. *Whether they are responding in this way to a work of grace is quite a different question.*

This is just one example of the difficulty in separating the spiritual from the phenomenal. They are particularly difficult to distinguish in the setting of charismatic experience.

Consequently this leaves a useful indicator, which is to distrust claims that *because* some phenomenon is inexplicable or peculiar, it must be a work of the Spirit.

History repeats itself when no one listens

We need to learn from the history of enthusiastic movements. Chapter 1 of this book has pointed out the significant links between the charismatic movement and those movements which were described as 'enthusiastic' in the seventeenth and eighteenth centuries. This provides useful insights into the assessment of charismatic experience.

It opens up a vast body of literature which is directly applicable to the charismatic movement. This work is often of a very high quality, because many of the best minds of the Enlightenment wrote pieces of work on enthusiasm. These provide insights which are directly applicable to the current charismatic movement.

One is struck by the force and intellectual quality of this literature when compared with much of what is written by many current writers. For example, an issue such as 'is it acceptable to have weeping, shaking and laughing in a charismatic meeting?' is currently addressed by seeing if such phenomena occur in the Bible and can be considered as 'Scripture based manifestations'.[27] Writers such as Edwards, Locke or Leibniz would not have spent the time on such a superficial question. Edwards argued that the odd phenomena of enthusiasm were merely *symptoms* of some emotional impact from a spiritual or human source. They were quite beside the point if one is aiming to determine whether an experience is a genuine or non-genuine 'religious affection'.

Using this literature has directed this whole book to ask questions which were raised by empiricism and rationalism. This leads to a concern as to whether what a person claims for their experience is *true*. The way in which we have attempted to resolve the issue is necessarily different from the solutions provided by empiricism or rationalism, but the questions of the seventeenth and eighteenth centuries still have the capacity to direct one's attention to the heart of the matter.

The detailed recurrence of enthusiastic movements provides a strong insight into the way in which the current charismatic movement is likely to develop. It provides useful leads in terms of how one may attempt to assess individual claims to have encountered God in charismatic experience, common traps into which enthusiasts are inclined to fall, examples of the strengths and weaknesses of such movements, how they develop and the ways in which they commonly deteriorate. There are powerful insights to be gathered from the charismatic movement's enthusiastic ancestry.

Be aware of the context of charismatic experience

The context of charismatic experience is a significant factor in an attempt at its assessment because this context creates a bias against fair appraisal. Chapter 2 argues that enthusiasm has always inspired fierce opposition because of its two-tier concept of spirituality, because of its reaction against the institutional, because of its dramatic forms of worship and because of the fearfully powerful phenomena with which it is accompanied. The resultant opposition leads to defensive and threatened reactions on either side of the charismatic/non-charismatic divide, which does not tend towards fair and unbiased assessment.

Chapter 2 also argues that another issue which creates a bias against assessment is that enthusiastic thinking is characteristically credulous. This is due to the use of distorted definitions of faith which treat as a virtue the ability to believe in the absence of evidence. Quality of faith is thereby made inversely proportional to evidence. Enthusiasm has an inherent tendency towards credulity because it focusses primarily on experience rather than on the mind, or on theology. It can substitute reason in favour of a claim to have received divine revelation.

These factors create an inherent resistance to reasonable appraisal. They must be borne in mind when an attempt is made to understand charismatic experience, because the context creates significant difficulties.

Look for counter examples

A more specific criterion of assessment than the above would be to look for counter examples as a means of assessing the reliability of charismatics' claims to knowledge.

For example, enthusiasm has an epistemology which substitutes reasonable appraisal in favour of a claim to be the recipient of divine revelation. Such an experience tends to leave the perceiver with a certain conviction that God himself was the direct cause of this experience. One of the difficulties with making claims to knowledge on such a basis is that it can justify the logically contradictory claims of different groups and individuals. The fact that though they could not all be right, their beliefs would all be justified if this method were adopted, provides a counter example which calls into question the acceptability of claiming certain knowledge on the basis of a claim to direct inspiration from God.

Another example of a useful counter example would be the claim that all Christians have the right to be healed on demand, and indeed have an entitlement to possess all that is of heaven in the immediate present, 'thy will be done on earth as it is in heaven'. One clear counter example to this is the fact that Christians die, and have been dying since the time of Jesus, and were indeed informed by the Bible that death ought to be expected: 'it is given to men once to die, and after that comes judgment' (Heb. 9.27).

In pointing this out one would need to look out for slippery redefinition of 'healing' so that one's enthusiast did not begin to define death as being 'the perfect healing' in mid-argument. One would also have to persuade the individual that his beliefs ought to be accountable to experience, as he may not accept this. However, if this could be done, one would be forcing a person to face up to a significant counter example, i.e. that the particular belief is being contradicted by empirical evidence.

Take account of the tendency to give emphasis to criteria which support one's own preferences

Constructing a cumulative argument demands the exercise of judgment, and so even when one has established acceptable criteria, one also needs to be aware of their relative significance, because the tendency is for one to attach significance to the criteria that suits one's own particular case. In the context of understanding charismatic experience, the individual sides have strong preconceptions, and so distorted arguments are to be expected.

Some writers simply consider observable physical experiences to be indicators of the work of the Spirit, such as falling, barking or shaking.[28] Others may want to emphasize the character of the person associated with the event.[29] According to Edwards, features such as Christ-likeness and holiness with a focus on 'Divine things' are the primary indication of a genuine religious affection.[30] One could argue, however, that significant character change is equivocal, on the grounds that it is not possible to distinguish a 'Godly pagan' from godliness in Christians. Others may prefer to emphasize mental and emotional features as being indications of an encounter with God.[31]

A pre-conceived emphasis can influence exegesis. For example the traditional arm of the church will argue that what is important in I Corinthians 12–14 is the section on love in chapter 13. However, the charismatic expositor prefers not to suppose that because chapter 13 is of special significance, chapters 12 and 14 are therefore unimportant.

There is one special feature of enthusiasm which creates an unusually strong preconception in the individual. This is that if a person believes that they have had a direct perception of God in an experience, then this conviction will often be given overriding emphasis above all other factors. Such is the history of enthusiasm.

As we have argued, however, this reliance on putatively direct perception is an unjustified basis for confidence. A general example of this is that the sensations of fear and elation are produced by the same hormonal system. This means that if a person does a parachute jump with a free fall, whether the experience is exciting or terrifying will depend on how the basic information is *interpreted*. At the time, though, it will *feel* like a direct perception of fear or elation, and one will be unaware of the interpretive processes involved. A person who has had a religious experience will respond in a similar way in the sense that he or she will be unable to distinguish aspects of the experience which are a consequence of interpretation from the raw, or basic, uninterpreted, subjective, emotional/physical sensations. Consequently he will have a tendency to give his own 'experience'/ interpretation primary emphasis and claim that he *knows* because he has experienced. As Kierkegaard put it, 'How can it be that Christ does not exist since I know that he has saved me.'

Edwards may have a useful check against personal bias. One of the features of genuine religious affections suggested by him is that 'they have a beautiful symmetry and proportion'.[32] This symmetry will be evident in the whole character of a genuine Christian. For example, if a person discovers that he has an increase in his love for God, he ought also to have an increase in love for his neighbour. Holy hope will be combined with holy fear, joy with trembling, public religion with private devotion, and so on. Such a criterion does not have conclusive force in isolation from other features, but since 'elegance' and 'simplicity' are also indicators of a good theory, a search for proportion may provide a more widely agreed indicator which could check on the tendency to give special emphasis to one's own preferences.

The potential that individual preferences have to distort one's argument does not negate the possibility of constructing a cumulative case in principle, but there are no easy practical ways to resolve all of these questions of emphasis. The situation must be accepted as part of the complexity of attempting to assess charismatic experience, and one of the difficulties inherent in the process of constructing a cumulative case argument. At least if one is aware that preconceived emphasis is a potentially distorting factor, then it is possible to attempt to examine the situation with all the objectivity that one can muster.

An assessment of internal logic

It is important to assess the internal logic of a set of beliefs because internal inconsistency is the one generally accepted way of rationally undermining a particular thesis. It is a means of assessment that can usefully function across differing paradigms, because all of the paradigms share this presupposition that thought ought to be consistent.

For example, in the application to enthusiasm, assessing internal logic would demand considering the way in which the Bible is being treated, because it would be irrational for a movement to reach conclusions which were contradicted by its premises.

Beyond this it is more difficult to find examples of internal inconsistency than one may expect. Wesley considered enthusiasts to be consistent with their presuppositions, but to have begun with a false supposition.[33] If a person is convinced that his message has been directly revealed to him by God, then he ought to submit his finite wisdom to this, however strange the content of the message may be. If this demands building an ark on dry land, then this is what he ought to do, and he would be quite consistent in performing such an action if it is a deed which is based on the orders of an omnipotent and omniscient God. Where there is logical inconsistency, however, this should be pointed out and corrected.[34]

Accuracy: how well does this theory fit all the available facts?

For example, if one states that 'God is love, and is in control of this world' then one will have to work hard to reconcile this statement with the fact of suffering. Theologians talk about the 'problem of suffering', not meaning by this that it is a problem for those who *suffer*, but that suffering provides empirical evidence which calls into question either the love or the omnipotence of God; it is an abstract theological problem. If the theory is irreconcilable with the empirical evidence, then the theory should be rejected on the grounds that it is inaccurate; it does not make sense of the available facts. The point is not to pass a judgment on the issue of suffering, but to indicate that suffering is a significant problem, because coherence with the available evidence is an important quality of a good theory, even in theology.

A more specifically charismatic example would be the 'name it and claim it' style of prayer which works on the theory that if one asks in the right way, it is possible to get anything that is demanded from God. The theory runs into difficulty when what is asked for does not arrive, and so the theory has to be supported with supplementary hypotheses. These take the form of attributing failure to lack of faith, 'God sometimes says wait', not using the right words, the prayer was foiled by demonic activity, there was a curse on your family, and so on.

Even with these qualifications, however, the theory is being called into question on the grounds that it is not making sense of all the evidence, and because it is in need of so much supplementary support. Testing whether a theory fits all the available facts is a useful criterion to assess charismatic claims.

Predictive capacity

Within enthusiasm an obvious example of a theory which can be tested by its predictive capacity would be the words of a prophet. If they contain some specific information about the future, and these events do come to pass, then one has an indication which provides positive support for the integrity of these words. This is a biblical as well as an epistemological test.

This would apply to other areas of experience. For example, if one's theology leads one to routinely expect significant organic healing in response to prayer, then the predictive capacity of the theory can (and ought to be) evaluated. Or if the doctrine of baptism in the Spirit leads one to expect such specific changes in character, then its predictive capacity can be evaluated. If it proves to be accurate then it is an indication that supports its claims. If it does not deliver what it promised, then the doctrine is called into question.

Fruitfulness

Fruitfulness is a useful test within charismatic experience, because it has a biblical as well as an epistemological basis. One is asking, 'How productive are the implications of a particular theory?' 'What kind of results does it yield?' The Bible also uses the image of fruitfulness in assessment and talks about the 'fruit' of the Spirit as an indication that a person has had a genuine experience of the Spirit.

In order to assess a claim to have had an experience which is caused by the Holy Spirit, then, one sees the kind of effects that it has in an individual life. One looks for unusual character changes, increasing Christ-likeness, a depth of devotion that was not there before, holiness, and the fruit of the Spirit. If this fruitfulness is not evident, then one would need to question the reality of the original claim to have encountered God in experience.

The same test could usefully be applied to an individual church, or to a whole 'movement' of the Spirit, by looking at the long-term effects of, for example, the 'Toronto Blessing'. In order to assess its 'fruitfulness' one would have to allow enough time to observe what kind of effects are produced by these phenomena. There is not enough evidence at present even to describe it meaningfully as a 'blessing'. Perhaps one could give it the benefit of the doubt for a while, let its 'fruit' develop, and then prune it to remove the dross. Given enough time one would be able to determine if there are beneficial results. A yield of 'good fruit' could take the form of dramatic healing, unusual character change, increasing holiness, a concern for the poor and downtrodden, depth in worship, growth in the church, and so on. 'Bad' fruit would consist of disillusionment, heresy, hollow emotionalism, superficiality, unfulfilled claims, divided churches, etc.

This does, however, raise the old problem of paradigm relative facts, and paradigm relative evaluative procedures. This is because the possibility of evaluating by using 'fruit' is complicated because what is considered to be 'good' fruit can be paradigm relative. Consequently, some of the 'fruit' which religious experiences produce may only be considered as beneficial within a religious framework. For example, increasing prayer is positive fruit when evaluated from within a Christian web of belief. However, if viewed from an atheistic paradigm it is not good at all, as the poor deluded person is talking more to himself than he was formerly.

Even with this proviso, other fruit, however, yields benefits which would be regarded as such by any paradigm's criteria. For example, benefits such as recognizing the intrinsic worth of all human beings, expressing love and care for the poor and those who have been abandoned by society, would be broadly accepted.

Caroline Franks Davis argues that religious experiences may also be conducive to good mental health and to promote a healthy, positive attitude towards death.[35] If a charismatic experience helps people to deal with crises, anxiety, sorrow, and guilt, and provide comfort, hope, courage, guidance and meaning, then these 'fruits' offer support to the theory that the experience was the product of divine activity.

Of course, the converse is also true, and the destruction of a personality or church would be a fruit which would support an interpretation that attributed the experience to a psychological or pathological state.

Generality

A theory which is applicable in more situations is preferable to one which has a narrow relevance to a limited situation. The law of gravity, for example, is shown to be strong because it seems to be applicable to that which can be observed throughout the universe. It is comprehensive, and embraces a wide range of phenomena and applications.

One could apply this to the differing theories which are invoked to explain the phenomenon of being 'slain in the Spirit'. The normal charismatic theory is that it is a direct work of the Holy Spirit. However, the weakness in this is that the theory has difficulties in explaining why such similar phenomena are observable in different religious settings, or in the context of psychiatric treatment, or during stage hypnotism. In order to cover these possibilities it must postulate a different cause for these experiences and attribute them to the work of Satan counterfeiting a genuine work of the Spirit.

If generality is a mark of a strong hypothesis, then the explanation for these phenomena as being ordinary human responses to a variety of emotional stimuli is preferable, because it offers a *general* explanation which could fit in with all the different situations in which these events occur. Of course, it is by no means 'proof' but it does allow us to give more weight to one interpretation over another.

Generality offers a useful criteria for assessment of charismatic experience.

Explanatory power of the theory

The ability of a theory to explain all the facts is a useful indicator of its force, and so could provide a useful criterion.

One point which does need care here is that explanations can be confused with labels. For example, why do apples fall down? The answer is 'because of gravity'. This is a good label and (sadly) would satisfy the majority of the population, but is by no means an *explanation*. What *is* gravity? The same is true of saying that some events were caused by God, and thinking that this answers all possible questions. This is inadequate, because it does not offer anything in the way of explanation.

There is an inherent problem with using this criterion with reference to a miracle, because by definition this is an event which does not have a natural explanation. This implies that the only way in which this could be used in the assessment of an enthusiastic experience would be to assess the quality of alternative explanations, and show the weaknesses of the alternatives on offer at the time. If one could do this it would not mean that miracle is therefore the best explanation, but it could contribute something to a cumulative argument.

Effectively this criterion is loaded against the miracle, as it can undermine, but rarely confirm. For example, the carbon dating of the shroud of Turin placed it to the twelfth century AD, and excluded the possibility that it was genuine. Even if it had turned out to be dated as first century AD, however, this would still not have proved that it was therefore the product of a miraculous event. The explanation only supplied a date.

In the context of charismatic experience, the provision of an explanation can be a useful means of assessment. However, a miraculous event such as God intervening in experience is, by definition, inexplicable by natural means, and so the provision of an explanation undermines a miraculous claim.

Take account of the complexities involved in choosing between competing paradigms

A cumulative argument is capable of producing complex and highly ramified religious beliefs. One could have a numinous experience of awe and reach a simple belief that there must be a God in this experience who is all powerful and magnificent. This much would be comparatively simple. However, the Christian concept of God moves well beyond this into significantly more complex beliefs. These beliefs have developed over the centuries in the context of theological debate, reaction against heresy, interaction with philosophy, claimed revelation, experience and new knowledge. Consequently, most current doctrines are the product of so much reflection on experience, and are so embedded in a web of interlocking beliefs, that religious experience alone could not provide a rational justification for holding them. Doctrines such as the nature of the Trinity, for example, the person of Christ, the doctrine of the work and person of the Holy Spirit, or the Atonement require such a complex cumulative argument for their justification that one could hardly begin to illustrate their construction here.

A particular understanding of experience is determined by such a conceptual framework and, as we have already argued, the decision between such frameworks needs to be made on the basis of cumulative argumentation. In order to assess the acceptability of each way of explaining the experience, one needs to judge the entire framework. This is an extremely complex task.

The complexity is increased because this is not a situation where there are wholly separate areas of unquestionable theory assessing a factual experience and using incorrigible methods. There is a constantly shifting dialectic between theory, fact, methodology and other paradigms, as they all jostle together to provide the most adequate understanding. In this setting the religious experience is assessed within a particular paradigm, but is also capable of becoming a piece of evidence which can contribute to the justification of that encompassing world view. Arguments which underestimate the complexity of this process are inadequate.

The use of Ockham's razor

Ockham's razor would be a useful means of eliminating false theory. It also sums up a number of the above criteria. To understand what this razor is we need to go back 2,400 years and think about Plato. Plato argued that as well as the world around us, there was a 'universal' world of ideas. So, for example, there is a 'universal' table which exists apart from the specific table on which I currently write. Plato also believed that the soul was pre-existent and that it used to dwell in the same world of the universals. The soul is placed into an earthly body at birth, but all the while it retains a sense of the reality beyond. Consequently this world is not our true home; we came out of the world of universals and that is where we really belong. It is as though birth placed us into a dingy cave chained to a wall in such a position that it is not possible to see the outside world through the cave mouth. All we can see are the shadows on the back wall of the cave cast by the bright light from the 'universal' world outside, a world which we wonder about and long for while we are forced to live in the shadowlands.

It is easy to see why Christians had a liking for Plato! His ideas have been taken up by many people throughout church history, including George Macdonald and C.S. Lewis.

Sadly all of this conceptual fun was spoiled by William of Ockham who argued the idea of 'universals' was not justified or needed, and was nothing but *flatus vocus*, or 'verbal flatulence'. Ockham's razor is a means of trimming down dubious, speculative and unnecessary ideas; *entia non multiplicanda sunt praeter necessitatem* (do not unnecessarily multiply entities).

Since then the general idea of this razor has been widely adapted and applied. Certainly within science one of the marks of a good theory is that it has an elegant simplicity, which avoids unnecessary complications. Even a paradigm can be overturned when it becomes overburdened by supplementary hypotheses to the point where the underlying theory becomes strained beyond credibility. This is using the original razor in ways not intended by Ockham, as the kinds of 'entities' being trimmed down are different, i.e. theories. However, this still involves a trimming down of possibilities to the most straightforward theory. In this sense, they are related.

If we are permitted to abuse Ockham's razor in this way, then we could apply it to theology. Essentially we are using it as a description of the simplicity, which is one of the marks of a good theory. 'God of the gaps' thinking is a theological equivalent of a lack of simplicity. Throughout church history there has been a tendency to 'multiply entities' by seeking a supernatural explanation for that which is beyond natural explanation at the time. Why do flowers grow? Because God makes it happen. Why do the planets revolve in the way that they do? Because God orders their paths. Why does this person exhibit such strange behaviour? Because he is possessed by a devil.

The difficulty with such thinking is that these gaps are gradually filled in with strong rational explanations, and so the apparently direct works of God are progressively squeezed out of the universe. This has reached the point where even *creatio ex nihilo* has a suggested explanation in terms of mathematics and physics. This would be the last foothold for a 'God of the gaps' explanation of reality.

Perhaps 'God of the gaps' thinking should not even be called explanation. It does little in the way of defining how cause and effect work in a particular instance. It is resorted to when an event is unexplained; 'what else could it be but a miracle?' Consequently it functions as a label which is applied to some phenomena which have no explanation at the time. Indeed, it is also given to some phenomena which do have a perfectly good explanation. Though they are often confused, to give a phenomenon a label is not the same as offering an explanation, or of understanding a process. The church is sometimes better at applying labels than at giving a full explanation.

The effect of this unwillingness to shave one's own theology is usually destructive. A good example of this would be the paradigm change initiated by the publication of Darwin's *Origin of Species*. The theory offered a natural understanding of the apparent design and complexity of the make-up of all animals in terms of natural selection and evolution. As is frequently pointed out, 'it is only a theory, it hasn't been proved yet'. This is true, but so obviously true that to point it out seems to qualify as *flatus vocus*. Scientific theories never can be 'proved', because it is always possible in theory that they will be undermined by future experiment. At least according to Popper, science functions by working with the best available explanations until they become too strained to be useful. Evolution may well be disproved at some stage; this will always be true in principle.

However, as an (admittedly tentative) theory, it has much to commend it, it is universal in application, simple, elegant, offers accurate prediction, it is capable of being tested using empirical evidence and it fits well into the web of other beliefs within science.

Many within the church have been less impressed, though. It certainly didn't fit with ease into a theological 'God of the gaps' web of belief, indeed it caused so much upheaval that it destroyed the web that many Christians had been content with. The effect was of widespread disillusionment with the Christian understanding of reality. It would have been less painful if the church had shaved itself properly before its overly hairy theories had been rather suddenly barbered by the strength of evolutionary theory.

When such a natural explanation turns up, the phrase which is sometimes used is not 'explaining', but 'explaining away'. This is curiously revealing. In superficial terms 'explaining away' means the same as 'explanation'; but the inference is that the person didn't like it. There is a sense that he has lost something which he would have preferred to keep; a grudging acceptance, and a distinct reluctance is implied. He would have preferred his original mistaken theory in preference to his new understanding.

The mystery is gone, and what seemed like a supernatural support within the person's web of belief has suddenly been eradicated, or explained away.

Within charismatic experience a tendency to offer supernatural 'explanation' is a particular danger. Entities are multiplied as the demonic is conjured up as an explanation for sin, illness, homosexuality, lack of money, general problems in life, and so on. The same process is also at work where the direct intervention of the Holy Spirit is used as an explanation for phenomena such as shaking, falling down, emotional reactions, healing, and so on.

Claiming that an event has a supernatural cause may be the best theory on offer. However, it is one theory in competition with other possible ways of understanding events, and it is important to be critical in one's thinking at this point. This is particularly so because the charismatic movement is often seduced into accepting a needlessly supernatural explanation by its desire to fill up the gaps in its understanding with certainty. In the short term this may be comforting and 'faith building', but in the long term it is a basis for disillusionment. The temptation not to doubt one's understanding of experience should be resisted wherever possible.

The charismatic movement needs to use Ockham's razor. If there is no obvious natural explanation for some phenomenon, it should not be too quick to jump into a supernatural web of belief for a label. This implies that one should look for a terrestrial understanding of events first. And even if it is not possible to come up with one, this does not necessarily imply that one has seen a miracle. On the evidence of history, it is more likely that one's understanding and imagination were not up to the demands of providing a full explanation.

The charismatic movement is in need of a good shave. It can do this the easy way by borrowing Ockham's razor and doing this itself, or the hard and painful way by letting itself be barbered by alternative and more coherent theory.

The use of the cumulative argument

If charismatic experience is either to be supported or to be opposed this can be done rationally by the force of a cumulative argument. A cumulative argument is not just an accumulation of evidence. The whole is greater than the component parts, and these 'parts', though individually weak as evidence, can provide mutual support when functioning in conjunction. This is one of the ways in which an arch provides a useful analogy of a cumulative case.

All of the criteria suggested in this chapter are, by implication, in the nature of leaky buckets which need to be combined into a relationship which offers mutual support. They are (questionable) guide-lines which assist in making a reasonable judgment, but do not individually provide grounds for certainty.

For example, a particular theory may be strong in one way, in that it can provide excellent explanation, but then be overly laden with supplementary hypothesis; it could be good at prediction, but poor in its fruitfulness, and so on. One must therefore use these *individual* indications in a cumulative fashion in which each is providing a degree of support for a theory, though none of them individually is adequate to provide proof.

Another example of the danger of isolating one particular criterion would be the criterion of coherence. This can be inadequate when isolated from other factors which could be used in the construction of an argument. Notoriously, a belief system based on coherence will have difficulty when it encounters another belief system which is also self-consistent. Consequently, in order that a self-consistent belief structure should be able to relate to other systems and to the world, it must use other criteria, such as making an attempt to reckon with experience.

A strong predictive capacity is another individual support for a theory, but one that must be balanced against other factors. In a charismatic context, for example, the phenomenon of 'slaying in the Spirit' could be predicted by using the theory that these events are the result of hypnotic techniques. One could also claim, however, that they are the result of direct intervention by God, on the grounds that it is possible to predict their occurrence in response to prayer. Both theories could be justified on the grounds of predictive capacity. Because of this other criteria are needed to make a decision between the two theories. On its own, 'predictive capacity' is not enough, and can be thoroughly misleading if it is assumed to provide proof. Only when it is incorporated into an argument that includes explanation, fruitfulness, generality, and so on, can it be given its correct epistemic force.

All the factors in a cumulative argument interact. For example, one could provide an explanation of conversion in terms of a psychological process. This explanation does not, on its own, undermine the acceptability of beliefs which are adopted as a result of this conversion. Conversely, however, an inexplicable conversion experience can contribute some support to the adopted belief system as a whole, and therefore if it is removed the support for these beliefs has weakened to some extent. There is a dialectic between the different parts of the cumulative system of belief.

A cumulative argument ought to be used throughout the web of belief. It can be applied to internal assessment within a Christian paradigm, as well as to more radical questions.

Take I John as an example of a cumulative argument which is situated within a Christian paradigm. It is a book which is written to a group of people who were infiltrated by Gnosticism. John offers suggestions as to the marks of a genuine Christian and the authentic Christian message. This is similar to the quest of this book, as it demands some kind of criteria which could sift out that which should be rejected. In order to assess Christian belief and experience, John does not give *one* answer, but offers a combination of factors: moral behaviour, doctrinal correctness (particularly about the person of Jesus), love for others in the fellowship, humility, an awareness of sin, a desire to be holy, a practical Christianity rather than one which is just evidenced in words 'he who *says* . . .', a love for God and not for the world, and an internal conviction which gives confidence to approach God. Each of these on its own does not provide a proof that the person is a genuine Christian believer; after all, Christians are sinners (I John 1.8). However, when all these attributes are evident together in one person there is a strong cumulative indication that this is a person who is 'walking in the light'.

A similarly cumulative approach is made by Edwards in his suggestion that genuine religious affections are indicated by a combination of distinguishing signs, rather than by individual proofs.[36]

Cumulative argumentation is also applicable to the more radical choices which must be made between a Christian paradigm and those with which it competes. In such a setting the questioning will be more extreme, and may have to include issues such as the problem of suffering, the evidence for the resurrection, or the reasons for adopting theistic belief. However, the way in which the issue is resolved is in principle the same. It is on the basis of a cumulative case.

All of this implies a doubly cumulative arguement, because (a) the argument appraises an entire collection of beliefs, rather than isolating the belief system into its individual components, and then (b) does this appraisal on the basis of an accumulation of the means of verification.

Firstly, then, the cumulative argument appraises an entire collection of beliefs. It is particularly useful to assess charismatic experience as a whole 'constellation' of beliefs, experience, and means of verification because, as we have argued, this enthusiastic pattern is one which recurs through church history as a whole jumble. As with any large-scale system of beliefs, the individual tenets of a religious paradigm rely on each other for mutual support, and are unable to stand up to epistemic evaluation when isolated from the rest of the conceptual system. It is therefore only fair that each should be assessed within the context of its interlocking web of belief.

Secondly, as well as a whole set of beliefs, there are also cumulative means of verification. As pointed out earlier, there is a difficulty in choosing rationally between conflicting paradigms because there are paradigm relative evaluative procedures and paradigm relative facts. Although difficult, this is a problem which is resolvable in principle because not all of the evaluative procedures are relative to a particular paradigm; there are usually significant areas of overlap between different large-scale conceptual systems.

This overlap exists in the conflict between charismatic interpretations of experience and those understandings which are rooted in different paradigms. Some means of assessment are internal; for example, the use of 'the gift of discernment' is only possible if one presupposes many charismatic claims, including the reality and availability of the gifts of the Spirit. This may be a useful contingent means of assessment as far as a charismatic believer was concerned, but is of limited use to a dispensationalist, and of even less use to an atheist.

Other means of assessment could provide the possibility of making a rational assessment even when the opposing interpretations of experience are situated in different conceptual systems. How this is done would depend on the type of claim that is being made. If one makes a historical statement, say that Jesus was born in Bethlehem during the time of King Herod, then this can be assessed by the methods used in historical research. A claim that a religious experience has been indicated by an unusual personality change could be assessed, to some extent, by means which are used in psychology or psychiatry. A claim that a person has been healed could have supporting evidence in the form of medical diagnosis. The same principle is true of literary interpretation, verdicts in a court of law, the use of induction or deduction to corroborate a scientific claim, existential evidence and biblical interpretation. The way in which a statement is assessed should be appropriate to the kind of statement that is under scrutiny.

The *accumulation* of such means of assessment could contribute to the construction of a cumulative case and thus provide an interpretation of a particular charismatic experience which is *generally* accepted as being rational.

In this way one is able to use means of verification which are accepted by different paradigms. This would allow a rational defence of a religious world view by showing that it made better sense of the available evidence even when assessed by using an opponent's criteria of verification.

Conclusions

The book has travelled a long road since setting out to determine how the cognitive claims made on the basis of charismatic experience could be evaluated. It has linked charismatic experience with enthusiasm, and because of this been pushed into the conclusion that a distinctive epistemology determines the shape of the charismatic movement. To assess this epistemology it has sifted through the options and concluded that the best available way in which this could be done is by the use of a cumulative case argument. The complexity of the question is magnified because the opposing interpretations of charismatic experience are the expression of conflicting paradigms. Even though it is a complex task, it is still possible to decide rationally between paradigms by the use of cumulative argumentation. Having established the way in which the question should in principle be resolved, the book criticizes much contemporary literature which relies for its means of assessment on too simple, or too few criteria of assessment. The final chapter has drawn together criteria from throughout the book which could be helpful, and suggested ways in which they could be incorporated into a cumulative case.

The question throughout the book has been, 'If a person claims that he has encountered God in his experience, how could it be known that this claim describes what has really occurred?' The question is not abstract in the sense it is detached from the realities of life in the church during the second half of the twentieth century. It is a question of both relevance and significance to the charismatic movement. There are strong historical grounds to suppose that if it does not sift ruthlessly its claims and experiences, then it will be destroyed by being pulled into confusion. Consequently, in order to preserve that which is worth retaining, one needs to be ruthless in sifting out that which should not be there. If this is so, then both those who are committed to this movement and those who oppose it ought to be united in seeking criteria which can interpret charismatic experience reliably.

This is not just a pragmatic issue for a Christian, it is an issue of spirituality. If one concedes that there is a genuine experience of the Holy Spirit, then such experience ought to be protected as rigorously as possible from fraudulence, superficiality, and misleading assessment.

As the Bible says, 'test everything, hold fast to the good'. Or as it was put by Jonathan Edwards:

And by what is seen of the terrible consequences of this counterfeit religion, when not distinguished from true religion. God's people in general have their minds unhinged and unsettled in things of religion, and know not where to set their foot, or what to think or do; and many are brought into doubts, whether there be anything in religion; and heresy and infidelity and atheism greatly prevail.[1]

The conclusion as to how this filtering may be achieved can be summarized in one sentence. The way to assess charismatic experience is by the use of a cumulative argument. In practice the construction of such an argument is multi-faceted and has wide implications.

The argument could be taken further forward, particularly because there is a need to examine the relationship between the tentative results of a cumulative argument, and the way in which Christian belief functions with such certainty in practice, and has thereby such a capacity to alter the life of the believer.

Alongside the road which has been taken are many areas which are interesting and worthy of exploration. These include the insights of sociology, psychology, church history, medicine and theology. The appendix points out how fruitful it may be to explore the relationship between hypnotic techniques and enthusiasm. There are other possible avenues of exploration. For example, there exists an obscure neurological disorder called Turette's disease which can afflict the basal ganglia. What is curious is that one of its symptoms is that people actually bark uncontrollably. The resemblance may be quite superficial, but it does bear a remarkable similarity to the observed phenomena of the 'Toronto Blessing'. The book has suggested how in principle charismatic experience could be assessed; with a cumulative argument. This needs to be applied to specific examples of charismatic experience.

The only way in which the integrity and direction of the central argument could be maintained and completed within limited space was to keep rigidly to that which is directly applicable to the main question. This has made it quite impossible to illustrate the argument with reference to all of the available examples, nor to dialogue with every writer along the road who has a comment to make on charismatic experience. This does not negate the main argument.

To use another analogy, the book has drawn an outline sketch of the epistemic structure of the charismatic movement. A sketch is a useful way to begin a painting, but such a sketch could always be criticized on the grounds that each of its component parts is not detailed enough. In spite of this incompleteness a sketch does provide a helpful framework within which an artist is able to place the detail in its correct relationship to the other parts of the picture.

One should not underestimate the amount of detail which is needed to paint in the structure of a cumulative case argument. Such a system of belief is extremely highly ramified, and will be too complex for any individual to complete. There are limitations on human understanding, even in the simple fact that life is not long enough for a person to explore thoroughly all of his or her beliefs. Any individual is forced to rely on a long history of thought.

The argument constantly makes reference to God, who is considered to be transcendent, infinite, dwelling in unapproachable light, beyond understanding. Consequently much of the data which is needed to complete the picture may be hidden in eternity. One needs a Kantian humility which recognizes the limits of human reason. Or as St Paul put it, we see through a glass darkly. To some extent we must end with the words of the Tractatus: 'What we cannot speak about we must pass over in silence.'[2]

Appendix

Enthusiastic phenomena and hypnotic techniques

One interesting explanation of the peculiarities of enthusiastic phenomena is that they can be the result of hypnosis. Although it is not argued in any detail, Peter Masters in his book *The Healing Epidemic* asserts that John Wimber's techniques are based on hypnosis. The same assertion is made by Professor V. Wright in an article assessing a signs and wonders conference in England.[1] The connection is not argued by him in any detail, but the suggestion is intriguing and warrants some exploration. Is hypnosis a plausible explanation for the phenomena of enthusiasm?

There is a vast amount written on hypnosis, and there are many theories which offer explanation of the phenomenon. Hypnosis even has its own journal, *The International Journal of Clinical and Experimental Hypnosis*. Consequently this appendix is by no means an attempt to cover comprehensively the relationship between hypnosis and enthusiastic experience, because to do so would be a thesis in itself. All that it does is indicate that, in my own experience, there seem to be evident similarities between these two areas. It is argued by Martin H. Katchen in his article 'Brainwashing, Hypnosis and the Cults'[2] that there is a lack of investigation into the link between hypnotizability as a possible variable which could predict successful cult recruitment. This lack is attributed by him to acceptance of the brainwashing model of coercive persuasion, and the preference for other sociological and psychological models. I would suggest that an exploration into the possibility that some *charismatic* experience could be attributed to hypnotic technique would also be a useful area of research.

The roots of hypnosis in Europe go back to the Austrian

physician Franz Mesmer (1734–1815), who developed his ideas in the early 1770s. In 1778 he visited Paris and made a sensational impact with his demonstrations of the effects of 'animal magnetism'. His method of induction was to use a tub full of magnets which supposedly focussed the 'magnetic fluid' in the ether which allowed 'animal magnetism' to enter the body and produce the various phenomena.[3] People stood around this in a circle, or 'seance',[4] then Mesmer would come in and touch people in the group. Some recovered from illness after collapsing to the floor in a state of delirium called 'the crisis'. Physical illness' such as skin rashes would disappear, or appear, people shook, screamed and experienced sensations of heat and cold.[5]

The idea of a 'magnetic fluid' was undermined, although hypnosis continued to work.[6] It became evident that it can be induced by a variety of methods; all that is needed is a conducive atmosphere with the right kind of psychological suggestion and stimuli.[7]

This is an interesting story for a number of reasons:

(i) It is a good example of a theory which had good predictive capacity and yet was wholly false.

(ii) It is possible to hypnotize a person without understanding the process one is using, and conversely it is also possible to be hypnotized without realizing that this is what is occurring. It would be conceivable that a person could use these simple techniques unintentionally in many different contexts.

(iii) The particular method of induction is of secondary importance; psychological force is the key.[8] This important point is confirmed by an experiment which explored the effectiveness of differing methods of inducing hypnosis.[9] The experiment controlled for suggestibility, and used four separate groups of subjects. Hypnosis was induced by using (a) traditional hypnotic induction, (b) alert induction, (c) relaxation technique, and (d) goal-directed imagery. Assessment of the depth of consciousness was gauged by self-report method and expert evaluation. The outcome of the study showed that the hypnotic state of consciousness was indistinguishable between the four groups, giving a clear indication that traditional hypnosis is just one method of altering thought patterns.

This is significant because it indicates that hypnosis can be induced without using traditional formal hypnotic induction, and also that it is possible to induce a level of hypnosis by using comparatively 'cold' techniques. The possibility of hypnosis being induced by informal methods in the context of a charismatic gathering is supported by these findings.

If we compare some of the common features in charismatic gatherings with hypnotic techniques, one finds that there are significant points of comparison.

(i) Both stage hypnosis and public charismatic 'ministry' times can induce individual responses within a crowd of people.[10]

(ii) Heightened expectation increases the effect of hypnosis.

> Expectation about the nature of hypnosis, for those who have not been hypnotized, tend to correlate with their subsequent hypnotic scores.[11]

This heightened expectation is evident in the charismatic movement. For example, it follows the 'Toronto Blessing' around and the expectation, for instance when a minister from Toronto is speaking, is breathtaking. The leaders of the gathering will claim verbally that you will see God at work directly and evidently during the 'ministry' time. You will expect to see things happen (and not be disappointed).

(iii) When hypnosis is being induced it is helpful if a person believes that something is going to happen to him or her. This is why scathing scepticism would make one unresponsive to hypnosis. It is consequently important not to implant negative ideas when inducing hypnosis because these can undermine the effectiveness of the process.[12] For example, one should not say 'Did you feel the prick of the pin?', but rather 'Will you let me know when the pin begins to feel blunt?'[13]

A positive expectation is also encouraged throughout the charismatic movement. The necessity for belief and faith can be tapped into by a leader in an evangelical context or charismatic meeting, because the ability to believe is considered to have intrinsic virtue. This applies particularly in situations where faith is considered to depend for its strength on excluding negative suggestions by which it could be undermined.

(iv) Suggestion is a mechanism which is arguably the main force in the production of hypnotic states.[14]

Suggestion is also in effect in a meeting where there are manifestations of charismatic phenomena. The participants are normally aware beforehand of the kinds of responses which will occur at the end in the ministry time. There is also the non-cognitive suggestion which is caused by being surrounded by many people who are responding to 'ministry' in dramatically physical ways.

(v) It is important to have confidence in the hypnotist. Hypnotic effect can be speeded up where there is a strong confidence in the hypnotist, a confidence which can be produced by the right kind of manner.[15]

This process could also be at work in, for example, a Wimber meeting, as he is a warm and likeable 'charismatic' character who approaches the issues in a gentle way, seeming to present an academic credibility along with a relaxed confidence in dealing with the supernatural. Someone who was a part of the signs and wonders movement would be aware of his powerful record and believe that here is someone who can handle charismatic phenomena with authority.

(vi) It is important for the one experiencing hypnosis to feel safe for it to be effective.

> The hypnotist establishes or reinforces some desultory conversation to put the subject at ease and allow time to adjust to the surroundings.[16]

Those who exercise ministry along the lines of the Vineyard movement will introduce ministry time with words such as, 'don't worry about the dramatic phenomena', 'feel comfortable', 'just watch if you prefer'. Any response is permissible, and people are encouraged to feel safe during the ministry time.

(vii) The atmosphere must induce relaxation.

> A dramatic tense sort of atmosphere is all right for a novel or film. In practice a kind of casualness – as if the treatment were the most ordinary everyday affair in the world – is better.[17]

Wimber talks about the 'natural supernatural'. When it comes to the 'ministry time' he will encourage people to relax, stretch their legs, feel comfortable. The hype is less, but in reality it is the perfect climate for hypnosis.

(viii) People respond best to hypnosis if they are led rather than pushed, and so the best manner is gentle and undomineering.

> Under most circumstances, therapeutic hypnosis is now carried out in an atmosphere of mutual co-operation, the hypnotist assuming the role of a teacher who can help his student to achieve a mutually sought goal.[18]

This non-authoritarian technique is also an element in Vineyard methodology. The approach is that here are some things we have learned, but we're all learning together. People split into groups and try things together, and learn by seeing how it works out as they lay hands on each other.

(ix) Suggestions are best in the indicative rather than the imperative, so that instead of 'lift your hand', we hear, 'your hand is lifting'. One encourages a 'passive attitude in which the subject neither strives to help nor hinder'.

My own experience of ministry times in different charismatic settings is that the same passivity is encouraged. 'You just relax, you don't have to do anything, we will pray for you. Just open your hands to receive from God.' The person is encouraged not to strive, but to accept passively.

(x) The essence of hypnotism is the ability to by-pass the critical mind in order to influence the subconscious, and so it is far easier to hypnotize if the 'critical threshold' is low.[19]

This is the essence of hypnosis, and also the central facet of enthusiasm and of current charismatic experience, i.e. to detach a person from the 'Western rational paradigm' and allow an acceptance of the realm of the supernatural.

This is significant as both hypnotic techniques and enthusiasm share the same central tenet, which is that the rational mind needs to be by-passed so that each should be effective.

(xi) Shared experiences are a part of inducing hypnosis. As the subject begins to respond the hypnotist often behaves as if he shares the subject's unusual experiences. This has the effect of reinforcing the unusual state of consciousness.

It is possible that in the charismatic movement people do simply fake this agreement about experience, but on my experience, this is unlikely to be common. However, there is a situation where all kinds of phenomena are being interpreted as being a sign of the work of the spirit: heat, cold, fluttering eyelids and so on. Those with experience in such phenomena may claim to be able to see such phenomena as a demon sitting on a person's shoulder, even though this will be invisible to people who are still 'limited by a Western paradigm'. It is also a situation where the participants do sincerely want to see God at work, and will be willing to believe that all kinds of effects are caused by the Spirit. This is what all involved want to happen, and so there is a mutual conformation created by a mutual trust and sincerity. Both sides will have a tendency to interpret experience in the same 'spiritual' way.

(xii) A common side-effect of hypnosis is a reduction of fear, and this is relatively easily achieved by hypnosis.[20] It also corresponds to the feelings of a person who has been 'slain in the spirit'.

(xiii) Memory can be distorted under hypnosis, and for this reason it is often used to enable an adult to regress and to re-experience events as a child.[21]

> Closely allied to the recall of buried memories is the phenomenon of age regression. In the somnambulistic state it is possible to take the subject back step by step to earlier periods in life.[22]

This is a distinct parallel with current charismatic practice, particularly the concept of 'healing memories'. Both have the same aim and effect, i.e. to dig up and reinterpret past traumatic events.

(xiv) A sense of time-distortion is associated with hypnosis, with little or no awareness or care of time having passed.[23]

The same experience can accompany being 'slain in the Spirit'.

(xv) Physical changes can occur during hypnosis, particularly where a symptom is the result of emotional distress, e.g. cold sores, feelings of heat and cold,[24] warmth in particular limbs, changes in heart rate and respiration, fluttering of eyelids.

The same changes are also associated with a 'ministry' time. Cold, for example, may be interpreted as an indication of demonic influence, fluttering eyelids as the coming of the Spirit.

(xvi) Post hypnotic suggestion is used so that someone will respond in a particular way after hypnosis, but is only largely effective where 'the posthypnotic suggestion is congruent with the individual's desires'.

The same condition applies to 'ministry' time, where there is a mutually sought goal, and it is emphasized that one must want God to do whatever is being suggested, as he would not force his will on to people.

(xvii) Feelings of 'heaviness, warmth and relaxation' are associated with both 'slaying in the Spirit' and hypnosis.

(xviii) There is a variation in hypnotic susceptibility, and consequently hypnosis induces varied responses in different individuals.[25] For example, some people seem hardly affected during hypnosis, yet show substantial alteration afterwards.

It is also true that in a given congregation who experience enthusiastic phenomena, one will soon be able to predict the separate ways in which different individuals are likely to respond.

(xix) 'Hypnosis is not, as is often thought, a power which is confined to some mysterious individual, but is a technique which needs little training and skill, and is easily taught.'

It would fit well into the signs and wonders 'workshop' setting where people learn from each other. It is also comfortable in a setting where the gifts of individual members are developed and encouraged.

(xx) It is difficult to hypnotize a person with a psychotic illness. Indeed, it is normal people in good mental and physical health who respond most positively to hypnotic suggestion.

Those who have tried to hypnotize the insane and mental defectives have found that in practically every case it has been impossible to influence mental defectives and the same difficulty may arise with certain types of insanity.[26]

From my own experience as minister of a church with three psychotic members, this is also true of charismatic phenomena. I have been unable to track down an instance of a psychotic person responding well to a ministry time.

(xxi) Hypnosis affects illness which is of the more apparently psychosomatic variety, and the same is true of the effects of signs and wonders. Many charismatic leaders such as Derick Prince, Wimber, Benny Hinn, Morris Cerillo, etc. have been criticized that, in spite of the claims, there is a distinct lack of evidence for significant organic healing. Both charismatic experience and hypnosis seem to have the same kinds of effects on the same kinds of illness.

(xxii) In hypnosis there is a bizarre technique called the 'confusional technique' which is reserved for those who retain a critical mental attitude and are consequently unable to accept suggestions of a straightforward nature.[27] For example, if it is suggested that the right arm is becoming heavy, then the person may think that there is no reason for it to do so, and so remains unaffected. To overcome this critical response, one may offer suggestions such as the following:

> Your right arm is becoming heavier. At the same time your left arm feels lighter and the right foot feels numb. Now your right arm feels lighter still while the left is becoming heavier and heavier and begins to fall. The left hand is also feeling numb and cold. At the same time you notice how warm your left foot is getting, while your right arm is becoming so heavy that you cannot lift it without considerable effort. All this while your left hand continues to feel warmer and, as it does so, it gets lighter and begins to lift in the air.[28]

Eventually the effort of trying to be critical towards all of the conflicting suggestions is too much, resistance is abandoned and criticism suspended.

I would be very surprised if anyone within the charismatic movement deliberately uses such blatant method. However, there are similar implicit mechanisms of confusion at play. The effect of a large group of people where individuals respond in dramatic ways can be disturbing, and creates confusion as one struggles to make sense of what is going on. The requirement to believe in a way that is disproportionate to the evidence creates a confusing mental double think as people try hard to believe. If one suggests that an argument doesn't make sense, the reply may be that God is mysterious and beyond our understanding, or that one is at fault for being limited by a Western rational world view. Logic is answered with a denial of logic as a means of assessment and the argument retreats into mysticism. Such an argument makes irrational belief seem rational, and the switches between logic and illogic are both subtle and confusing. There seems no way to sift through the confusion.

(xxiii) *Flexibilitas cerea* may be present.

> Another curious phenomena is what is known as *flexibilitas cerea* (waxy flexibility). In this condition a limb may be moulded into certain rather bizarre positions at the joints because of the great increase in relaxation of the surrounding muscles. There is also an apparent increase in the strength of some muscles. This may be because any conscious restraint normally imposed upon muscular activity is removed during hypnosis so that the muscles are able to contract with their full force and to the maximum extent.[29]

We can compare this with phenomena reported to have occurred during charismatic meetings. In one instance people were

> Moving backward and forward or from side to side, and their arms and sometimes even their legs flailing in the wake of their moving bodies. I doubt that any ballet dancer or gymnast could reproduce the movements.[30]

> Sometimes the bodily shaking is on a vertical axis, the body leaving the ground in a series of bounces. Since the body remains more or less rigid, it looks like someone bouncing on a pogo stick.

The physical energy used must be considerable, especially when one considers that pogo-sticking is no respecter of persons.[31]

The bodily rigidity mentioned above is also a feature of hypnosis:

One of the most striking phenomena is catalepsy; a limb may be made perfectly rigid by suggestion and held for a long time in a given position without apparent effort or fatigue . . . Not only may an arm or leg be thus affected, but the process can be extended to other muscles of the body; in extreme cases the subject's whole body can be made so rigid that he can be supported quite well by supports placed only under his head and heels, just as if he were a plank of wood.[32]

Conclusions

In the light of all this, one can conclude that there are significant parallels between enthusiastic phenomena and hypnotic technique. In terms of physical, psychological, and after effects, the same phenomena occur in the same atmosphere. It is most unlikely that such close parallels could be coincidental.

One does not need to conclude that leaders are therefore consciously practising hypnotic techniques. As has been pointed out, hypnosis is a simple technique which can be done without realizing how the process is working. Wimber, for example, developed his approach by trying things out and seeing what worked. If it was effective he retained it. It is just as likely that people have accidentally stumbled on these old techniques which have been understood as hypnotic.

All of this leaves us in a situation where there are three currently available alternative theories to chose from:

(i) Hypnotism is an occult technique, and the effects are due to evil forces. This is what is tapped into by those who experience charismatic phenomena.

(ii) Signs and wonders are a pure work of the Spirit

(iii) Both the occult and the charismatic movement have

(intentionally or unintentionally) tapped into a psychological technique.

As we have already argued, while it is theoretically possible, there are no good reasons to assume (i). In respect of (ii), one would have to be prepared to attribute these same effects to the Spirit acting directly on a person who is in the psychiatrist's chair, or part of the occult, or visiting the theatre to see a stage hypnotist. The parallels are too close to be simply coincidental. One would need to start on the supplementary hypothesis road, and attribute the similarities to satanic counterfeit. The Spirit creates these effects in church, and Satan counterfeits the same phenomena on command everywhere else.

This leaves us with the third option. As a theory it has much to commend it. Significantly, it allows a detailed explanation to be constructed; it can predict the kind of responses, e.g. influence on psychotic illness, why there are more peculiarities in the charismatic gatherings than the dramatic healing one would expect if this was the Creator at work. It has an elegant simplicity that makes sense of all the available evidence in differing contexts, and it avoids an unnecessary 'multiplication of entities'. It is also quite congruent with both a Christian and atheistic paradigm. Certainly there is no biblical reason why such phenomena should be attributed directly to the Spirit.

It is, of course, an unprovable argument, but if one applies the criteria which select the best of different theories, then this is the option which has most to commend it.

To describe the phenomena occurring in charismatic worship as 'signs and wonders' is often dubious. As signs, they are ambiguous, and pointing more in the direction of the hypnotist or psychologist than to the Creator. There are wonders, but even these seem to be more explicable than at first sight. Even if they are helpful in themselves, they should not be described as 'signs of the Kingdom'.

The best of the options is to see what is occurring as the result of psychological forces, which does not necessarily undermine their use. An experience of charismatic phenomena such as falling to the ground or shaking could be as acceptable as any other form of hypnosis.

The question which would need to be resolved is whether hypnosis is acceptable for a Christian. In the modern charismatic movement, hypnosis is generally viewed as being dangerous, since it is considered to have the potential to open a person up to evil forces which can get direct access to a person's mind. It is quite unacceptable (in spite of being practised unintentionally by the same people). Other Christians have recommended its use.

If we treat such experience in the way that it was treated by Edwards, enthusiastic phenomena become a neutral psychological irrelevance. This is the way that people sometimes react to particular stimuli, and so to determine whether this is 'good' or 'bad', one needs to ask, 'To what is the person responding?' And, 'In what way are they affected?' It is one thing to be so overwhelmed by the truth and by the Spirit that one falls to the ground in wonder; it is quite another to respond to a lie or to the occult in this way. If hypnosis is indeed a means of by-passing the conscious mind to get access to the subconscious, one needs to ask, 'What has been placed in the mind when it was in this state?'

The argument that the physical phenomena associated with enthusiastic phenomena have a parallel with hypnosis is a strong one. However, as a means of assessment, it is still questionable. It does demand that the term 'sign and wonder' should be used with caution, but if a person responds in a strongly physical and emotional way, then one still has to ask, 'To what are they responding?' In other words, the phenomena themselves need to be assessed because on their own they could indicate the work of the Spirit, or some other force. Consequently, one should not say that *because* a person has fallen down or shaken during prayer this is a sign of the Spirit. Such experience is too ambiguous to be a reliable criterion of assessment.

Glossary

A priori   Latin for what comes before. An *a priori* statement is one that can be known to be true or false without reference to experience, except in so far as experience is necessary for understanding its terms. An argument is *a priori* primarily in so far as it attempts to deduce conclusions from *priori* propositions.

Epistemology   The branch of philosophy concerned with the theory of knowledge. What is the nature of knowledge? What is the scope of knowledge? How can you justify a claim to know?

Fideism   A view which has recurred throughout Christian history, that essential doctrines cannot be established by rational means, but must be accepted by an act of faith. One could be moderately fideistic; for example according to Pascal reason is not automatically opposed to faith, but lays an auxiliary role in formulating or elaborating what must be first accepted by faith. The more extreme end of the spectrum would find writers such as Kierkegaard and Bultmanm. According to Kierkegaard religion requires the acceptance of doctrines which are absurd or contrary to reason. Fideism considers it acceptable to have beliefs which are detached from evidence.

Incorrigible   An incorrigible statement would be directly and conclusively verified, not subject to any further tests. 'Basic beliefs' such as 'I have a sore foot' are generally regarded as being incorrigible because they can be justifiably believed without support from other evidence.

Jansenism   A seventeenth-century Roman Catholic movement which was outlawed by the church. They revived a form of Augustinian theology and were noted for a harsh moral rigourism.

Manachians   A gnostic sect founded by Mani (216–276). They were a zealous missionary group with a strong duelist theology and a belief in reincarnation. Jesus, along with other religious leaders, came to release souls of light from the prison of their bodies. Mani was decapitated for heresy in 276.

Quietism   Quietists were noted for condemning human effort in religious matters. To obtain perfection one must abandon oneself to God, to the extent that one does not even care about one's own salvation. When this state is reached it is impossible to sin, even by performing actions which would be sinful to others. Because a person no longer has a will, his or her actions are no longer sins.

Bibliography

Only works cited in the text have been included here. Standard reference works such as concordances and lexicons have been omitted.

Abraham, William J., *An Introduction to the Philosophy of Religion*, Prentice Hall Inc. 1985

Adams, R.M., 'A Criticism of Richard Swinburne's *Faith and Reason*' in *Nous*, vol XIX, March 1985

Allan, John, *Dealing With Darkness*, Handsel Press 1986

Alston, W.P., 'Religious Experience and Religious Belief' in *Nous*, vol XVI, 1982

Alston, W.P., *Perceiving God*, Cornell University Press 1991

Ambrose, G. & Newbold, G., *A Handbook of Medical Hypnosis*, Balliere Tindal, 4th edn, 1980

Angel, Gervais, *Delusion or Dynamite?* MARC EUROPE 1989

Ayer, A.J., *The Concept of a Person and Other Essays*, Macmillan 1963

Ayer, A.J., *The Problem of Knowledge*, Macmillan 1956

Barbour, Ian G., *Myths, Models and Paradigms*, SCM Press 1974

Barth, Karl, *Church Dogmatics*, I/I, T. & T. Clark 1960

Benn, Wallace and Burkill, Mark, 'A Theological and Pastoral Critique of the Teachings of John Wimber', *Churchman*, vol 101, no 2, 1987

Bennett, D. and R., *Nine O'clock in the Morning*, Logos International 1974

Black, Max, *Models and Metaphors*, Cornell University Press 1962

Bobgan, M. and D., *Hypnosis and the Christian*, Bethany House Publishers, Minneapolis, Minnesota 1984

Boyle, Mary, 'Schizophrenia and the Art of the Soluble' in *The Psychologist* magazine, vol 7, no 9, 1994

Braithwaite, R.B., *An Empiricist's View of the Nature of Religious Belief*, CUP 1956. Reprinted in B. Mitchell (ed), *The Philosophy of Religion*, OUP 1971

Bridge, D., *Spiritual Gifts and the Church*, IVP 1973

Brown, Colin, *Philosophy and the Christian Faith*, IVP 1968

Brunner, Emil and Barth, Karl, *Natural Theology*, Bles 1946

Bultmann, Rudolf, *Existence and Faith*, Hodder 1961

Bultmann, Rudolf, *Faith and Understanding*, SCM Press 1969

Bultmann, Rudolf, *Kerygma and Myth* ed H.W. Bartsch, SPCK 1961

Calvin, John, *Institutes of the Christian, Religion*, ed John T.
McNeil, LCC vols XX and XXI, SCM Press and Westminster Press 1960

Canty, George, *The Practice of Pentecost*, Marshall Pickering 1987

Carothers, Merlin, *Bringing Heaven into Hell*, Coverdale 1979

Carothers, Merlin, *Praise Works!*, Coverdale 1974

Carter Stapleton, Ruth, *The Gift of Inner Healing*, Hodder 1976

Chauncey, Charles, *Seasonable Thoughts on the State of Religion in New England*, Boston, Rogers and Fowle (US) 1743

Chauncey, Charles, *A Caveat Against Enthusiasm*, Boston, Rogers and Fowle (US) 1743

Chisholm, Roderick M., *Theory of Knowledge*, Prentice Hall Inc. 1977

Chisholm, Roderick M., *The Problem of the Criterion* (The Aquinas Lecture), Marquette University Press 1973

Cho, Paul Yonggi, *The Fourth Dimension*, Logos International 1980

Clarke, S.R.L., *From Athens to Jerusalem*, Clarendon Press 1984

Cole, M., *What is the New Age?*, Hodder 1990

Collingwood, R.G., *Essay on Metaphysics*, OUP 1940

Coltman, N. (ed), *Songs of Fellowship*, Kingsway Publications 1985

Copeland, Gloria, *God's Will Is Prosperity*, Harrison House (US) 1978

Copeland, Kenneth, *Voice of Victory* magazine. Published by Eagle Mountain International Church Inc. (Kenneth Copeland Ministries Inc.)

Copleston, Frederick, *A History of Philosophy*, Vol V, Burns Oates and Washbourne Ltd. 1959

Cragg, Gerald R., *The Church and the Age of Reason*, Penguin 1970

Craston, Collin (ed), *The Charismatic Movement in the Church of England*, CIO 1981.

Darwin, Charles, *The Origin of Species*, John Murray 1888

Davis, Caroline Franks, *The Evidential Force of Religious Experience*, Clarendon Press 1989

Dearing, Trevor, *Exit the Devil*, Logos International 1976

Descartes, R., *The Principles of Philosophy* (1644), Dent Everyman Edition 1986

Dowley, Dr Tim (ed), *The History of Christianity*, Lion n.d.

Dunn, J.D.G., *Baptism in the Holy Spirit*, SCM Press 1970

Dunn, J.D.G., *Jesus and the Spirit*, SCM Press 1970

Edwards, Jonathan, *The Religious Affections*, Banner of Truth Trust 1961

Edwards, Jonathan, *The Works of Jonathan Edwards*, Banner of Truth Trust 1990

Eliot, George, *Scenes of Clerical Life*, 1858; many editions

Fiddes, Paul, *Charismatic Renewal. A Baptist View*, Baptist Union Publications 1978

Fielding, Henry, *Joseph Andrews*, 1742; many editions

Flew, Antony (ed), *A Dictionary of Philosophy*, Pan Books 1979

Flew, Antony and MacIntyre, Alasdair (eds), *New Essays in Philosophical Theology*, SCM Press 1955

Flew, Antony, *God and Philosophy*, Hutchinson 1966

Foster, Richard, *Celebration of Discipline*, Harper and Row 1978

Fox, George, *The Journal of George Fox*, CUP 1952

Fredrick, S., *Voice of Victory* magazine, vol 16, no 6, 6 June 1988. Published by Eagle Mountain International Church Inc. (Kenneth Copeland Ministries Inc.)

Fromm, Erika and Shor, Ronald E. (eds), *Hypnosis Research Developments and Perspectives*, Paul Elek 1972

Gardner, Rex, *A Doctor Investigates Healing Miracles*, Darton, Longman and Todd 1987

Gibbons, D.E. and De Jarnette, J., 'Hypnotic Susceptibility and Religious Experience', *Journal for the Scientific Study of Religion*, vol 11, 1972

Glock, C.Y. and Stark, R., *Religion and Society in Tension*, Rand McNally & Company 1965

Gordon, Jesse E. (ed), *Handbook of Clinical and Experimental Hypnosis*, Macmillan 1967

Green, M., *I Believe in the Holy Spirit*, Hodder 1979

Grudem, W.A., *The Gift of Prophecy in I Corinthians*, University Press of America 1982

Hacking, Ian (ed), *Scientific Revolutions*, OUP 1981

Harper, Michael, *As at the Beginning*, Hodder 1965

Hendry, G.S., *The Holy Spirit in Christian Theology*, SCM Press 1957

Hobbes, Thomas, *Leviathan – The English works of Thomas Hobbes*, vol 3, London 1839

Hampshire, Stuart, *Spinoza*, Penguin 1957

Hodges, H.A., *Languages Standpoints and Attitudes*, OUP 1953

Hodgkin, Thomas, *George Fox*, Methuen 1906

Holmes, A.F., *All Truth is God's Truth*, IVP 1979

Horrobin, Peter, *Healing Through Deliverance*, Sovereign World International 1991

Houston, J. (ed), *Is it Reasonable to Believe in God?* Handsel Press 1984

Houston, J., *Reported Miracles*, CUP 1994

Hughes, Selwyn, *Ye Shall Receive Power*, Crusade for World Revival, n.d.

Hume, David, *An Enquiry Concerning Human Understanding* (1748), OUP 1990

Hunt, D. and Mcmahon, T.A., *The Seduction of Christianity*, Harvest House Publishers, Oregon 1985

Jackson, J.L., *Remarks on the Vaudois of Piedmont During an Excursion in the Summer of 1825*, London 1826

James, William, *The Varieties of Religious Experience*, Collins 1960

Jenson, P. and Payne, T. (eds), *John Wimber Friend or Foe?*, St Matthias Press, Stanton Road, London 1990

Katchen, Martin H., 'Brainwashing, Hypnosis and the Cults' in *The Australian Journal of Clinical and Experimental Hypnosis*, November 1992, vol 20

Kelsey, Morton, *The Christian and the Supernatural*, Search Press 1976

Kenny, A., *Rationalism, Empiricism and Idealism*, Clarendon Press, 1986

Kirsch, I., Mobayed, C.P., Council, J.R. and Kenny, D.A., 'Expert Judgements of Hypnosis from Subjective State', *Journal of Abnormal Psychology*, November 1992, vol 10

Klaassen, Walter, *Anabaptism in Outline: Selected Primary Sources*, Herald Press, Kitchener, PA 1981

Knox, R.A., *Enthusiasm. A Chapter in the History of Religion*, OUP 1950

Koyre, A., *From the Closed World to the Infinite Universe*, John Hopkins Press, Baltimore 1957

Kuhn, Thomas S., *The Structure of Scientific Revolutions*, University of Chicago Press 1962; 2nd edn 1970

Küng, Hans and Tracy, David (eds), *Paradigm Change in Theology*, T. & T. Clark 1989

Lakatos, I. and Musgrave, A. (eds), *Criticism and the Growth of Knowledge*, CUP 1970

Lampe, G.W.H., *God as Spirit*, Clarendon Press 1977; SCM Press 1983

Latourette, K.S., *A History of the Expansion of Christianity*, 7 vols, 1937–45; reissued Zondervan, Grand Rapids 1976

Leibniz, G.W., *New Essays on Human Understanding*, CUP 1981

Leibniz, G.W., *Philosophical Writings*, Dent Everyman Edition 1987

Lewis, C.S., *Miracles*, Collins 1980

Lewis, C.S., *The Magician's Nephew*, Bodley Head; 1955; Penguin 1963

Lewis, C.S., *The Screwtape Letters*, Collins 1980

Lewis, Dr David, *Healing: Fiction, Fantasy or Fact*, Hodder 1989

Locke, John, *An Essay Concerning Human Understanding* (1690), OUP 1991

Locke, John, *The Reasonableness of Christianity* with *A discourse of miracles*, A. and C. Black 1958

Lovelace, R.F., *Dynamics of Spiritual Life*, Paternoster Press 1978

Macnutt, Francis, *Healing*, Ave Maria Press 1974

Major, R.H., *Physical Diagnosis*, 8th revd edn by M.H. Delp and R.T. Manning, W.B. Saunders 1975

Masters, Peter, *The Healing Epidemic*, Wakeman Trust 1988

Mcbain, D., *Discerning the Spirits*, Marshall Pickering 1991

McGuinness, Brian, *Wittgenstein: a life*, Duckworth 1988

Moore, G.E., *Philosophical Studies*, Routledge and Kegan Paul 1922

Newman, John Henry, *An Essay in Aid of a Grammar of Assent*, e.g. University of Notre Dame Press 1979

Mitchell, Basil, *Faith and Logic*, Allen and Unwin 1958

Mitchell, Basil, *The Justification of Religious Belief*, Macmillan 1973

Mitchell, Basil (ed), *The Philosophy of Religion*, OUP 1971

Moltman, Jürgen, *The Church in the Power of the Spirit*, SCM Press 1977

Nott, George Frederic, *Religious Enthusiasm Considered*, Oxford 1803. Eight sermons (Bampton Lectures) preached at Oxford in 1802

Owen, John, *The Works of John Owen D.D. Vol III*, 'A Discourse Concerning the Holy Spirit', Johnstone and Hunter 1852

Packer, J.I., *Keep in Step With the Spirit*, IVP 1984

Payne, Leanne, *The Healing Presence*, Kingsway 1991

Plantinga, A., 'Epistemic Justification', in *Nous*, vol XX, March 1986

Plantinga, A. (ed), *Faith and Rationality*, University of Notre Dame Press 1983

Plantinga, A., *The Reformed Objection to Natural Theology*, Proceedings of the American Catholic Philosophical Association 1980

Plantinga, A., 'Is Belief in God Properly Basic?' in *Nous*, vol XV, 1981

Plantinga, A., *Warrant: The Current Debate*, OUP 1993

Plantinga, A., *Warrant and Proper Function*, OUP 1993

Popper, Karl. R., *The Logic of Scientific Discovery*, Hutchinson 1959

Prince, Derek, *From Curse to Blessing*, Derek Prince Ministries, n.d.

Pytches, D., *Come, Holy Spirit*, Hodder 1985

Quine, W.V.O., *From a Logical Point of View*, Harvard University Press 1953

Quine, W.V.O., *Theories and Things*, Harvard University Press 1981

Quine, W.V.O. & Ullian, *The Web of Belief*, Random House 1978

Rhaner, Karl, *The Spirit and the Church*, Burns and Oats 1979

Reese, William L., *Dictionary of Philosophy and Religion*, Harvester Press, Sussex 1980

Rhees, Rush (ed), *Recollections of Wittgenstein*, OUP 1984

Ryle, Gilbert, *The Concept of Mind*, Hutchinson 1949

Wise, Robert et al., *The Church Divided*, Bridge Publishing 1986

Sargant, William, *Battle for the Mind*, Heinemann 1957

Sargant, William, *The Mind Possessed*, Heinemann 1973

Scobie, G., *Psychology of Religion*, Batsford 1975

Smart, Ninian (ed), *Historical Selections in the Philosophy of Religion*, SCM Press 1962

Smail, Tom, Walker, Andrew and Wright, Nigel, *Charismatic Renewal. The Search for a Theology*, SPCK 1993

Smail, T.A., *Reflected Glory*, Hodder 1975

Springer, Kevin (ed), *Riding the Third Wave*, Marshall Pickering 1987

Stapleton, Ruth Carter, *The Experience of Inner Healing*, Hodder 1977

Stapleton, Ruth Carter, *The Gift of Inner Healing*, Hodder 1976

Stayger, James M. and Packull, Werner O. (eds), *The Anabaptists and Thomas Muntzer*, Kendal/Hunt Pub. Co, Dubuque, Iowa 1980

Stevenson, J., *A New Eusebius*, SPCK 1977. Revised 1987

Swift, Jonathan *A Tale of a Tub* (1704); many editions

Swinburne, R., *The Coherence of Theism*, OUP 1977

Swinburne, R., *The Existence of God*, OUP 1979

Swinburne, R., *Faith and Reason*, OUP 1981

Tomberlin, James E., 'A criticism of *Faith and Rationality*' in *Nous*, vol XX, March 1986, pp. 401–412

Toulmin, S., *Foresight and Understanding*, Indiana University Press 1961

Tucker, Susie I., *Enthusiasm. A Study in Semantic Change*, Hodder 1979

Urquhart, Colin, *Anything You Ask*, Hodder 1978

Urquhart, Colin, *When The Spirit Comes*, Hodder 1974

Walker, Andrew, *Restoring the Kingdom*, Hodder 1989

Walker, W., *A History of the Christian Church*, T. & T. Clark 1918

Wallace, B. and Kokoszka, A., 'Experience of Peripheral Temperature Change during Hypnotic Analgesia', *International Journal of Clinical and Experimental Hypnosis*, July 1992, vol 40 [3]

Walsh, W.H., *Metaphysics*, Hutchinson University Library 1963

Warfield, B.B., *Counterfeit Miracles*, Banner of Truth Trust 1986

Watson, David, *I Believe in the Church*, Hodder 1978

Weatherhead, Leslie D., *Psychology, Religion, and Healing*, Hodder 1963

Wesley, John, *Sermons*, Vol I, London 1825

Wesley, John, *Journal*, Many editions eg. Isbister, London 1902

White, John, *When the Spirit Comes With Power*, Hodder 1988

Williams, B. and Montefiore, A. (eds), *British Analytical Philosophy*, Routledge and Kegan Paul 1966

Willyams, Jane Louisa, *A Short History of the Waldensian Church*, London 1855

Wimber, John, *Power Evangelism*, Hodder 1985

Wimber, John, *Power Healing*, Hodder 1985

Wimber, John, *The Dynamics of Spiritual Growth*, Hodder 1990

Wise, Robert et al., *The Church Divided*, Bridge Publishing Inc. (US) 1986

Wittgenstein, Ludwig, *Philosophical Investigations*, OUP 1968

Wittgenstein, Ludwig, *Tractatus Logico-Philosophicus*, tr. D.F. Pears and B.F. McGuinness, Routledge 1993

Wright, Nigel, *The Fair Face of Evil*, Marshall Pickering 1989

Yolton, John W., *The Locke Reader*, CUP 1977

Notes

Full publication details for the works cited will be found in the Bibliography.

Introduction

1. John Locke, *An Essay Concerning Human Understanding* (1690), Book IV, Chapter XIX, section 1. Introduction to the discussion 'On Enthusiasm'.
2. Tom Smail, Andrew Walker and Nigel Wright, *Charismatic Renewal. The Search for a Theology*, p. 40.
3. For example, Derek Prince, *From Curse to Blessing*.
4. For example, Paul Youggi Cho essay in Robert Wise et al, *The Church Divided*.
5. Jonathan Edwards, *The Religious Affections* (1746), p. 15.
6. Ibid., p. 17.
7. Ibid., p. 20.
8. Ludwig Wittgenstein, *Tractatus Logico-Philosophicus*, p. 74.

1. History Repeats Itself

1. Susie I. Tucker, *Enthusiasm*, p. 15.
2. Cited in ibid., p. 30.
3. John Wesley, *Sermons*, Vol I, 'The Nature of Enthusiasm', p. 467 (Preached in 1750).
4. Ibid., p. 468.
5. Henry Fielding, *Joseph Andrews* (1742); T. E. Owen, *Methodism Unmasked* (1802).
6. Samuel Johnson, *A Dictionary of the English Language*, first published in 1755. The dictionary was principally remarkable for its definitions of the meanings of words.
7. Tucker, *Enthusiasm*, p. 15.
8. Tim Dowley (ed), *The History of Christianity*, p. 483.

9. For example: Sir William Temple, *Essay Upon Heroic Virtue*, (1690); Dryden, translating St Evermond's essays, (1692); Swift, *The Mechanical Operation of the Spirit* (1704); George Lavington, *The Enthusiasm of Methodists and Papists Compar'd* (1749–1751); George Eliot, 'Amos Barton' in *Scenes of Clerical life* (1858); Coleridge, *The Friend*, 1, 432 (1809–1810); Daniel Defoe, *The Review*, VIII, 94 (1704–1713); William Tong, *The Nature and Consequences of Enthusiasm Considered* (1720); Charles Chauncey, *A Caveat Against Enthusiasm* (1743), *Seasonable Thoughts* (1743); John Owen, *A Discourse Concerning the Holy Spirit* (1674); Jonathan Edwards, *The Religious Affections* (1746), *Thoughts on the State of Religion* (1742); John Locke. *An Essay Concerning Human Understanding*, (1690); Richard Baxter, *The Certainty of the World of Spirits* (1691); Thomas Ludlam, *Four Essays* (1797); John Milton, *Defensio Prima* (1650–1), *Defensio Secunda* (1653). Henry More, *Enthusiasmus Triumphatus* (1646); George F. Nott, *Religious Enthusiasm Considered* (1803); T.E. Owen, *Methodism Unmasked* (1802); Joseph Priestly, *Institutes of Natural Religion* (1782); Alexander Pope, *Letters of Mr Alexander Pope and several of his Friends* (1737); Shelley, *Preface to the Revolt of Islam* (1817); John Wesley, *An Answer to the Rev. Mr Church's Remarks* (1745), *Letter to the Author of the Enthusiasm of the Methodists and Papists Compar'd* (1750) *Sermon on Enthusiasm* (1750) Sermon XXXII in Standard Sermons.

10. John Locke, *An Essay Concerning Human Understanding*, Book IV, Chapter XIX, section 7.

11. Ibid., section 14.

12. Jonathan Swift *A Discourse Concerning the Mechanical Operation of the Spirit*, in *A Tale of a Tub* (1704). The title is often shortened to *A Tale of a Tub*.

13. R. A. Knox, *Enthusiasm*, p.1.

14. Ibid., p.1. This section is based on a summary of the traits outlined in Knox's authoritative book, p.1–8.

15. Ibid., p.2.

16. Ibid., p.3.

17. Ibid., p.4.

18. Ibid., p.105.

19. *Restoration*, (Nov/Dec), 1983 p.40. This magazine is published by Harvestime and is the official voice of the Bradford House Church movement.

20. Andrew Walker, *Restoring the Kingdom*, p.142.

21. Chauncey, *Seasonable Thoughts*, (1743) p.xxiii. Comments on enthusiasts by a critic of Edwards.

22. Andrew Walker, *Restoring the Kingdom*, p.142

23. Ibid., p. 140.
24. Peter Masters, *The Healing Epidemic*, p. 12.
25. Opatus, *On the Schism of the Donatists*, I, 15–19. Cited in J. Stevenson, *A New Eusebius*, p.314.
26. John Wesley, *Journal*, 11/8/1774.
27. John Wimber, *Power Evangelism*, p.101.
28. George Cantey, *The Practice of Pentecost*, p.182. This book is written from the stand-point of traditional Pentecostalism.
29. Nigel Wright, *The Fair Face of Evil*, p.14.
30. All of these examples are in a tract from 'Upper Room Tracts', Great Yarmouth, Norfolk, England (1989).
31. Peter Horrobin, *Healing Through Deliverance*, p.89–105.
32. Jonathan Edwards, *Thoughts on the Revival*, in *The Works of Jonathan Edwards*, p.374.
33. Ruth Carter Stapleton, *The Gift of Inner Healing*, p.9.
34. Wesley, *Journal*, 29/11/1761.
35. Assemblies of God, *Statement of Fundamental Truth*, date and publisher unknown.
36. Gervais Angel, *Delusion or Dynamite?*, p.21–22.
37. George Fox, *The Journal of George Fox*, i,33.
38. Ibid., i,56.
39. Susan Fredrick, *Voice of Victory* magazine, vol 6, no 6, 6 June 1988, p.10.
40. George Fox, *The Journal of George Fox*, i,33.
41. Locke, *Essay*, Book IV, Chapter xix.
42. John Wimber, *Power Healing*, p.192.
43. P. Jensen and T. Payne (eds), *John Wimber Friend or Foe?*, p.14.
44. Ibid., p.21.
45. Peter Horrobin, *Healing Through Deliverance*, p.87.
46. Ibid., p.82.
47. Charles Chauncey, *Caveat Against Enthusiasm*, p.4.
48. John Wimber, *Power Healing*, p.71.
49. Thomas Muntzer cited in Stayger and Packull (eds), *The Anabaptists and Thomas Muntzer*, p.124.
50. Andrew Walker, *Restoring the Kingdom*, p.128.
51. Chauncey, in a letter to Mr James Davenport, pastor of the church at Southold at Long Island, now Boston, 17 July 1742. Stored on microfilm at the British Library.
52. Cited in Walter Klassen, *Anabaptism in Outline, Selected Primary Sources*, p.321.
53. Jonathan Edwards, *Thoughts on the Revival*, in *Works*, p.381.
54. Ibid., p.381.
55. Ibid., p.382.

56. Andrew Walker *Restoring the Kingdom*, p.137.
57. John Wesley, *Journal*, 7/7/1735.
58. Philip Seldon in P. Jensen and T. Payne (eds), *John Wimber Friend or Foe?*, p.34.
59. David Lewis, *Healing: Fiction, Fantasy or Fact*, p.169.
60. Ibid., p.185.
61. See *Baptist Times*, 1 Sept 1994, p.2.

2. Criticism and Credulity

1. R.A. Knox, *Enthusiasm*, p.1.
2. Charles Chauncey, *Seasonable Thoughts* (1743) p.166.
3. Cited in John White, *When the Spirit Comes With Power* pp.40–41. G. Campbell Morgan (1863–1945) was a Congregationalist writer and preacher. R.A. Torrey (1856–1928) was an American Evangelist, writer and academic who had a long association with D.L. Moody.
4. Peter Masters, *The Healing Epidemic*, pp. 13, 41.
5. Jonathan Edwards, *Thoughts on the Revival*, in *Works*, p. 377.
6. Ibid., p. 390.
7. Ibid., p. 398f.
8. Ibid., p. 396.
9. Ibid., p. 396.
10. Described in 'Amos Barton', the first of George Eliot's *Scenes of Clerical life* (1848). See also Thomas Hardy, *Under the Greenwood Tree* (1872).
11. Chauncey, *Seasonable Thoughts*, p. 207.
12. Ibid., p. 208.
13. Masters, *The Healing Epidemic*, p. 16.
14. For example, Acts 5.5; 5.11; 19.17.
15. Edwards, *Thoughts on the Revival*, in *Works*, p. 376.
16. Chauncey, *Seasonable Thoughts*, p. 77.
17. White, *When the Spirit Comes*, pp. 84–104.
18. Masters, *The Healing Epidemic*, p. 17.
19. Knox, *Enthusiasm*, p. 4.
20. Ibid., p. 585.
21. Tucker, *Enthusiasm*, p. 16. My italics.
22. Cited by W. Benn and M. Burkhill in 'A Theological and Pastoral Critique of the Teachings of John Wimber'.
23. Stevenson, *A New Eusebius*, p. 114. My italics.
24. Masters, *The Healing Epidemic*, p. 182,
25. Colin Urquhart, *Anything You Ask*, p. 101.
26. Ibid., pp. 108, 106.
27. Ibid., p. 100.

28. Thomas Ludlam, *Four Essays* (1797), essay IV, p. 68.
29. Knox, *Enthusiasm*, p. 2.
30. Ibid., p. 3.
31. Chauncey, *Seasonable Thoughts*, p. 207
32. Margaret Magdalen, *Renewal* magazine, July 1990.
33. Chauncey, *Seasonable Thoughts*, p. 100.
34. T. Smail, 'The Cross and the Spirit'. Essay in T. Smail, A. Walker, and N. Wright, *Charismatic Renewal, The Search for a Theology*, p. 49.
35. Ibid., p. 49.
36. Edwards, *Religious Affections*, p. 102.
37. Argued in ibid., p. 100ff.
38. Wimber, *Power Evangelism*, pp. 56, 74ff, 49, 59. It would be a distortion of Wimber's view to suggest that he wishes to reject all aspects of rationality. His aim is to reject the elements of a Western paradigm which would exclude the supernatural (ibid., pp. 75ff.). All that is being pointed out is that this effectively makes reason secondary to experience.
39. Edwards, *Religious Affections*, p. 102.

3. Theological Surf-Boarding

1. C.S. Lewis, *Miracles*, p. 7.
2. John Locke, *An Essay Concerning Human Understanding*, Book IV, Chapter IXI, section 10.
3. Ibid., section 14.
4. Karl Barth, *Church Dogmatics*, 1/1, 'The Doctrine of the word of God', p. 350.
5. Locke, ibid., section 14.
6. Karl Barth, in Brunner and Barth, *Natural Theology*. Cited in William J. Abraham, *An Introduction to the Philosophy of Religion*, p. 78.
7. R. M. Chisholm, *Theory of Knowledge*, p. 120.
8. R. M. Chisholm, *The Problem of the Criterion*, p. 1.
9. Leanne Payne, *The Healing Presence*.
10. R. A. Knox, *Enthusiasm*, p. 579.
11. See Appendix.
12. John Wimber, *Power Evangelism*, p. 80.
13. Ibid., p. 15.

4. I Dreamed God Spoke to Me?

1. Thomas Hobbes, *Leviathan* (1651), pp.361f. (my italics).
2. Locke, *Essay Concerning Human Understanding*, Book IV, Chapter xviii, section 11.

3. John Locke, *The Reasonableness of Christianity* (1695), *Works*, VII, p.140.
4. Locke, *Essay Concerning Human Understanding*, Book IV, Chapter xix, section 14.
5. Ibid., Chapter xvii, section 6 (my italics).
6. Ibid., Chapter xvi, section 13.
7. Ibid.
8. Ibid., section 14 (my italics).
9. David Hume, *An Enquiry Concerning Human Understanding* (1748), section XII, part III, p. 165.
10. For example, R. Descartes, *The Principles of Philosophy* (1644), 'Human Knowledge', section XLV.
11. Cf. Stuart Hampshire, *Spinoza*, pp. 67ff.
12. G. W. Leibniz, *Philosophical Writings*: 'Necessary and Contingent Truths' (c. 1686), p. 96.
13. G. W. Leibniz, *New Essays on Human Understanding*, Book IV, chapter xix.
14. Ibid., p. 505.
15. Ibid., 506.
16. Ibid., (my italics).
17. Ibid.
18. This is an interesting point because it is similar to the approach taken by N. Wolterstorff, i.e. an attempt to demonstrate that enthusiasm could be shown to be an unreliable method of belief formation. The point about contradictory revelations is made by Flew in *God and Philosophy*, p. 127.
19. *New Essays on Human Understanding*, book IV, chapter xix, p. 507.
20. This agreement illustrates incidentally the artificiality of classing Locke as an 'empiricist' who is polarized from 'rationalism'.
21. Swinburne, *The Existence of God*, p. 1.
22. Ibid., p. 3.
23. For example, Alvin Plantinga, 'Is Belief in God Properly Basic?', p. 49.
24. Nicholas Wolterstorff has a chair of philosophy at Yale University. He could be described as a 'Reformed Epistemologist'.

5. Do We Know Already?

1. G.E. Moore, *Philosophical Studies*, p.163.
2. Much of the argument on these issues is contained in A. Plantinga (ed), *Faith and Rationality*.

3. Chisholm, *The Problem of the Criterion*, p.19.

4. N. Wolterstorff, 'Can Belief in God be Rational?' in A. Plantinga (ed), *Faith and Rationality*, p. 177. What he considers to be 'adequate reasons' will be discussed in more detail later.

5. Ibid., p.163.

6. Ibid., p.163.

7. Ibid., p.166 (Part VII).

8. Charles Chauncey, *Seasonable Thoughts*, p.180.

9. Wolterstorff, 'Can Belief in God be Rational?' in Plantinga (ed), *Faith and Rationality*, p.177.

10. Ibid., p.172 (my italics). NB. 'Ought' would be enough for Wolterstorff's argument.

11. Precisely what kind of 'certainty' Descartes means is open to question. This could be logical necessity or perhaps phenomenological. 'Clear and distinct perception' implies a psychological certainty.

12. Plantinga, 'Reason and Belief in God' in *Faith and Rationality*, pp.16ff.

13. Ibid., p.90. This assertion is questioned by James E. Tomberlin, in *Nous*, vol XX, 1986, p.406. 'Classical foundationalism is no doubt reeling as a result of sustained attacks from Plantinga and others. But the assessment that it is self-referentially incoherent is abortively premature.'

14. Alvin Plantinga, 'Is Belief in God Properly Basic?', p.46. The meaning of being 'appropriately appeared to' is briefly illustrated below (p. 77) at the end of the section on 'Enthusiasm and Empiricism'. See also footnote 23.

15. Ibid., p.50.

16. Ibid.

17. Ibid. (my italics).

18. W.P. Alston, 'Reason and Christian Belief' in Plantanga (ed), *Faith and Rationality*, p.112.

19. Locke, *Essay Concerning Human Understanding*, Book IV, Chapter XIX, sections 8–9 (my italics).

20. Edwards, *The Religious Affections*, p. 102 (my italics).

21. Plantinga, 'Is Belief in God Properly Basic?', p. 50.

22. Plantinga, 'Reason and Belief in God' in *Faith and Rationality*, p. 34.

23. See footnote 14. The phrase 'Being appeared to' is an attempt to describe an event without adding any interpretation to what is directly being experienced. See R.M. Chishom, *Theory of Knowledge*.

24. Plantinga, 'Is Belief in God Properly Basic?', p. 47.

25. Plantinga, 'Reason and Belief in God' in *Faith and Rationality*, p. 34.

26. Plantinga, 'Is Belief in God Properly Basic?', p. 46.

27. For example, A. Plantinga, *Warrant and Proper Function*, pp. 50, 89.

28. Ibid., p. 50.

29. John Locke, *Essay Concerning Human Understanding*, Book IV, Chapter XIX, section 14.
30. The following section owes its direction to Basil Mitchell, *The Justification of Religious Belief*.
31. John Calvin, *Institutes of the Christian Religion* (1535), Book 1, chapter III.
32. Ibid., Book 1, chapter VI, section 4.
33. Ibid., Book 1, chapter VII, section 4.
34. Ibid., Book I, chapter VII, section 5.
35. Karl, Barth, in Brunner and Barth, *Natural Theology*, p. 76.
36. Karl Barth, *Church Dogmatics*, I/I, p. 135 (my italics).
37. Ibid., p. 165.
38. Ibid., p. 282.
39. Basil Mitchell, *The Justification of Religious Belief*, p. 144.
40. Ibid., pp. 144–145.
41. R. Bultmann, *Kerygma and Myth*, pp. 210–211.

6. *Can Leaky Buckets Hold Water?*

1. Basil Mitchell, *The Justification of Religious Belief*, p. 31.
2. R.H. Major, *Physical Diagnosis*, p. 56.
3. Ibid., p. 59.
4. Ibid., p. 59. One could question whether such 'knowledge', should be called knowledge if it is uncertain (my italics).
5. Ibid., p. 63.
6. Ibid., p. 69.
7. By Dr David C. Lewis of the Religious Experience Research Project, Nottingham University and the Alister Hardy Research Centre, Oxford. This was published in an Appendix in J. Wimber, *Power Healing* (1985).
8. Ibid., p. 252.
9. Ibid., pp. 257–58.
10. Although being applied to charismatic experience, parts of the following argumentation are based on Mitchell, *The Justification of Religious Belief*.
11. Ibid., p. 45.
12. A. Flew, *God and Philosophy*, p. 141.
13. Cf. Caroline Franks Davis, *The Evidential Force of Religious Experience*, p. 109.
14. John Henry Newman, *An Essay in Aid of a Grammar of Assent* (1870).
15. R. Swinburne, *The Existence of God*, p. 277.
16. Ibid., p. 13.

17. Ibid., p. 289.
18. Ibid., p. 290.
19. Ibid., p. 291.
20. W.P. Alston, *Perceiving God*, p. 306.

7. *Can Ducks Turn into Rabbits?*

1. John Wimber, *Power Evangelism*, p.89.
2. Ibid., p.89.
3. D.E. Gibbons, and J. De Jarnette, 'Hypnotic Susceptibility and Religious Experience'. See also the discussion in G. Scobie, *Psychology of Religion*, chapter 7.
4. Cf. Caroline Franks Davis, *The Evidential Force of Religious Experience*, pp. 203 ff.
5. C.S. Lewis, *The Magician's Nephew*, p.116.
6. Thomas S. Kuhn, *The Structure of Scientific Revolutions*, p.25. Page refs are to the first edition.
7. A.J. Ayer, *The Concept of a Person and Other Essays*, p.27 (my italics).
8. Cited in Kuhn, *The Structure of Scientific Revolutions*, p.18.
9. W.V.O. Quine, *The Web of Belief*, pp.67 ff.
10. A. Flew (ed), *A Dictionary of Philosophy*, p.261 (my italics).
11. These writers are not all people who use the word paradigm themselves, but there is some commonality between them. They are certainly used as examples of different concepts of paradigm by other writers.
12. R.G. Collingwood, *Essay on Metaphysics*, chapter 5.
13. R.B. Braithwaite, *An Empiricist's View of the Nature of Religious Belief*.
14. R.M. Hare, contribution to 'Theology and Falsification' in Flew and MacIntyre (eds), *New Essays in Philosophical Theology*, pp.96–103.
15. A. Koyre, *From the Closed World to the Infinite Universe*, p.192.
16. S. Toulmin, *Foresight and Understanding*, pp.56, 47, 101.
17. H. Küng & D. Tracy (eds), *Paradigm Change in Theology*, p.7.
18. Thomas Kuhn *The Structure of Scientific Revolutions*, p.175.
19. Ibid., p.25.
20. Ibid., p.154.
21. Ibid., p.155.
22. Ibid., pp.121 f.
23. Ibid., pp.110 f.
24. The accusations of extreme relativity would be denied by Kuhn, but at least in the first edition of *The Structure of Scientific Revolutions*, it is easy to see why he has been criticized in this way. He does clarify his views in response to criticism, and in the postscript to the second edition of *The Structure of Scientific Revolutions* (1970), he gives more

prominence (a) to the control that experiment has over theory; and (b) to the role of criteria which are independent of the particular paradigm.

25. Kuhn, *The Structure of Scientific Revolutions*, p.157.
26. Cf. H. Küng & D. Tracy (eds), *Paradigm Change in Theology*. Argued by Charles Kannensgiesser in the essay 'Origen, Augustine, and Paradigm Changes in Theology', pp.113 ff.
27. John Watkins, 'Against Normal Science' in Lakatos and Musgrave (eds), *Criticism and the Growth of Knowledge*, p.33.
28. Quine, *The Web of Belief*, p.67.
29. Ibid., p.75.
30. Kuhn, *The Structure of Scientific Revolutions*, p.110.
31. Ibid., p.121 (my italics).
32. Quine, *The Web of Belief*, pp.66–69.
33. Ibid., p.77.
34. Kuhn, *The Structure of Scientific Revolutions*, p.158.
35. Ibid., p.110.
36. What I mean by 'absolute presuppositions' here is not the sense in which the phrase was used by Collingwood, i.e. presuppositions that are relative to a specific community. What is meant are the most central parts of the web of belief; that which is beyond question from the point of view of any paradigm or community.
37. William Sargant, *Battle for the Mind*, p.xi.
38. Charles Darwin, *The Origin of Species*, pp.305–306.

8. Attempting to Build an Arch with a Brick

1. *Healing* 92; information from Vineyard Conferences, 297 Chapel Street, Manchester, M3 5JG.
2. Edwards, *Thoughts on the Revival*, in *Works*, p. 378.
3. B.B. Warfield, *Counterfeit Miracles*, p. 58.
4. Ibid., p. 122.
5. Ibid., p. 123.
6. John Locke, *A Discourse of Miracles*, p. 84.
7. P. Jensen and T. Payne (eds), *John Wimber Friend or Foe?*, p. 7.
8. Kenneth Copeland in *Voice of Victory* (magazine) vol 17, no 2, February 1988, pp. 5, 8.
9. Edwards, *The Religious Affections*, p. 59.
10. Ibid., p. 19.
11. Kenneth Copeland in *Voice of Victory*, vol 17, no 11, November 1989, p. 6.
12. Ibid., p. 5.
13. Kenneth Copeland in *Voice of Victory*, vol 13, no 2, 1985, p. 4.

14. Edwards, *Thoughts on the Revival*, in *Works*, p. 368.
15. P. Jensen and T. Payne (eds), *John Wimber Friend or Foe?*, p. 10 (my italics).
16. Edwards, *Thoughts on the Revival*, in *Works*, p. 378.
17. Edwards, *The Religious Affections*, p. 16.
18. D. Hunt and T.A. Mcmahon, *The Seduction of Christianity*, pp. 73ff.
19. Gloria Copeland (the wife of Kenneth Copeland), *God's Will Is Prosperity*, pp. 48–49.
20. Hunt and Mcmahon, *The Seduction of Christianity*, p. 101.
21. Ruth Carter Stapleton, *The Experience of Inner Healing*, p. 17
22. Richard Foster, *Celebration of Discipline*, p. 27.
23. Francis MacNutt, *Healing*, p. 183.
24. Foster, *Celebration of Discipline*, p. 26.
25. Hunt and Mcmahon, *The Seduction of Christianity*, p. 163.
26. Ibid., p. 123.
27. Yonggi Cho, *The Fourth Dimension*, p. 44.
28. Hunt and Mcmahon, *The Seduction of Christianity*, p. 150.
29. Ibid., p. 184.
30. Edwards, *The Religious Affections*, Part II, Section II.
31. Ibid., pp. 59–60.
32. William Sargant, *Battle for the Mind*, p. 41.

9. How to Shave Hairy Theology

1. Caroline Franks Davis, *The Evidential Force of Religious Experience*, pp. 108–109.
2. Probably none of these people would accept the label 'fideist', as it has become something of an insult. I would argue that it is still a justifiable description of their theology.
3. D. Pytches, *Come Holy Spirit*, p. 109 (my italics).
4. R. Bultmann, *Existence and Faith*, p. 57.
5. R. Bultmann, *Faith and Understanding*, p. 121.
6. Ibid., p. 330.
7. Ibid., p. 331.
8. Houston, *Reported Miracles*, p. 97.
9. Colin Urquhart, *Anything You Ask*, p. 117 (my italics).
10. R. Bultmann, 'New Testament and Mythology' in *Kerygma and Myth*, p. 5.
11. Sofia Richmond, untitled feature, *The Independent*, Thursday 4 August 1994, p. 15.
12. Ibid.
13. Ibid.

14. Gilbert Ryle, *The Concept of Mind*.
15. Cf. Luke 21.4–11 and W.A. Grudem, *The Gift of Prophecy in I Corinthians*, p. 79.
16. Grudem, ibid., p. 229. It is argued in the same thesis that it is the apostle who has taken on this role in the New Testament, and that the reason for the change in description was that in first-century Greek culture, the understanding of the word 'prophet', would have been so ambiguous, that it would have been misleading.
17. B.B. Warfield, *Counterfeit Miracles*, p. 120.
18. By this I mean to refer to the ambiguity of the word 'unbelief'. In reality this is a belief in the antithesis of a belief. For example, to say 'I don't believe in ghosts' is to believe that there are no ghosts. Perhaps 'non belief' would be preferable.
19. Davis, *The Evidential Force of Religious Experience*, p. 206.
20. M. and D. Bobgan, *Hypnosis and the Christian*, p. 52.
21. T. Smail, A. Walker and N. Wright, *Charismatic Renewal*, pp. 82–84.
22. Ibid., p. 129.
23. David Lewis, *Healing: Fiction, Fantasy or Fact?*, chapter 4.
24. John White, *When the Spirit Comes With Power*, pp. 60–61.
25. Edwards, *Thoughts on the Revival*, in *Works*, p. 176.
26. Edwards, *The Religious Affections*, Part II, Section II.
27. For example, David Blake, 'Is there Scriptural Evidence for the Toronto Blessing' in *Direction* magazine, March 1995, pp. 12ff.
28. For example, D. Blake, 'The Toronto Blessing' in *Direction* magazine, February 1995, p 12.
29. George Canty, *The Practice of Pentecost*.
30. Edwards, *The Religious Affections*, Part III.
31. For example, Leanne Payne, *The Healing Presence*.
32. Edwards, *The Religious Affections*, Part III, Section X.
33. John Wesley, *Sermons*, Vol I, 'The Nature of Enthusiasm' (1750), p. 467.
34. This is not to deny that God may appear paradoxical and beyond understanding. The discussion applies to logical contradiction.
35. Davis, *The Evidential Force of Religious Experience*, pp. 207–209.
36. J. Edwards, *The Religious Affections*, Part III.

10. Conclusions

1 Edwards, *The Religious Affections*, p. 20.
2 Ludwig Wittgenstein, *Tractatus Logico-Philosophicus*, p. 74.

Appendix

1. Appendix by V. Wright in Peter Masters, *The Healing Epidemic*, pp. 202–27.
2. Article by Martin H. Katchen, 'Brainwashing, Hypnosis and the Cults' in *The Australian Journal of Clinical and Experimental Hypnosis*, November 1992, vol 20, pp. 78–88
3. Essay by Gordon, Pattie, Frank, 'A Brief History of Hypnosis' in Jesse E. Gordon (ed), *Handbook of Clinical and Experimental Hypnosis*, p. 14.
4. The word 'seance' should not be confused with spiritualism, as Mesmer pre-dates the development of spiritualism in the 1840s. It straightforwardly describes a circle.
5. Gordon, Pattie, Frank, 'A Brief History of Hypnosis' in Jesse E. Gordon (ed), *Handbook of Clinical and Experimental Hypnosis*, p. 13.
6. Ibid., p. 19.
7. Ibid., p. 21.
8. Essay by Perry London, 'The Induction of Hypnosis' in Gordon (ed), *Handbook of Clinical and Experimental Hypnosis*, p. 49.
9. I. Kirsch, C.P. Mobayed, J.R. Council, and D.A. Kenny, 'Expert Judgements of Hypnosis from Subjective State', *Journal of Abnormal Psychology*, November 1992, vol 10.
10. Essay by Theodore Xenophon Barber, 'Suggested ("Hypnotic") Behaviour: The Trance Paradigm Verses and Alternative Paradigm' in Erika Fromm, and Ronald E. Shor (eds), *Hypnosis Research Developments and Perspectives*, pp. 132 ff.
11. Essay by Ernest R. Hilgard, 'Individual Differences in Hypnotizability' in Gordon (ed), *Handbook of Clinical and Experimental Hypnosis*, p. 430. See also essay by Theodore Xenophon Barber, 'Suggested ("Hypnotic") Behaviour: The Trance Paradigm Verses and Alternative Paradigm' in *Hypnosis Research Developments and Perspectives*, p. 168.
12. Theodore Xenophon Barber, 'Suggested ("Hypnotic") Behaviour: The Trance Paradigm Verses and Alternative Paradigm' in *Hypnosis Research Developments and Perspectives*, pp. 133 ff.
13. G. Ambrose and G. Newbold, *A Handbook of Medical Hypnosis*, p. 41.
14. Essay by E. Eugene Levitt and Hennessy Chapman, 'Hypnosis as a Research Method' in *Hypnosis Research Developments and Perspectives*, p. 93.
15. Essay by Perry London, 'The Induction of Hypnosis' in *Handbook of Clinical and Experimental Hypnosis*, p. 51.
16. Ibid., p. 59.
17. Leslie D. Weatherhead, *Psychology, Religion and Healing*, p. 127.

18. Ibid., p. 119.
19. Ibid., p. 119.
20. Essay by E. Eugene Levitt and Hennessy Chapman, 'Hypnosis as a Research Method' in *Hypnosis Research Developments and Perspectives*, p. 94.
21. See also ibid., p. 96.
22. Ambrose and Newbold, *A Handbook of Medical Hypnosis*, p. 28.
23. See essay by Theodore X. Barber, '"Hypnotic" Phenomena: A Critique of Experimental Methods' in Gordon (ed), *Handbook of Clinical and Experimental Hypnosis*, p. 453.
24. For example, a sensation of coldness is common under hypnosis. This is attributed by Wallace and Kokoszka to an association between numbness and coldness which lead to this experience. B. Wallace, and A. Kokoszka, 'Experience of Peripheral Temperature Change during Hypnotic Analgesia' *International Journal of Clinical and Experimental Hypnosis*, July 1992, vol 40 [3], pp. 180–193.
25. Essay by Ernest R. Hilgard, 'Individual Differences in Hypnotizability', in Gordon (ed), *Handbook of Clinical and Experimental Hypnosis*, p. 400.
26. Perry London, 'The Induction of Hypnosis' in *Handbook of Clinical and Experimental Hypnosis*, p. 25.
27. See also ibid., p. 67.
28. Ibid., p. 47.
29. Ibid., p. 27.
30. White, *When the Spirit Comes with Power*, p. 92.
31. Ibid., p. 94.
32. Ambrose and Newbold, *A Handbook of Medical Hypnosis*, p. 26.

Index